Chronicles of a Million Dollar Trader

Chronicles of a Million Dollar Trader

MY ROAD, VALLEYS, AND PEAKS TO FINAL TRADING VICTORY

Don Miller

WILEY

Library of Congress Cataloging-in-Publication Data
Miller, Don, 1961-
    Chronicles of a million dollar trader : my road, valleys, and peaks to final trading victory / Don Miller.
        pages cm
    Includes index.
    ISBN 978-1-118-62789-1 (cloth); ISBN 978-1-118-62773-0 (ebk);
    ISBN 978-1-118-62779-2 (ebk); ISBN 978-1-118-62778-5 (ebk)
 1. Stocks. 2. Investments. I. Title.
    HG4661.M55 2013
    332.6092–dc23
    [B]
                                                                    2013005316

Printed in the United States of America

10 9 8 7 6 5 4 3 2 1

Contents

Preface

For years, I said no to numerous requests to write a book on trading for many reasons. First, I believed that my online trading journal at donmillerblog.com was a better way to get my thoughts across to the trading community on a current basis, initially as a detailed trading diary and then in a manner that shifted focus away from me and more toward intensive trader education, motivation, and industry activism. A book, on the other hand, unless properly crafted, runs the substantial risk of becoming dated the minute the ink dries. So, the first hurdle to be overcome by any bona fide author is to create lasting content that will forever stand the test of time.

Second, even though the title of this book, *Chronicles of a Million Dollar Trader*, accurately depicts my 2008 through 2009 journey in which I earned more than $2 million in 18 months by trading equity index futures intraday—largely as the result of a self-imposed one-year $1 million challenge—I didn't want to write a book that was a story primarily about success, nor did I want to put something forth that might encourage prospective readers to leave behind their current pursuits and talents to follow in my footprints. This is because as you'll read in the coming chapters, the virtual feet that created such prints have been bloodied, battered, and bruised as I stumbled and tripped my way through my own humanity toward a goal that seemed ever-elusive. And although I did ultimately reach my objective and beyond, the journey didn't come without a certain degree of personal and family sacrifice and hardship.

Third, there is substantial risk when writing what is largely an autobiography that despite best intentions, personal ego and pride will slip in. Yet, as any successful trader will tell you, both character flaws are among the leading causes of failure in the trading world, just as they are in life. Plus, any success I've been granted over the years has been largely rooted in the foundation of failure. *Read that last line again and you may have unlocked several secrets to life itself!* So, another challenge I'd have to overcome as an author would be to put forth content that would focus as much—if not more—on my failures than my successes.

Fourth, from a pure business perspective, a good trader can make far more profit from directing his or her energies toward trading than by writing. Any author of a trading book will tell you that the royalties are minimal at best and that the resulting "distraction" usually isn't worth the financial loss.

Finally, in terms of intended educational benefits, it's impossible to teach anyone to trade solely via a book. As is the case in any performance-based field, successful trading requires intensive education, years of experience, and the ability to hone and maintain the skills necessary to navigate the ever-changing seas of the financial markets. As such, for these reasons and more, for years I've turned down requests to write such a book.

The Call

Then came a call from Laura at John Wiley & Sons—a leading publisher in the financial world with a reputation for quality and high standards—who encouraged me to formally document and supplement my existing journal in permanent book format. As publishing ideas and discussions began, though, I was reluctant, as I made it clear from the outset that if we did something, it would have to be done in such a way to hold true to the values I've tried to maintain since beginning trader educational and advocacy efforts in the late 1990s.

Then the parallels began. Here was an opportunity to write a nonfiction version of my entire trading journey along the lines of the classic *Reminiscences of a Stock Operator* (Lefevre [1923] 1994), another Wiley book long regarded as one of the top trading books ever published. Much had changed since then, including the increased abundance of shorter-term trading opportunities, improved technologies, market access advances, and evolving regulation. Then, there was the opportunity to tell that rare story of someone who quietly but ardently prepared for years, reaped a substantial reward, and *didn't subsequently give it back.* Too often, we hear of investors, celebrities, professional athletes, and lottery winners who let it all slip away, sometimes as quickly as they earned it. There are also the modern-day real-life versions of Gordon Gekko (the lead character in the movie *Wall Street*) who have added new wrinkles to the long-running objective of ensuring that the market doesn't take your money, as now we have the game of ensuring that your *broker* doesn't abscond with your hard-earned money.

Suffice it to say that as time and discussions progressed, my thoughts slowly shifted from concerns of *whether* my story should be told to the growing possibility that my story *must* be told, if only (1) to prove once and for all that successful trading *is* downright possible with the proper mix of education, experience, patience, focus, and motivation; and (2) to chronicle my footprints in such a way that doing so might help just one person *avoid* the bloodied footprints that had disappeared into crevices.

I've often said that I wouldn't choose trading as a first career choice for my children given the necessary pain and hardship that is a fact of life in this field because (1) most small businesses fail, and (2) most traders fail. As such, every prospective trader begins with two strikes against him or her with a small remaining margin for error. Conversely, I've also said that (1) there is *zero* doubt in my mind that consistent and abundant success in the markets *is* possible, and (2) if, after weighing all the attributes of this field, my children or others made their own decisions to follow my pursuit, I'd do whatever I could to help make their way less painful. So, after many years of saying no to authoring a book on trading, I finally said yes.

So, welcome aboard as we journey together through a trip of a lifetime. Our journey will take us through the lowest valleys of despair that seem endless to beautiful bamboo forests that seem to grow to the sky before your very eyes. We'll travel through time and place, starting in my early years of immaturity. We'll travel through the puddles of tears, witness the self-inflicted wounds, see how I often poorly managed ongoing battles with interruptions and focus, and revisit battles with personal spirituality and life's true priorities. Through it all though, you'll see the path was forever moving forward.

One note of caution: As you begin reading, I strongly encourage you not to jump ahead and get right to what I call the "bamboo" years, where the fruits of time, effort, and grace finally blossomed. Although I recognize that traders by their nature can often be impatient beings and thus prefer to cut to the chase, Part I provides a necessary foundation for the later chapters.

Yes, this true story includes a certain level of accomplishment in the financial trading world, which will show that despite the

tremendous imperfections of humanity—and this trader specifically—anything is possible when years of extreme dedication, preparation, and motivation collide with that special window of
opportunity. Far more important however, is that these pages
describe a tale about passion, humility, tears, triumph, redemption,
and the constant struggle between humanity and the pursuit of ever-
elusive perfection. Just as trading mirrors life, life mirrors trading.
Succeed at one, and you'll likely succeed at the other. And if, when we
reach the end of our virtual journey together, these words increase
your perspective on life as much as it does on trading, we'll call it a
mission accomplished.

Hold on tight as we witness the good, the bad, and the ugly. In the
end however, as with the gift of life itself, it was and remains all good as
you witness the unrelenting grace of God.

Acknowledgments

Where do I begin? I'll start with the two easy ones: my lord and savior Jesus Christ and my beloved wife, Debra, who so often bore the risk, brunt, and reward of my decisions. Without this incredible team, I wouldn't be breathing today. Together, they held me up during my most difficult times and stood beside me during better days.

Yes, I'm a follower of Jesus Christ. Perhaps better said, call me a forever bumbling, stumbling, always-battling-with-his-own-humanity, too-much-left-to-work-on Christian. And although you won't find me "bible-thumping" my way through these pages, I've lived long enough and have personally witnessed specific life events such that there is no debate in my mind as to whether God exists and who Jesus truly is. For those with differing religious views, I love you beyond that which you'll ever know and look forward to our virtual journey together.

As for my wife, Debra, although I touch on her incredible love, support, and patience in various segments, I could easily write another book about what she's meant to my life. Simply put, I've been richly blessed with the ability to journey life's ups and downs alongside my best friend and confidant, one who loves me despite all my human flaws.

The next two acknowledgments are also easy: our two daughters, Courtney and Chelsea (listed sequentially by date of arrival only!). They've likely taught me more than I've taught them. And yes, the apples don't fall far from the tree, which as we all know can be both a blessing and a curse, depending on which of my characteristics were passed on and to whom. They've both reached incredible heights in their young lives, while persevering through their own struggles as they continue to discover their place in this world. In Chelsea's case, she was diagnosed with type 1 diabetes at age 10, which was a devastating blow to us all and meant that she'd be forever dependent on doctors, needles, and insulin pumps. Since then, she's provided an incredible inspiration to me and others, as she's persevered to become valedictorian and an accomplished musician despite her hardship. She's also been the direct inspiration for our work with the American Diabetes Association and other charities, which receive a portion of the proceeds from our trading educational videos and services.

None of this, of course, would be possible without my parents, Betty and Burnie, who reared and guided me through some difficult early years, as well as my grandparents. In particular, my maternal grandfather, Frederick, had an especially strong influence in my young life prior to his passing in 1983, as did his wife, my grandmother Miriam, who—through my parents—would later provide me with a gift in her dying days that would provide a safe harbor for me and my family when life's sea got stormy.

On the industry front, although I admittedly learned the business through personal experience and trial and error, a few standouts have accompanied me during various phases of my journey. This list includes Dr. Brett Steenbarger, whose *The Psychology of Trading* 2003 work I consider to be among the best trading books ever written and who supported my initial efforts to begin publicly blogging my daily trading journal. Others include Larry Connors, Linda Raschke, Damon Pavlatos, and Pat Lafferty, all of whom have supported me over the years either by providing necessary infrastructure or simply as peers and friends.

With respect to the latter, there's an interesting dilemma for those of us who have found ourselves inadvertently placed in positions of perceived industry leadership, either through performance or other credible means. Although many look to us for guidance, it can be quite challenging and, frankly, a bit lonely when we find ourselves in need of our own sympathetic ear or shoulder on which to lean. At those times, a strong peer network of those who truly "get it" becomes a lifesaver.

I'd also like to acknowledge the initial 2009 "Jellie" trading team— which you'll read about more in Part IV—for their help in refining one of the more unique educational trading experiences ever crafted. Simply putting up with me for eight weeks (336 hours!) should earn them some kind of medal of valor.

Last, this book would not be possible, nor its final chapters complete, if not for the herculean efforts of James Koutoulas, John

Roe, Greg Collett, and the Commodity Customer Coalition, which was created in late 2011 as the result of the MF Global bankruptcy that adversely affected tens of thousands of small business ranchers, farmers, hedgers, and traders. This team, and James in particular, was directly responsible for speeding the safe return of our assets that had been wrongfully taken during a very unfortunate time in this wonderful industry's life. Special heartfelt thanks go to Sandy Meyer and John Norquay, two dear friends who were placed in my path just prior to that tumultuous period and who helped me maintain some sort of personal and spiritual balance. Were our meetings simply happenstance or coincidence? Not in a million years.

To you all, I am eternally grateful for the gracious love and support you've provided me.

Introduction

In December 2007, at the age of 46 and after numerous starts, failures, restarts, and distractions, I decided to take a drastically different approach to my on-again off-again passion of trading equity index futures. Although successful by most standards, I believed that my results were simply not reflective of a far deeper potential, similar to an iceberg that has a significant proportion of its mass below the water's surface. Further, because I was only a few years away from the half-century mark with a retirement nest egg that in my view was less than optimal due primarily to a splintered focus over the years, I had a growing need to maximize opportunity in such a way that would provide longer-term financial security for my family.

In addition, as a multitasking trader, columnist, and trading educator with a deep personal conviction that people should develop self-sufficient financial management skills to the extent time and circumstance permit, I believed that I was becoming the proverbial jack of all these trades as it related to the financial markets yet master of none. Add a growing irritation with naysayers who didn't understand the true *business* of trading and suggested that trading was irresponsible gambling or that any degree of market success was either impossible to attain or due solely to dumb luck, and I felt a growing desire to "walk the talk."

The "Race"

My solution? Dedicate myself for an extended period of time—in this case, one year—in such an extreme and intense manner that I would eat, sleep, drink, dream, and live the world of intraday index futures trading with the goal of increasing my retirement fund by $1 million. The purposes of this "Race," as I would later label it and how I often refer to it throughout this book, were threefold. First, if accomplished, it would exponentially grow that modest nest egg such that financial security would be in reach and allow me the time and resource to pursue endeavors later in life that I truly enjoyed, including trading itself. Second, striving toward such a goal would provide a deep personal challenge to see how far I'd evolved my trading skills after roughly a decade of development. Third, doing so would provide a large sample size of factual data to show that successful trading was indeed possible, plausible, sustainable, and real.

As important as it is to understand the above contexts, it's equally important to consider what the Race *wasn't* intended to accomplish. It wasn't a means to get rich, nor was it a self-promoting publicity stunt. The first point will become clearer as you read through these pages because it relates to my view on money. Simply put, I believe that we're simply temporary stewards of whatever assets we've been blessed with and that financial gain or loss does only two things: it allows us to earn or spend "time" for both ourselves and others. At the same time, I believe that we have a responsibility to maximize and share the gifts with which we've been bestowed. Given an age in which it seems that we often can't trust anyone other than a select few to effectively grow and protect our assets, the burden of such responsibility often falls to oneself.

They say that time is money? Well, I'll turn the tables and say that money is time. For example, gains in the midst of one's trading career provide the time to withstand interim periods of equity drawdowns and plateaus as well as illnesses and loss of focus or ambition. Far more importantly, though, is that cumulative gains—once locked in and set aside—can provide the time to pursue other interests that can more directly affect and improve human life. Losses, on the other hand, simply turn the clock back. A modest loss might set one back a few days, whereas an occasional larger loss—a natural and expected part of life for those engaged in a business based on statistical probability and in which imperfect humans are involved—might set the calendar back several months. And although it took me many decades to more fully understand this way of perceiving time, it helped me immensely during periods of both rapid asset accumulation and financial hardship.

A Motivational Carrot

With respect to the effort being a publicity stunt, nothing can be farther from the truth. Before my million dollar exploits, I was already a public figure in the industry, with writing, speaking, and mentoring efforts resulting from earlier successes. Although I thoroughly enjoyed them, the result was often a divided market focus that never allowed me to reach my fullest potential as a trader. So, I temporarily went "off the industry grid" for a few years to prepare life, career, and body in such a way that I didn't have such distractions. As such, the Race and its goal became nothing more than an internal motivational carrot for me.

Despite the benefits of this self-imposed seclusion, it soon became clear that there were several substantial drawbacks to pursuing my objective in a vacuum. First, I had no day-to-day accountability of my actions to others. Second, I had no readily available means of peer support. Third, as I realized that my true grasp of trading was reaching a state where several critical light bulbs were clicking simultaneously, I had a growing desire to share my observations with others *in real time*. The chosen solution was to begin an unadvertised online journal in the spirit of the movie *Julie & Julia* (2009) that, although released more than a year after I'd begun my journal, tells a similar tale of an individual who set a specific and personal challenge, and then invited the world to watch her failures and successes through her daily blogging. In the movie, Julie Powell (played by Amy Adams), decides to cook in one year every recipe Julia Child (played by Meryl Streep), included in her 1961 book, *Mastering the Art of French Cooking*, and in doing so decides to write a blog to motivate herself and document her progress. As I would later describe in my journal, the post of which is included in these pages, I found the similarities to my life downright eerie.

As such, the second half of this Race—as well as life beyond it—was chronicled live in painstaking detail beginning in July 2008 and witnessed by thousands of traders who read daily journal entries, watched a live countdown clock, and interacted with me at donmillerjournal.blogspot.com, a website that would later evolve into donmillerblog.com. And although the journal picks up the effort in midform, the remaining six months and continuing tailwind will take us on a $1.5 million journey of their own, the magnitude of which I didn't fully realize or appreciate until I began compiling the material for this book.

How This Book Is Organized

The content of this book is, for the most part, laid out chronologically, beginning with a never-before-seen overview in Part I of my early life experiences and career successes and misfires that formed necessary building blocks for my later years. The rest of the story is told primarily through approximately 100 detailed trading journal entries made between 2008 and 2012. Part II contains more than 70 detailed journal entries written during the latter half of 2008. Parts III through VII then highlight subsequent periods, including additional key entries made from 2009 to 2012 that reflect continued trading, further discoveries, my plan for *not* joining the majority who let significant short-term income disappear, a desire to give back to the industry through charity and trader education, some fun with various recorded trading sessions, and the MF Global saga that shook the futures industry—and this trader—to its very cores.

To illustrate and get us started, here's my initial journal post from July 2008.

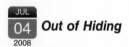

Out of Hiding

Where does one begin after a $2\frac{1}{2}$ year break from the public eye? As some of you may know, February 2006 was my last public post after years of teaching traders and writing for various trading publications and websites. Two and a half years. Gas prices were a heckuva lot lower, and the Celtics were pre-Garnett.

And while I had planned on remaining "off the radar" until the beginning of 2009, I want to begin sharing the revelations I've discovered that have taken my trading to a completely new paradigm, as well as start a formal logging of daily thoughts, trades, and results. And yes, as I've always done in the past, I'll post actual results . . . good, bad, ugly, **and fully supported by trading records**.

As has been the case in my past "public" life, this will be a completely no-hype site. I hate it, period. I'm a trader . . . pure and simple . . . and consider the ethical portion of this business to be more important than any other aspect of trading. The sole purpose of my posts will be to share observations from one person's perspective for those who choose to follow my journey to consider. So let the journey begin anew.

Although the journaling effort was intentionally unadvertised, it soon became evident how avalanches begin. What started as a small snowball of onlookers would quickly grow into a full-speed avalanche that would later propel the site toward one of the top-visited trading sites, landing it on two industry top 10 lists of trading blogs.

To this day, I'm not sure why interest grew the way it did. Perhaps it's why reality shows do so well on TV. For a while, I even thought that it might be because—like watching NASCAR races—some enjoyed watching octane-fueled high-risk and high-reward efforts that include periods of crashes and carnage. Yet although I can tell you, based on interactions with journal onlookers, that a tiny handful did come with such motives or, even worse, challenged my intentions, integrity, or actual results, or tried in various ways to mentally defeat me, the vast majority—and they numbered in the thousands—were supportive beyond belief. As it would turn out, and this may seem highly ironic, I soon discovered that I needed *both* groups if I were to have a legitimate chance of successfully reaching my goal. Further, as I now look back, it's clear that I needed that small number of detractors even more, as they clearly served to strengthen my resolve. To all of you, I thank you and wish you well.

Intention and Use of the Trading Journal Entries

As you review the journal entries, which span a five-year period, here are a few critical points to put them in proper perspective and help maximize their use. First, like this trader and author, there will be imperfections. For example, I'm confident that the moment the electronic or tangible ink of this book is dry, I'll wish I had included something else, said something in a slightly different way, or included different journal entries. Frankly, choosing from among more than 1,100 journal entries to include in this book was difficult at best, and I went to painstaking levels to try to provide a representative balance of varied market days, performance results, and topics. Some of the selections were chosen based on feedback from readers who found certain passages to be particularly useful, and others were selected based on timing that matched the intensity level at which I was trading that varied over the years as market conditions and life priorities evolved.

You'll also notice a general evolution of the blog over time. For example, the initial posts were intended to provide a foundation and perspective for future detailed notes, and they include my thoughts on several "light bulb" moments that had occurred in recent times and taken my trading to a new level. Then, in later years, you'll see a general shift in content as I began to increase my focus on trader motivation, education, and advocacy. In the end, any gaps before, during, or after any of the chosen selections can be filled by accessing the online blog.

In addition, keeping in mind that the journal entries are just that—entries in my personal diary intended primarily for my own use and concept reinforcement—may be the best advice to provide proper perspective. Years ago, I remember an episode of M∗A∗S∗H in which Sidney Freedman, played by Allan Arbus, wrote a letter to Sigmund Freud as a form of self-therapy. Similarly, my diary entries— including those that seem to address the public—were primarily directed inward and intended to keep me focused, centered, and on track. Another relevant analogy appears in *The Psychology of Trading* (2003) when Dr. Brett Steenbarger refers to the notion of an "Internal Observer" to help objectively view one's mind-set and stay balanced. My "observer" just so happened to have access to a keyboard. And, if no one had ever stumbled across the blog, I'd have likely written most entries exactly the same way.

The journal entries are for the most part identical to those initially appearing in the online journal, corrected for typos and condensed in some cases for brevity or clarity. The entries also include a newly inserted 15-minute chart of the Standard & Poor's E-Minis (U.S. day session with a 15-period simple moving average) for each day on which market action is referenced to provide a general idea about the day's rhythm and put any price-related comments in at least some perspective. In such cases, you'll notice that each chart actually shows *three* days of action—including the day prior and the day subsequent to the one journaled—to increase perspective of the day's price action. Keep in mind that each chart merely provides a backdrop for general reference and that it would be a futile and dangerous exercise to try to precisely match comments or trade rationale with such limited information because (1) I don't always elaborate on why I did what I did (remember, I was largely writing to myself); (2) I use other tools, such as the NYSE TICK and Three Line Break charts, that space simply doesn't permit to be printed here; (3) many other resources are available that address the technical aspects of trading; (4) some of the notes reflect trading that occurred on the Eurex Exchange or outside of the U.S. day session for which I haven't reproduced charts here; and (5) there may be nonmarket issues and priorities, or simply an unfocused or tired mind-set, that didn't allow me to make certain trades that, based on the chart, may in hindsight appear obvious. *If you've ever traded while living any sort of a life, you'll thoroughly understand that last point!* Nevertheless, the charts should provide some perspective about the type of day discussed.

In many instances, I wrote the journal entries at the end of the day; at other times, I kept time-stamped shorthand notes during the trading hours. The Appendix at the back of this book lists some of the shorthand and acronyms that I use. You'll also find various journal entries that are more topic-oriented or introspective than others— I wrote those on the weekends—as well as witness an evolution of creativity over time, including portraying the month-end equity graphs in such a way as to reinforce both motivation and humility. (Note: I began to use video for many journal entries beginning in 2009, which obviously don't appear here but remain accessible on the site.) Also, and with apologies to my fifth-grade grammar teacher, you'll often come across various grammatical "licenses"—including the lack of complete sentence structure and omission of the term *I*— because my primary concern was to simply document my thoughts. Again, keeping in mind that you're simply viewing my diary "over my shoulder" should help place each journal entry as well as the entire compilation in proper perspective.

Last, as should be the case when viewing any market data relating to shorter intervals, I strongly encourage you to keep the "micro" writings of each hour and day in perspective as they relate to the larger "macro" views of events and rhythms occurring in the market and in my life. Otherwise, like a market chart, any single entry will be completely meaningless unless placed in the proper context. After all, it's the balancing of micro and macro events that will tell the complete story and help you better understand my mind-set as we journey together through time.

Journaling and Performance

As I look back, I see that the journal helped me stay more focused and disciplined than I would have been otherwise. At the same time, documenting my thoughts often seemed to neutralize the intense market focus by allowing me to use a different part of my brain. Maintaining the journal also provided me with a highly productive outlet with which to vent during times of frustration, which undoubt-edly helped me constructively redirect any negative energy toward improved focus and performance. And although journal onlookers may have grown weary of an abundant use of sports and movies analogies at the time, my occasional comparisons to boxers, Olympic swimmers, and other athletes or competitive endeavors provided me with a strong motivational mechanism that helped me rise from failure and keep pushing myself.

I can't emphasize these benefits of the journal enough. There is no doubt in my mind that the most optimal trading periods in my career occurred specifically during those times when I had the discipline and time to journal my trading thoughts every day.

With respect to any perceived educational content relating to specific trading techniques, it's simply impossible and naive to believe that one could learn to effectively trade by simply reading a book, just as it's ridiculous to try to learn how to fly a plane by watching *Top Gun*. Such a task is better left to quality trader development programs designed for just that purpose. And although one tool includes the trader training videos documenting the trail of the beta "Jellie" trading team discussed in Part IV—with a portion of any proceeds continuing to go to charity—there are, of course, other reputable programs as well. These chronicles are in no way intended to infer that any particular program—including the Jellie program—is best.

Balancing Credibility and Humility

A primary concern when deciding whether or not to write this book was that despite the best of intentions, personal ego or pride might slip in. Although I've gone to great lengths during the editing process to refine and filter content to minimize such risk, it's possible that some such residue remains, even if simply inferred. An extremely fine line separates the good that comes from documenting the lessons learned from a credible experience from the bad, where such sharing, if gone unchecked, could morph into an internal self-indulgent exercise with no outward benefit. Similarly, there's a thin line between a trader's confidence that is required to successfully profit from the markets and a cockiness that over time leads to complacency and losses.

Because I believe that author integrity and the credibility of these chronicles are paramount, I've taken some unique steps in compiling these materials. For example, I believed that it was paramount to share specific financial performance results at both the macro and micro levels so that readers can place the events in proper perspective, including the entire 10-year period beginning in late 2001 when I began trading futures to October 31, 2011. My reasons for doing so are threefold. First, because much of my journal accompanies a period and fund in the late 2000s that we will appropriately micro-analyze at times in terms of performance in Parts II through VI, I believe that it is necessary to also provide an overview of (1) all accounts and (2) the early periods of my futures trading, including those during which I suffered losses due to the typical learning curve "tuition" that most experience, an imbalanced career mix, and an inappropriate transaction cost structure as discussed in Part I. Second, providing a full view would minimize any risk of inadvertently cherry-picking funds or periods relating solely to positive results while ignoring the rest. Third, providing complete disclosure is simply the right thing to do in an industry in which transparency seems to be sorely lacking at times.

Further, to ensure the validity of the performance data contained in this book and given that we now apparently live in an unfortunate era in which even brokerage statements can be doctored without detection (as occurred at PFG Best in 2012), I've provided the publisher with an affidavit supporting the content contained in these pages. I've taken all these steps because in my view nothing less should be acceptable from those of us who—willingly or unwillingly—have found ourselves in a position of perceived industry leadership, for we must hold ourselves to a higher standard of integrity and account-ability. Of course, in the end, we'll all stand accountable one day before God, and He won't care one iota about bravado, book sales, or blog viewer volumes. And that will be the only opinion that matters.

Finally, just to ensure that I cover all appropriate bases, please note as you read my journal that *past performance is not necessarily indicative of future performance,* which as we'll see will hold true for both extraordinary and suboptimal results during smaller time intervals.

Bamboo Trees and Windows

Before we begin our journey, it's important to emphasize that although it's technically correct that my peak career performance period occurred during a relatively brief period when several windows of opportunity opened simultaneously—including career, family, market conditions, and trading skill evolution—the deeper truth is that untold years of preparation ultimately allowed me to open and step through the window. This concept is not unlike that of a professional gymnast, whose Olympic routine may only last minutes yet requires years of frustrating sweat and toil with little immediate tangible result. Another analogy is that of the Chinese bamboo tree, which doesn't break ground for several years; then, it finally breaks the surface and proceeds to grow at a highly accelerated rate, often exceeding dozens of feet in just a few weeks. For the bamboo, though, those early years were necessary to establish a strong root system that could both propel and support the eventual growth. We see this concept again and again throughout our lives.

Likewise, much of a trader's career can be spent "underground," which was certainly the case for me, and a trader can experience periods of slowing growth near maturity. Fortunately, trading the financial markets—as we explore in later chapters—is all about maximizing opportunity when the window opens while minimizing the downside when it closes. And unlike other endeavors or professions where monetary rewards are spread evenly over time, much of a trader's peak earnings come in spurts when those windows of opportunity open. The rewards come when, after years of mental and physical preparation, the trading "gymnast" is focused and, after hundreds of falls and bruises or broken bones, finally nails that gold-medal-winning triple twist before his or her body outgrows the ability to handle the required dexterity or before a personal choice is made to pursue other endeavors.

So it was with this journey. There were hundreds of virtual broken bones before, and a few sprains after. Included in the latter are the effects of the May 2010 "Flash Crash" and the 2011 MF Global broker meltdown as well as a personal choice to protect accumulated gains and balance my life and income stream with endeavors unrelated to trading performance.

A Book about Trading?

This journal is as much about life as it is trading, and you'll see this theme reinforced again and again throughout these pages. Although it took me many years to understand how intertwined life and trading are, my hope is that you'll grasp these connections far sooner than I did and at far less cost in the context of lost time or resources.

If you've stumbled across this detailed journal looking for trading insights, I hope you won't be disappointed. Yet don't be surprised if the book you thought you'd read solely to try to become a better trader instead helps improve your perspective of trading as it relates to life itself, even if just a little bit.

Before we can talk about bamboos, windows of opportunity, and trading journals, we must first begin with a brief overview of how all this came to being, including some initial life gifts and obstacles.

PART

I

Beginnings

March 10, 1961. Yes, to put these chronicles of recent trading years in proper perspective, we must first go back to the day I took my first breath. Long before we can talk about the failures and redemptions of my trading life, we must first journey through the years that would shape my view on life and mold a certain degree of perseverance that would become paramount in later years.

Actually, we must go back two additional years, to 1959, because although we all came into this world through no asking or effort of our own, I consider myself particularly blessed given that two years prior to my arrival, my parents had experienced a devastating stillbirth. And although they've never discussed those trying days much with me, I do know that the baby was male and that my mother carried him to full term.

For many parents, such a devastating life event would understandably end attempts to further expand the family tree right there. Yet largely because my parents didn't want my sister, Judy, who had been born two years prior, to be an only child as my mother had been, they set aside their doubts and fears to try once again. Of course, life is never easy, and as they prepared for my arrival, my mother had the bad fortune of coming down with the chicken pox, which would complicate the delivery. Nevertheless, on March 10, 1961, and certainly through no effort of my own, I was brought into the world via a cesarean section in such a way that I was effectively isolated from the virus. Of course, I had no inkling at that time as to the events that led to that day, but later discoveries of my brother's premature death and my parents' subsequent perseverance would clearly help shape my views on life and its accompanying struggles.

Early Tunnels of Life

It soon became evident that a mix of struggles, accomplishments, and setbacks would accompany me throughout my life, with most of the setbacks during my youth surfacing in the form of health battles due to a compromised immune system. Although I survived the birth without complication, my first 10 years would include multiple visits to doctors and hospitals as the result of an asthmatic condition and various allergies that required frequent shots and occasional stays in oxygen tents. Of course, I also picked up all the typical childhood illnesses at that time, including the mumps, measles, and—yes, finally—the chicken pox in the second grade.

My teen years were equally challenging for my parents and myself as I seemed to be a magnet for a variety of obstacles, setbacks, and embarrassments, some self-inflicted, others outside of my control. Although I hated going through what my future wife would later call these "tunnels of life," the experiences served to install a certain degree of perseverance and perspective pertaining to the concept of "time" that would later serve me well in my future trading years. Examples of my early "tunnels" include:

- Repeatedly being ridiculed as the son of the assistant superintendent, often having to sit on the floor on the bus.
- Shooting at the wrong basket in a junior high school basketball game. *One not-so-funny aspect of that event was that I missed the first shot, rebounded it, and made the next one. Imagine the official scorer trying to figure out if I should be credited with a rebound!*
- Being hazed as a high school freshman during basketball road trips.
- Bombing in front of a full auditorium while performing a trumpet solo for which I hadn't adequately practiced. *(This one was clearly a self-inflicted wound that would later have strong trading parallels.)*
- Having any degree of success, including winning the sixth grade science fair, challenged by a few nitwits as being illegitimate due to my father's position. *(Another eerie parallel to later trading successes.)*

- Missing half of my junior and senior high school years due to an unrelenting mononucleosis-type virus.
- Tearing my ankle ligaments as I tried to return to basketball during my senior year only to miss our school's run toward the state championship.
- Being ridiculed again, this time in college because I refused to drink or do drugs in an era when many attended school solely for that purpose.

I could list more, yet my point is like so many others, I was faced with various challenges that felt so very painful at the time, yet in later years would seem nothing more than insignificant bumps in the road thanks to the combination of time and perspective. Although I could list various successes such as honor societies, eagle scout attainment, and others, I prefer to emphasize those aspects that most contributed to shaping my future years: the tunnels.

A Late Bloomer

Another aspect to my life that would become clear was that I seemed to be what many would call a late bloomer. Perhaps it was because my mind or body simply needed more time to mature than others or perhaps because I underestimated the required preparation time required to accomplish anything significant in life. *With respect to the latter, one of my greatest weaknesses to this very day is a general lack of patience, and this Achilles' heel has repeatedly gotten me into trouble over the years, especially as I began my trading career.* It would also become clear that I'd typically emerge from each tunnel stronger and with greater vibrancy and desire to succeed as well as an improved perspective on life.

Said another way, I loved coming back from defeat. For example, years after shooting at the wrong basket, being hazed on road trips, tearing my ankle, and essentially lacking any innate basketball talent, I'd eventually worked my tail off to become a fairly decent player in my college years. One example occurred during the summer of 1982, when I returned to my hometown to score 27 points on a "couldn't-miss" 13-for-14 shooting night where I outscored, outhustled, and generally outplayed some of my very peers who had hazed me in prior years, a few of whom left the court that night in utter disbelief. This late-blooming trait would go on to accompany me throughout my life and especially throughout my trading career.

Early Vocations

From the outset, I was a finance guy. As early as age 10, there are pictures of me at our kitchen table helping my father balance his books with a giant calculator that took up half the table. I also loved brainteasers and jigsaw puzzles, and I was pretty good at them. *To this day, both my mother and wife will tell you that I can find a missing puzzle piece in seconds.* As high school evolved into college and college evolved into early career years, finance would dictate much of my life in the context of initial vocations. In 1983, I graduated from a business college summa cum laude with a major in accounting, and after rejecting offers from a number of large accounting firms, I accepted a position with a large corporation in the telecommunications industry that emphasized the early and continuous development of future executive leaders.

From there, I spent approximately 16 years climbing the corporate ladder in two firms and living in a variety of places, and at 37, I was blessed to have reached a career level with a high degree of scope and responsibility. From a corporate perspective, I had it all, including position, stature, a company car, and an executive home. I had even recently completed an aggressive two-year Executive MBA program at a leading university. Still, I felt that something was missing. The professional spark that had ignited my earlier career years was no longer there, and I felt that if I was going to make a career change, I'd better do it soon before time as age would zap the energy required to pursue a new field.

It was during these soul-searching years that the Internet and access to the financial markets were combining to provide an inviting combination for one who embraced the combination of finance, computers, numbers, brainteasers, and challenge. The more I learned about the challenges and possibilities of trading the financial markets for a primary or secondary career, the more I realized that doing so would reflect in the ultimate pay for performance endeavor, where one could be compensated solely based upon one's ability. *As I would later tell people, though, it's also one of the only fields where if you perform poorly, you pay your employer!* I'd grown tired of modest cost-of-living raises amid occasional promotions, and getting paid 100 percent based on performance seemed to be an optimal compensation structure for one who was confident of his abilities while also satisfying a strong entrepreneurial craving that had accompanied me throughout my life. Said another way, "I was bitten by the bug."

Don't Quit Your Day Job

*At this point in our journey, if you feel a similar urge to leave your current stable vocation to pursue trading the financial markets, **think long, hard, and long again**. The rocky path I'm about to lay out is meant to fully disclose the ramifications of my choice, which although ultimately leading to success in later years, resulted in a difficult, soul-searching journey that included believing I'd made the worst decision of my life.*

In 1999, at the age of 38 as primary wage earner and father of a young family I had established a six-month track record to prove to my wife that I could make at least as much as I was making in my current career as the result of part-time trading. Believing that my trading results had been suboptimized due to the lack of full-time focus, I made the decision to leave my safe career as a corporate executive to enter the world of trading on a full-time basis.

The immediate result? Well, in financial terms, during the first month, I lost everything I'd earned from trading in the previous several months as I broke every rule in the book trying to force profits. Far more importantly, in life terms, I felt I'd lost anything and everything I gained in 38 years, including the near-term and long-term future of those most dear to me: my wife of 14 years and my two children, ages 7 and 10.

I can't stress enough the inner turmoil that I experienced during those initial months, which was **only** countered by the even greater powerful support of love, family, and God. Despite my personal selfishness and shortsightedness that placed my own career aspirations ahead of what was likely best for my family at the time, grace and support abounded everywhere and forever changed my life's priorities. And although much of that time was admittedly a blur, I do recall hitting my lowest low—what I call my personal abyss—one night as I fell on my knees in tears and asked God to help a soul who had gotten too far ahead of himself for his own good.

Out of the Abyss

The good thing—if there is one—about feeling that you've hit rock bottom, is that it's, well, the **bottom**. In other words, there's only one direction one can move from the bottom, and that's up. And although I believed at the time that the climb out of the abyss was slower than I'd like, I can now say with the utmost confidence that the series of events that would ultimately pull me out of life's low began to occur at startling speed.

These events begin and end with my family, and specifically, with my wife, Debra, who had always supported every one of my career decisions, regardless of relocation and personal uprooting. She was—and continues to be—my rock and my best friend. And what a rock she was during that time as she convinced me all was not lost, that she would still love me even if we were dirt poor, and that things would work out. Then came a call out of the blue from my parents, who sensed something was wrong, and who offered me their vacant house on Cape Cod *(or as known in these parts, simply the Cape)* should I choose to downsize and return to my New England roots. The home had actually previously belonged to my grandparents, yet it had stood vacant in recent years, with my aging grandmother living with my parents during her final years. Ironically, it was also a home that Gram wanted to keep in the family, yet one that she knew my folks would likely sell upon her passing.

As I was still digesting my self-served humble pie, and despite an ironclad son-versus-parent independence streak I had intentionally forged, I considered the offer and chose to fly back to Boston in the dead of winter to check out the house which had been closed for a few years. The next sequence of events simply border on indescribable, if not surreal.

First, the day was a Friday, and as I had traded poorly that day, I just wanted to sulk. Second, I hate flying, and the two Midwest cities from which I'd have to depart and change planes were experiencing near-blizzard conditions. Nevertheless, just as I was about to postpone the trip for these reasons and more, I felt a Presence that just said, "Get on the darn plane." And so, I did, cursing internally all the way.

I somehow managed to make it to Boston that night without ripping the armrests out of their sockets, and once I landed, I decided to see Gram at my parents' home before heading to the Cape the next morning to check out the house. Although healthy most of her life, Gram had gone downhill quickly in recent days, and I had to communicate with her via a whiteboard that simply said something like, "house" and "checking it out." And although I didn't know if she fully understood me, she seemed to grasp at least some of what I was saying.

The next morning, I headed to the Cape house, which was small and musty as expected. As we were pulling back the carpets and I was internally deciding to make the move, the phone rang with news that Gram had passed away at the age of 98, but not before—according to firsthand accounts—smiling for the first time in weeks and waving good-bye. Simply put, she was at peace, and to this day, I sense with great conviction that she held on until she could give her grandson and his family her most prized possession.

Yes, this book is about trading. Yet none of these remaining pages would be possible had it not been for the "rescue" team that circled and rallied around me, a team that would forever change my views on the importance of a strong network of family and friends.

Evolving Perspectives

The next few years would bring about additional challenges, including selling our newly built executive dream home for a loss, relocating my family to an older house about one-third the size, and dealing with two major health crises. On the health front, during one four-month stretch, we almost lost Deb to a massively burst appendix and subsequent infection, and then we learned that our younger daughter, Chelsea, would have to spend the rest of her life dealing with type 1 diabetes. There were also the continual starts and misfires of my trading career as stress, lack of focus, commitment, and skill refinement combined to produce inconsistent results that didn't really amount to much and that led to a growing sense that trading would perhaps best be suited as a secondary pursuit with a reduced stress level versus primary source of income.

I soon discovered that, for me, optimal trading had its strongest probability of success if I had another revenue stream—such as my spouse's wages or other supplemental income—to put food on the table as long as such effort didn't impede on my ability to monitor and participate in the markets. *Over the years, I've frankly found that balancing the need for undivided trading focus with managing a separate income stream to lessen any performance-related stress to be one of a trader's greatest paradoxes.* As such, I chose to maintain my corporate connections and often found myself consulting or working part-time in my former industry as I continued to hone my trading skills. And such was the case throughout the early to mid-2000s as we were able to better balance trading and nontrading income flows and resurrect our former years of stability and hope for the future.

During this time of improved balance and perspective, the earlier seeds of trading failure and frustration were slowly but steadily beginning to establish a root structure that would later bear fruit.

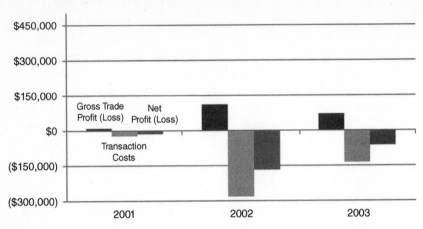

Past performance is not necessarily indicative of future performance.

FIGURE 1.1   Futures Account Performance (All Accounts), 2001–2003

Along the way, I'd also "graduated" from successful stock and exchange-traded fund trading—where I'd earned more than $300,000 in 2000—to equity index futures in 2001. The move to futures trading, although reflecting a natural progression, was clearly my most difficult largely due to an inappropriate transaction cost structure for one who traded frequently and who used multiple trade entries and exits to manage risk. Specifically, as shown in Figure 1.1, although my precommission results were positive, my net results in the first three years of futures trading were negative.

The negative net results were due to implementing an effective "wholesaling" business approach, yet doing so while incurring transaction costs (commissions) at retail prices. As any business manager will tell you, this is the sure ticket to net financial loss. As such, I researched various options to reduce costs and eventually discovered a startling fact that wasn't widely disclosed to the trading public by brokers: the ability to substantially cut costs by (1) leasing an exchange seat and (2) negotiating volume discounts. So, in early 2004 I began leasing an exchange seat and negotiating lower brokerage commissions. The result on my bottom line was immediate and profound, and by the end of the 2004, the results of the same strategy employed in the previous three years were as shown in Figure 1.2.

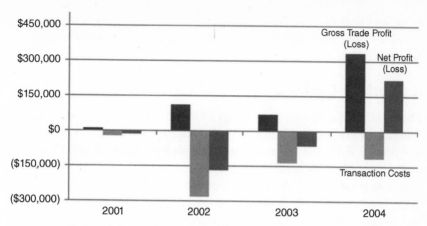

Past performance is not necessarily indicative of future performance.

FIGURE 1.2   Futures Account Performance (All Accounts), 2001–2004

As satisfied as I was with the cost structure changes and results, I admit I was equally dismayed that I had to discover the solution much on my own and at great initial cost. The last thing brokers want to see is reduced commission revenue, so wholesale pricing isn't typically something that's advertised. Yet, as will be the theme throughout these pages, **please learn from my mistakes**. If learning the details of my journey does nothing other than encourage current traders to pursue lower-cost options via negotiated commissions and exchange leases, these writings will have paid for themselves in spades.

During this time I also learned of another little-known fact: the ability to actively manage one's retirement fund via a self-directed futures option provided by various custodians. Although I clearly don't advocate such an option for traders who haven't acquired the skill, such an alternative may be a bona fide alternative for proven traders who desire to take control of their longer-term portfolio. In my case, I believed that my skill had evolved to a point where I could do just that, and as such, my investment strategy evolved into one that emphasized having a nonmarket income stream to provide immediate cash flow and pay bills while using my improving trading skills to actively manage my retirement fund for the future. In fact, such a strategy is similar to the one used by comedian Jay Leno, who once indicated that he used income received from stand-up comedy to pay expenses, while using his television revenues to build his retirement nest egg.

A Sporting Chance

The next few years would result in a fairly effective mix of trading and non-market-related income, and the balance seemed to be just what the doctor ordered after the turmoil and misfires of 2001 through 2003. Nevertheless, as 2007 was drawing to a close and the trading motor seemed to be running smoothly, I still believed that I wasn't living up to my true potential as a trader as the result of various distractions and thus chose to significantly step up the pace, intensity, and motivation. My solution was to dedicate myself in an extreme manner to see how far and fast I could grow my retirement fund, which by that time had grown slowly but steadily from about $247,000 at the beginning of 2001 to just over $700,000 by the end of 2007. My goal was simple: Put whatever trading skill I'd acquired squarely and fully on the line and aggressively grow my fund by $1 million in 12 months, as a part of a longer-term objective of attaining a $2.5 million balance from which we could draw in our waning years, while not relying on such income for immediate cash flow needs. Simply put, for someone who had taught, spoken, and written extensively about the financial markets, it was time for me to put up or shut up. Or, in the context of my earlier basketball struggles and ultimate success, it was time for me to set aside all the prior peer criticism, internal questioning, lack of preparation and discipline, initiation hazing, and torn ankles to have that 13-for-14 shooting night, if nothing else than to prove to myself what I believed I knew all along. It was time for me to take that sporting chance, synchronize my internal rhythm with that of the market, and leave it **all** on the court.

Speaking of sport, as we prepare to review the journal entries that make up much of the rest of this book, you'll notice that I firmly believe that trading the financial markets is highly analogous to a competitive performance sport, albeit a mental one. *In fact, we could likely take any sports axiom and by twisting a few words apply it to trading.* As such, I often used various sporting terms such as *races, fights,* and *comebacks* throughout 2008 to keep my mind appropriately focused and motivated. I also uncovered a few additional motivational tools and techniques as the result of playing poker and other life experiences that you'll discover as we move ahead. And although such references may at first appear on the corny side, you'll quickly learn how important these perspectives were in generating a sustained level of motivation that can often only come from within.

Ultimately, I believe that one has to discover what best drives one's inner self. For example, I know that in my case, I trade far better when energized, focused, motivated, aggressive, and at least slightly ticked off, even if it means manufacturing reasons to be ticked off. One strong example includes intentionally exaggerating the mental effect of losses, which are perfectly normal and an expected expense in a business where the lesser probability outcome will occur at times, whether that probability is statistical or simply the result of occasionally being off our game. This exaggeration and resulting personal anguish allows me to tighten up my game such that I can nip bad habits quickly, and you'll see this tendency throughout the journal. Said another way, I want to be the frog that's dropped in boiling water and jumps out versus the one placed in cool water that dies a slow death as the heat is slowly turned up. Although such a position may go against the traditional grain in the industry that dictates not trading on emotion, I can say with full conviction and based on years of records that I personally trade far worse when emotion and aggression are absent as opposed to channeling such aggression in a positive manner that's fully aligned with the market and counter to those trading **incorrectly** on emotion. *My guess is if you ask quarterback Tom Brady how he prepares for each game, he'll probably tell you that he's still ticked off at being a low draft choice and thus he has something to prove each and every day. For him, such a mind-set has paved his personal road to consistent greatness.*

Further, I firmly believe that if and when a trader has moved past the difficult learning curve stage, the only three things preventing success are focus, motivation, and simply showing up, especially during those "inconvenient" times when others are getting that extra hour of rest. *Been there, done that, and still visit the neighborhood from time to time.* For me, approaching trading as a mental sport isn't just a convenient analogy; rather, it's an absolutely necessary frame of mind. Otherwise, I'd simply be going through the motions and leaving far too much on the table, as I did at various points in my career.

So, let's lace up the shoes and review the detailed journal entries beginning in July 2008, at which point I was slightly ahead of the required $1 million pace and the game was beginning to heat up.

The 2008 "Race" Progress to Target

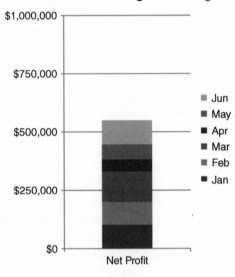

PART II

Journaling the Million Dollar Race

July 2008 Journal Excerpts

We'll begin with a few key journal entries that summarized recent discoveries and set the foundation for my trading at that time, as evidenced by the first post appropriately titled "The Cornerstone." Please take particular note of the referenced visualization chart, as it will be repeated at various times throughout these pages, including at the very end of the book. Consider it my metaphoric alpha and omega.

 **The Cornerstone**

JUL
04
2008

One of the things I did at the beginning of this year was to take a hard look at all my trading shortcomings. In doing so, I discovered that one of my greatest weaknesses was getting sloppy and away from my game plan after a period of significant equity growth. On most occasions, the result was a drawdown and equity ceiling—both real and perceived.

Yet a decade of history also showed that one of my greatest strengths has always been refocusing and coming back from such times, which is when I'd experienced my greatest levels of focus and performance. So, heading into 2008, I decided to do two things:

1. Get myself in the "comeback" mind-set in every moment of every trade of every day; and
2. Not look at my actual equity balance until June 30 and December 31.

For #1, I created the visualization chart shown in Figure 2.1.

What does the chart reflect? Well, the solid line reflects my actual equity curve over a period of time leading up to January 1, 2008—and this is key—**up to the point of the peak**. The subsequent sharp retracement line reflects a **fictional** and **exaggerated** significant drawdown, and the dotted line "rebound" reflects how I've traditionally traded after a drawdown.

So, as I entered the Race, I trained myself to believe that I had just experienced a devastating loss and was refocusing for the greatest comeback of all. Then day after day, I mentally placed myself at the trough of the "V" bottom just above "technical support" in every moment of every trade of every day. And although it took some training to turn fiction into firm belief, I can truly state that I believed this low point is where I would always stand on my equity curve.

As far as #2 and not looking at my balance, it was a pure cold-turkey move as I had always booked my P&L daily and reconciled my brokerage statement balance to my internal records. So, effective January 2008, I made it a point to simply view only the portion of my daily statement that contained the trades (to ensure I was flat) and the daily gain/loss and commissions (for booking purposes). Paraphrasing

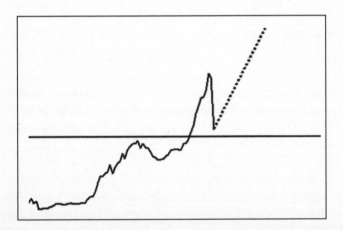

FIGURE 2.1   Visualization Chart

Dr. Brett Steenbarger in *The Psychology of Trading*, it's difficult—if not impossible—for one to trade **and** keep score. And yes, it was **extremely** difficult and painful at first, before eventually becoming routine.

Looking back, I can't begin to overstate what these two actions did to slay my inner demons and improve trading performance, and I encourage you to find your worst weaknesses in trading or life, acknowledge them, and **then take action to correct them**, no matter how crazy the tool may seem.

Why Has It Worked?

My midyear sanity check has my brain in high gear, especially as it relates to the chart mentioned in my last post in terms of "Why has it worked?" Here are a few thoughts in response:

- The bounce is similar to actual performance after draws. Essentially it's "been there, done that" and thus reflects concrete evidence that has evidently been burned into my brain to support the expected performance bounce.
- The chart reflects one of my all-time favorite setups: a reversion toward the mean—a.k.a. an initial pullback following a break to new highs—in a clear uptrend, albeit at ridiculous proportions. The fact that the chart is an equity curve and not a market chart makes no difference, for I've often found that life's charts are extremely similar those of the market. Consolidation breakouts, doldrum days, peaks and valleys . . . you get the point.
- By believing that the "eventual day from hell that's just around the corner" that used to plague my trading **has already occurred**, the likelihood that I'll self-implode due to some silly subconscious income-limiting belief has been greatly reduced. In fact, at this very moment, I'm looking at the chart frustrated that I just drew down that badly on Friday to prepare for the coming week. "How could it happen?" "What did or didn't I do?" "Back off from the next trade until darn sure it's the right high probability setup!" All soul-searching for Monday.
- It just "feels" right. I can't explain it, but it has made my trading feel more natural and unforced, and as a result I find myself holding good entries longer, withstanding more wiggles, and

trading larger sizes more naturally. Perhaps it's because I know—even without viewing the scorecard—that there's an underlying growth in capital such that has alleviated much of any former capital-related fear component. Who knows? All I can say is that it just feels as if the world is as it should be.

Someday, I'll share the actual results of this week, but that's for another day. I've got a comeback to focus on.

 *Poker Impacts*

Filling in some more missing pieces of the 30-month gap, I began playing small-stakes no-limit poker about a year ago, partly because I've always wanted to and partly because I thought I'd learned enough watching and studying it that I'd have a decent shot at winning from time to time. *Yes, I'm still competitive in the worst way . . . that hasn't changed over the last few years.* What I didn't realize, however, is that the subsequent experiences would have positive effects on my trading.

So, last summer, I started playing in a local league that awards points in weekly tournaments for final table players, with the winner getting 500 points, second place getting 250, and so on. Then, at the end of each quarter, the person with the most points gains entry into a Foxwoods tournament with the chance to win a few thousand dollars. It's a fun group led by a great guy *(thanks Jeff)* who taught me some of the early ropes.

Which leads me to my first poker/market comparison: Even in a small group of 20–30, the players reflect all segments of humanity, with strong parallels to market participants. Examples include the gamblers, the self-proclaimed know-it-alls, the bluffers, the sore losers, the sore winners . . . just like the market. And although I've always advocated that any serious trader read *The Tao of Poker* (Phillips 2003), it took experiencing cards firsthand to have some of the notions sink into this trader's stubborn brain.

Many of you know my trading strategies. However, at the poker table, I consider myself to be a simple, inexperienced amateur with one basic strategy: Play tight, quality hands the majority of the time, and vary from that only on occasion. It's essentially up to the other guy to figure out when I'm varying. And it's worked fairly well as I ended up winning this year's 1st-quarter event, and then finished in the money at the subsequent Foxwoods tourney, finishing 13th of about 120. *The winnings pretty much paid for gas and a few meals as the real money is finishing in the top five.*

OK, so what does this have to do with my trading? Here are a few reflections:

- Poker has magnified my personal trading weaknesses and in some way has transferred potential market blunders from my large S&P trades to small-scale poker losses (as in largest career S&P loss: $80K; largest poker loss to date: $650). Example: I stink when I'm tired. Period. Happens in poker all the time. I remember a few weeks ago when I was up strong in a cash game and then gave much of it away in one hand at 3am on a poorly read hand after a six-hour stint. And it seems that rein-forcement has subsequently reduced the number of times I've tried to trade tired in the market.

- You can't expect to win at poker—or the market—if you limit your time exposure, as probability requires time to play out in both cards and in the market. I still struggle with this in the market given nonmarket obligations, but I can say that I trade less now when I'm faced with a limited trading window vs. before I began my poker journey.

- Bet strong and **add to your position** when you have a strong hand, especially the "nuts," which in poker lingo means you have the best hand possible. This notion has had the greatest positive influence on my trading, as size at the right time matters in both poker and trading and can generate a month's worth of income on a single trade or hand. However, I will say that I'm better at this in my trading vs. poker, giving the occasional necessity to hide one's hand strength in poker. At the table, I still struggle with deciding when to go for it vs. hiding. *No need to hide hand strength when trading the S&Ps electronically!*

  In fact, I credit poker reinforcement directly for my size and trade management last Thursday, when I bought heavy within a point of the market's morning puke point and had my best take in several years in about a 10-min window. *I could almost hear Jeff saying, "Bet those trips strong."*

  Of course, **sensing** with high probability that one has the nuts and **actually having it** are two different things. At least in trading, there are position-reducing stop actions that can take effect when wrong. In no-limit hold 'em, if you're wrong . . . see ya. *I still find myself calling a poker all-in with what often turns out to be the second-best possible hand. Happened yesterday when I had Aces over Kings and didn't put my opponent on three Jacks. Lost a bit on that one. Another time yesterday, I had A–K and the flop—I kid you not—came A–A–A. Once-in-a-lifetime hand. The problem was there was no money in the pot and just two of us . . . one was the Big Blind with a likely lousy hand, who checked it down to the river where I couldn't even get a small value bet called. Imagine, having one of **the** best hands you can have and getting zippo for it.* Which brings me to another thought . . .

- Tilt. It happens at both the table and market. Advantage unemotional pros. Enough said. And lastly . . .

- Playing poker has made trading "feel" easy **in comparison**. Any decent card player knows that the element of short-term luck is a key factor in poker. "Short-term luck/long-term skill" is the winning combination cited by most poker pros. And although on **rare** occasions "luck" occurs in the markets, such as being long when a surprise interest rate cut is announced, the "luck" factor is pretty much absent in the trading world.

   This luck factor still aggravates me to death in my poker game. Like anyone, I've drowned at the river *(losing on the last common card dealt)* in noncash tournament games by some amateur who called my trip Aces with a 1 percent hand but catches runner-runner to fill out his 2–6 straight. I've then seen myself morph into the very "sore loser" that I used to criticize, spewing something like "You called with that garbage?"

   Yet those are the gamblers playing with either none of their personal cash at stake in free tournaments, or playing cash games for a very short time before they bust. Thankfully, the market is a true cash game where the gamblers usually donate their chips to the pros. I'd hate to try to earn my living at the table, but will keep playing for the trading benefits.

JUL
11
2008

Wouldn't You Know It

This is a good one. Once there was a well-known trader who went into public exile for $2\frac{1}{2}$ years to—among other things—focus his market energies 100 percent on **trading**. In doing so, he crafted a renewed and proven comeback mind-set effective at the beginning of the year with a fictional equity drawdown to minimize the risk of an actual drawdown. And the mind-set worked incredibly well . . . for six months, six days, and about 14 hours. Then, he made his first and worst sloppy trade sequence of the year . . . right after he started his online journal. Wouldn't you know it.

Yes, it happened. I got sloppy on Monday afternoon with respect to size management in a highly volatile market and got caught as the squeezee vs. the squeezor. *Now although it's true that those of us who provide market liquidity do get caught from time to time in squeezes, that's not an acceptable excuse.* As I said last week and throughout the last decade, I'll always share the God's honest truth including the good, the bad, and the ugly.

Then, as has often happened during most drawdown phases, the start of the next day started poorly as I was pressing. **Yet here's where the tide turned**. In the middle of day two, I said "enough" and went immediately into "Emergency and Extended Scalp Mode" ("EESM"), which essentially means, "Get size down and scalp like heck until you get your rhythm back and restore the drawdown." It's sort of like a self-imposed trip to the penalty box and shower for a high-sticking major and game misconduct, and includes beginning with a trade-by-trade profitability log on day one, followed by tracking the percent comeback day-by-day until 100 percent is reached.

Now early in my career, it might take a month or more to restore the drawdown. Every successful trader has been there, and I mean **EVERY**. Yet here I sit at 3:15 on Friday afternoon—a mere three days after EESM started—and I've recovered 53 percent. *By the way, thanks for those last two PM shorts Mr. Bernanke . . . nice closing trades for the weekend.* Day 1 of EESM was typical of comeback mode: 24 trades; 21 winners; average ES point gain a tiny 0.40; net take for the day over $9K.

Conclusions? Perhaps even despite the best of safeguards, it sometimes takes that one **real** experience to reinforce intent. Nevertheless, the chart still did the trick as the draw was far less than that shown in the fictional chart as the fictional draw is meant to be earth-shattering beyond that which should ever happen. And as history has shown that the comeback **will** occur, it's simply a matter of doing everything possible to ensure that the time frame is as short as possible.

It's also a reminder that risk in this business can be minimized, but never eliminated.

The Intraday Journal Begins

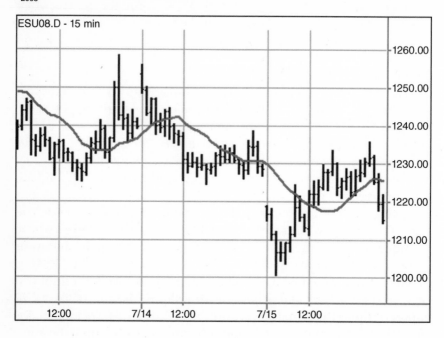

11:06am   I'm going to try something new in terms of intraday blogging. *Remember, Don, this is your personal trading journal that you're writing to yourself.* When I feel the market settling into consolidation/chop/etc., I'm going to head to the sidelines and post my observations. Based on the 5-min chart, we're settling into a tight chop. Decent start to the week trading long for scalps premarket before having a definite short bias once the U.S. bell rang with stops above Friday's high. Took 2–3 points and reentered on some pops. Keeping sizes very modest to start the week and letting volatility drive the P&L.

11:18am   Just scratched a short sequence on another postbreak pullback; confirms the meat is off the bones for now. Decent job protecting AM gains . . . only gave back about $500 on a $11K morning. ES has breakdown potential heading into the PM but watching for now. Next trade might be long on capitulation. In capital preservation mode.

11:48am   ES hanging on to 1235 by a thread. Look out below if that dam gives way. VIX climbing and primed for another push up.

11:58am   Still on sidelines watching. Longs are clearly stuck from the morning buys and puking . . . going long at 1226.

Wow, exited for 1.5 on pop but underestimated the extent of the postpuke bounce. Need better hand/eye coordination in this volatility. Next move short.

12:04pm   Shorting 31.75 for scalp and will take it out on drop. Out 29.25. *Still good reads, Don.* 25.50 now the new puke point. *This intraday blogging to self will either help or hinder. So far, seems to be helping. Going to evaluate end of day. Back on sidelines.*

Tough day for "investors." And the VIX **STILL** hasn't passed the magic 30 mark. Investors way too complacent.

12:17pm   Have short entries queued up in the 32s, not sure we'll get there, though. 5-min trend down.

12:20pm   Got 3225 and 3250; Want 1 point for half and hold rest.

12:22pm   OK, getting tired and feeling personal greed setting in a bit. Took 1 point on most and scratched rest. 1-min 3-Line Break just turned long, which is a warning. Might still get another push south on 5 min but back on sidelines.

12:55pm   Definitely left some money on the table on that last one. Oh well. I'll be shocked if the VIX doesn't spike this afternoon.

1:12pm   VIX 29.20. Tick, tick, tick. Watching only; tough to find good entry points.

1:25pm   zzzzzzzzzzzz. No trades for last hour.

1:48pm   Nice scalp sequences, long on 1-min turn then short off 35 resistance. Flat for now. Clear resistance at 35 until broken. Keeping contract sizes extremely moderate (below 50) for the most part. Definitely want to do an end-of-day recap of the blog's impact on my trading today. So far, it's keeping me focused and respecting all key indicators. I do know I'm leaving $$ on the table, but that's the largest negative of the day so far.

2:24pm   I doubt I'll take another trade. I'm tired, had a decent day, and it had better be a ridiculously good entry. VIX coming back down. I know this much: My historical record of last hour trading is clearly net negative.

OK, did this intraday experiment work? Perhaps. Stayed out of trouble by playing defense, and have been on right side of market for most part. Day profits at $17K+ and EESM recovery now at 74 percent in under a week. Not sure I'll do this every day though . . . maybe from time to time if I need to refocus. Time will tell.

JUL 17 2008   *Planning and Trading a Premarket Bias*

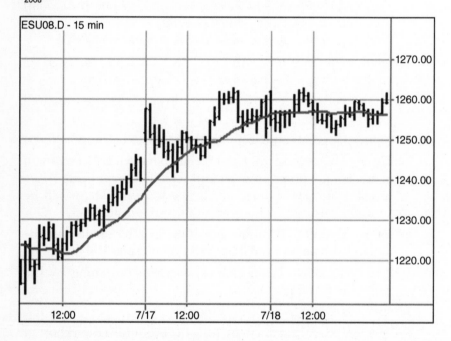

9:08am   I'm going to take advantage of this journal to discipline myself with holding a premarket short. Shorted 30 ES at average of 51.50 premarket and plan on covers at 44 and 45 OR by 10:30am. Will let that stand on its own and wiggle as a midterm intraday swing trade. Managing risk with very modest size. Will also establish separate short positions on any clear confirmation or further climb. Looks like a major gap and trap after yesterday's earnings short covering rally. Will short any approach to 58 with stops above 60. ES 50 points off Tuesday's low and nothing goes straight up. Stayed away from shorting yesterday but timing is now. Philly Fed the remaining news item at 10am. *Focus, Don.*

10:13am   Whew! Underestimated the extent of the postopen run. I hate it when the market is obvious BUT the whole world sees it. Too early on shorting the approach to 59 (along with the rest of the market . . . duh!!) and scrambled a bit, but the read was right on. Day-after-trend day is usually my favorite. Ironically, my best profits came on buying the first dip heavy to 47s and exiting 49s. Taking a breath here. Will short any approach toward 56 or buy next hard dip and that may be it for day.

10:50am   Nabbed that last dip in the 46s and already took it out. Want to buy and hold any further dip into the strong 15-min uptrend support.

11:02am   Turning out to be a good rhythm today for 2-point scalps. Strong resistance to the north and strong support to the south. Very good volume and market pace today, and it was worth staying on the sidelines for much of yesterday.

11:26am   Rebought on the nice dip to the low 40s and took it out on the rebound.

OK, here's my view of today's performance thus far. The early morning blog entry helped me get focused. I knew how the market was likely to act and had convictions to trade the expectation. Even though I was early on the initial short and had to improvise a bit, I feel good about my trading, which for the most part was in lockstep with the market. And unlike the last two days, I feel my P&L thus far is a fair representation of my trading decisions, as I'm up $25K for the morning.

At this point, I'm likely done for the day. No reason to overtrade *(is there ever, Don?)*. Nice to see a premarket plan work.

Current-Day Note: The day subsequently ended +$22.6K.

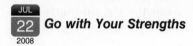

Go with Your Strengths

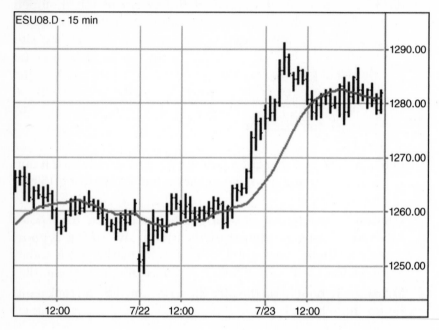

I just took a peek at the close after I'd shut things down for the day around 2pm, due in part to nonmarket commitments, and noticed the post-3:30pm moon shot. Now there are two ways to look at this: (1) Damn, I missed the move! or (2) get immediately in the day-after-trend mind-set to prepare for tomorrow's opening trade sequences.

Now before we choose the obvious preference, we must first immediately revise the phrasing for #1 to reflect "OK, I missed part of that move!" given that most traders don't catch—or intend on catching—the full move. That alone should neutralize any emotional baggage associated with not participating in a market move.

Nevertheless, the clear choice of mind-set #2 for this trader reflects:

- Stewing does no good. Been there, done that.
- My strength and the vast majority of my earnings comes prior to 3:30pm.
- My greatest losses come from trading after 3:30pm (*especially fading extreme trends*).

- My greatest gains typically come from the day after trend.
- All I care about is tomorrow's trade potential. *OK, this only works in tandem with effective execution\tomorrow . . .*
- *The planning of which must now be my top priority.*

Yes, I know this all sounds preachy—even if I'm just talking to myself—but I easily have a few hundred thousand dollars' worth of scars validating these simple truths that are on page one of any generic Trading 101 textbook. So, it's not lip service . . . it's **conviction**. And although I stayed pretty sharp today scalping and feeling the market's pulse, I'll need to be even sharper tomorrow to maximize potential. I'll need to read and sense the other poker players' hands, many of whom were experiencing capitulation big-time at today's close. Did the market call their final bluffs? Did their Kings get cracked by today's Aces? If so, will Kings take tomorrow's pot? *Likely yes, as it sure felt like short-term capitulation panic buying at close.*

But that's not a prediction. All I know is I'm going with my strengths tomorrow.

JUL
23
2008
Textbook Morning-After Prior-Day Trend

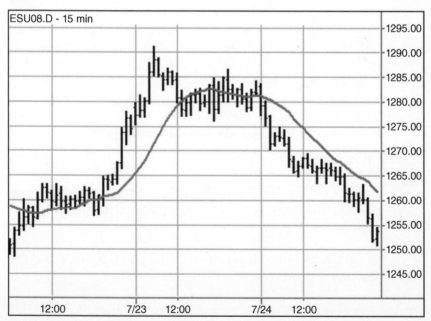

11:37am   OK, backing away from the keyboard after an OK morning as the market pauses. One of the benefits of this journal was supposed to be keeping me out of trouble when the market stopped moving, so it's time to type. Thus far, my reads carrying over from yesterday have been strong, and I'd give myself an A for reads and entry, and a B for holding time. I didn't hold the post-10:30am ES short as long as I would have liked, but am OK with the result. The decrease in volatility and resulting change in pace is admittedly taking a bit of getting used to. Got a few nuggets trading the DAX in the wee hours as well with a similar sequence by shorting into the first climb. Gotta love the morning after the prior-day trend!

I'd love to see a strong breakdown from this midday consolidation to buy any overreaction to the downside (strong 15-min trend support), but it would have to be near 1275 as the new prime objective for the rest of the day is to protect the $18K in morning profits. *Don't screw up the rest of the day, Don!*

12:20pm   *Geesh,* if I knew that all I had to do was ask. Nice drop to 1278 where I picked up a nice long scalp sequence. Not being overly aggressive down here given the extent of the recent run, but expecting support for the moment. Flat on the scalp but will buy one more push down if we get it.

12:24pm   Love that 15-min chart!! Bought the last push down and taking it out on the climb. Preparing for **major gain preservation mode** shortly. Outstanding market pace and I'm dancing with it cheek to cheek. Expecting the oscillations to begin narrowing. This could be it for the meat. Watching now. 1-min 3LB still south into the larger time frame supports, but that's often a trailing indicator on the day after trend.

12:33pm   Took 1-pt stop on small 15 lot. First stop of day. *Careful, Don.* VIX climbing.

12:40pm   OK, support held and made up for initial stop on reentry. That may be it for the day. $25K in profits and don't want to get sloppy.

As I've said in the past, I'll always share the good, the bad, and the ugly. Today was a good day.

Current-Day Note: The day subsequently ended +$24.8K.

Market Bias

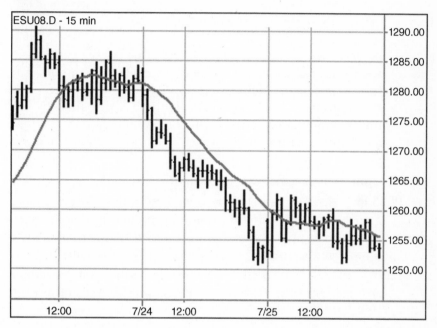

11:17am OK, let's start blogging for today. Not as much on my game as I was yesterday, yet I'm having a decent day given the early intraday bear trend that began evolving immediately after market open . . . the 10:30–11:00 chopfest notwith-standing. Shorting 5- and 15-min downtrend retracements and covering on the extensions (or the same thing contra-trend in reverse). Immediate trend is extended a bit so watching to see if we get lunchtime capitulation toward the 1264 support area. Buy orders queued in the 64s if we get a spike down and will go to market if it gets close on a pause. Want one more push here (11:29am).

Like every trader, my entries and trade executions are full of imperfections. And some days, they downright stink. A bit early, a bit late, too small size, too large size, system outages, missed fills, distractions, yadda yadda yadda. This is where market bias comes to the rescue, which seems to be the case in today's early trade. Nothing like market bias confirmed by half a dozen indicators on multiple time frames to make up for what will always be imperfect executions.

11:35am   Nice. Best fill 65.50 on the pause and out on the reflex spike. VIX at HOD; 5-min trend and 3LB still south. Could get strong support here from Tuesday's range break. Some TICK vs. price strength divergence (TD) on that last drop. Prefer to see a 1-min turn though to hold longer off that support. Any turn likely to be tricky given approaching lunchtime pace. Resistance now in the mid-1270s for next strong short opportunity, which is my main focus for reentry. 15-min oversold and want a deep retracement. Want some meat on sizing there if we get it.

12:12pm   zzzzzzzzzzzzzzzzz. No decent retracement to short.

12:35pm   Not as interested in longs here unless we get a clear 1-min turn. 2pm should be interesting if volume comes in. Does this support hold? 5-min 3LB has had no turns since open. Needs a period close above 1267.75 to change.

12:52   Nibbled on a short sequence at 68. Still want a stronger move up to short size. Keeping sizes very modest thus far.

1:30pm   Stuck my toe into a long tester and stubbed toe for $^{3}\!/_{4}$ point. Fortunately, it was only the little toe testing the water. **Note to self: Resistance trend lines approaching from north, so shorting further move up may be troublesome**. Now we seem in more of a breakout mode heading into the PM. *Stay flexible, Don.* Will retry long on trades going off at 68. Could squeeze shorts toward 72. Not interested in breakdown shorts at these levels. Dow –164; ES –17 on day. VIX potential further move north on 15 min. Conflicting signals = stay on sideline. Plus, I'm a terrible breakout trader.

2:08pm   VIX winning for now. 5-min 3LB **still** short. 13 consecutive short bars. Rare.

2:16pm   Volume spike on breakdown and VIX pop Lack of long-trend change triggers kept me out of intraday trend reversal trade. *Strong reads, Don.* On sidelines and watching. Tough to short down here, but better flat than long! Maybe one tidy short scalp on a move toward 63. Won't stick around long if we get it with tight stop.

2:23pm   ES ticked 62.50 . . . I'm sitting at 62.75 and won't chase. Only want ¾ pt on scalp. Will cancel if not filled.

2:25pm   Pulled order. There's the imperfect market at work. Scalp would have been good for 1.75 max, but fills would have been tough and I would have had to be wholesale on both sides. Maybe one point was doable. If it implodes further, I don't care as that would queue up tomorrow's posttrend sequence yet again. Not going to get cute. 90 mins to go.

2:35pm   So much for Tuesday's support. Investors gritting their teeth again . . . if they have any left. Glub, glub, glub. In hindsight, a bit conservative on that postbreakdown short miss, but I'd rather let an extended trend extend further than get caught the majority of the times when there's quick intraday capitulation and turn. That's my excuse anyway. *I hate afternoon trading!*

Updated 5-min 3LB: 19 consecutive bars.

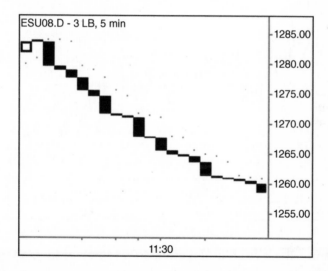

3:00pm   Bar count now at 20! Needs a period close above 61. Watch them frustrate all the bottom pickers by turning in the last hour. I see lots of cute/heroic scalp entries, but that's what they are . . . cute and heroic. No thanks. Too much slop and starting to think about tomorrow's plan but that depends on how we close. Still sitting on AM profits.

3:09pm   Finally got that short sequence from 63.25 with a nice wholesale fill as someone panic covered at the wrong time. 5-min 3LB finally turned up. Keeping sequences tight. Doubt we'll see the lows again now . . . if we do, all the better for the morning. Eyes now on tomorrow. Chip count +$11.0K on the day on only 565 contracts, which is extremely low volume for me.

Naptime.

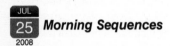

Morning Sequences

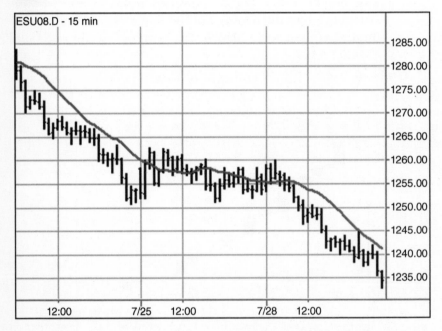

8:00am   Back from a nap after doing some early DAX trading.

8:39am   Low liquidity ES Globex spike to 1260 on the Durable Orders data release. Scalped a small short sequence. Best entry fill 59.75 and covered on the drop toward 58. Going to wait for normal session open to attempt any sizes. *By the way, I rarely look at news. Right now, I have no idea what the # was, or whether it met or beat expectations (I assume so). I do have Briefing.com and the TV talking heads accessible, but usually only* *peek if the market is acting completely out of the ordinary. Gets back to how irrelevant news really is unless it's something catastrophic. However, I **am** aware of the economic calendar. Don't forget, Don that we have Michigan Sentiment and New Home Sales today at 10am.*

8:55am   Entering my personal no-trade zone of 9:00am–9:30am, which has gotten me in a lot of trouble over the years, similar to 3:30pm–4:00pm. Yet I'm getting better at simply not trading then.

9:01am   I bent my rule a bit after looking at yesterday's closing charts again *(Mother always said to look both ways before crossing the street)*, shorting on the small pop back to 57.50. Navigating the no-trade zone by keeping sizes small. Covering on the drop. Flat; best cover 56.00. That should be it for me until open. Going with the strong short bias after we open though with resistance in the low 1260s. Need to refocus for that. Hope the 10am data doesn't ruin the plan.

9:25am   Rule bend #2 as I shorted a small lot at 58.50 "just in case" that's it for the pop. Wide leash and will let it run toward 61. Managing risk with size. Target cover 55s. Want better entry during liquid session but who knows if we'll get it. Feels like it may shoot straight down at the bell, but we'll see.

9:30am   Added to short 58.25. This should plummet.

9:38am   Flat . . . best cover 55.25. Got 2 solid points on the meat. Can still run more but probability questionable. I want Aces or Kings.

9:50am   So far, a repeat of yesterday where I underestimated the extent of the barf-a-thon. Could have held some until the TICK went negative, which I was watching. Oh well, solid read, strong entry points, and got initial target. Maybe the DAX didn't gap up into resistance, but **ES sure did**. Economic data coming up shortly.

9:57am   Took restroom break. Wowzer 8-point pop. Cover looking pretty good now. Eying potential short 62ish if we pop on news.

10:01am   Short avg 61.50; best entry 62.25; stop 63.

10:05am   Looking for a Wile E. Coyote dive toward 57.

10:17am   Bit of a rough ride during that 10:11 to 10:17 window, but finally getting the drop. A few covers, scratches, reentries, along the way to manage risk and P&L. Still expecting 57ish. Free-rolling on partial lot with 62 stop.

10:22 Feels like it for the upside wiggles. Sitting in 57s for final covers.

10:25 Flat at 57.50. Can't complain. Again, there could be more, but do I care? Will take 4 points any day. Still underestimating the runs a bit, though. Look at this 30-min ES chart and compare to the DAX one at the top. Love it when both plans work.

10:34 That may be it for the day. Increased chip count by $16K to end a very solid week. Don't want to give it away.

Current-Day Note: The day subsequently ended +$16.2K.

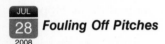

Fouling Off Pitches

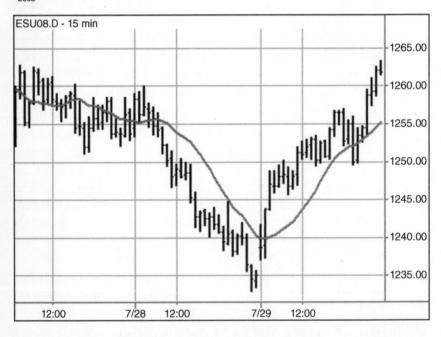

Today was interesting, for it seemed that my body kept telling me all day that it's still Sunday as I felt a bit lethargic throughout the session and could never get the blood pumping. Oh, I traded here and there, but between not feeling particularly energized and not having much chart conviction—aside from the 2:40pm pop to short—I felt like David Ortiz in last night's Sox-Yanks game where he simply kept fouling off tough pitches until he found that pitch he could drill into the stands, which, of course, he did.

Yet if you've been reading much of this journal at all, you'll know that it's not today that invigorates me, but tomorrow. It's frankly becoming a bit scary to see as many trend and posttrend days as we've had lately, especially for summer trading. A bit "scary," of course, and falling in the "Too Good to Be True" category in terms of Day 2 probability. Call it the gift that keeps on giving, or hammering those fighting each day's trend (Day 1) or oscillation (Day 2) rhythms.

So, we'll keep it short and sweet tonight as I enter tomorrow with the bat on my shoulders with a 2–2 count waiting for a pitch I can drill. How about a nice hanging curveball over the middle of the plate in the context of an 8-point overnight futures pop?

The week has yet to begin.

Current-Day Note: The day subsequently ended –$2.8K.

Work Remains

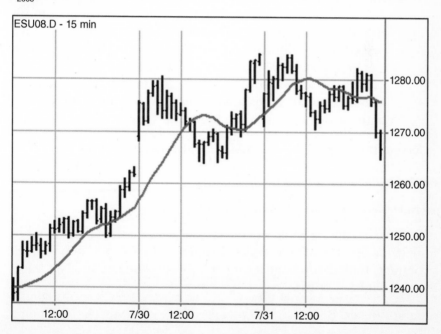

6:08am   OK, this is getting a bit frustrating. Pitcher and batter been going at it for 2+ days now, and this batter keeps going to the rosin to get a better grip. The DAX indeed had that pullback toward closing supports in the Europe sessions, but essentially got table scraps as the pace has been tough. Got myself into a hole 4:30am–5:00am, but slightly positive on the day now. Nothing like a squiggly/wiggly 5x bottom on the 3-min chart into strong 30-min support to frustrate dip-buying traders before the turn. Fairly tight overnight range and ES holding the 1260 area for now. Would love ES long in the high 1250s after open, but haven't gotten it in the overnight session . . . thus the early DAX trading. Noticing I'm holding the bat tight; am a bit early on the swing . . . sort of like trading with scared capital. Going to focus on making contact and letting the wood do the work in the main session.

7:08am   Planning ahead, game plan will be looking for the first decent dip with rock solid support in the low 1250s as the wind beneath my wings. Second choice will be to short any approach to 1270 on a high TICK reading, but I prefer the trend pullback option!

4:02pm   First, yes this is a **nine-hour gap** between posts. In-between went something like this: Had to adjust plan to yet another gap and run; nailed the first top; had to leave my station when the first primo bounce came so missed that; got chopped up a bit midday and gave back some gains; and closed on a couple of decent scalp sequences on the PM climb. All in all, a positive day, but I'm still not at all satisfied with my management in this dog-pile in/out summer market.

Current-Day Note: The day subsequently ended +$3.2K.

July Grades and Observations

Trade Execution and Management: **C**

It's been a long while since I gave away more than 50 percent of my gains by end of day, which happened today. Not good. 1,445 contracts traded: too large a sum considering the market. Not selective enough on entries.

Market Reads: **B**

Reading well, even with executions still missing by a beat or two. It's very much been a summer market in terms of start/stop pace. I've also noticed that I've had to adjust more times than not to an opening rhythm, which was somewhat different than expected.

It's interesting that both the DAX and ES had ugly-paced bounce points into their respective 30-min supports. Ugly meaning multiple bottoms with somewhat volatile bottom-building that made clean entries a bit tough. It's also extremely interesting to see yet another closing trend run, which makes ES closing with strong trends for **three straight days**. One thing is certain: That won't keep happening forever.

I should actually be satisfied with this month's performance heading into the last day. Started strong; had the infamous brain cramp; rebounded faster than I ever had and then some; and now some less-than-optimal results in three strong trend days. The P&L will show very strong #s for the month, yet as usual it won't reflect opportunity loss and I'm not pleased. Simply put, a great deal of work remains. The chip pile continues to grow, but I won't accept less than optimal results.

The chart says a lot.

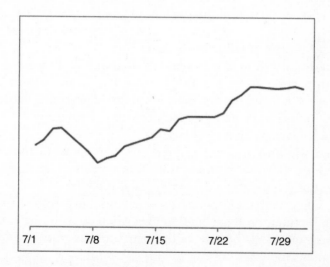

No, it's not yesterday's ES 5-min chart or the Boston fans' preference for trading Manny Ramirez. Rather, it's my actual July daily equity curve. And if you've been following this journal, you'll see the performance in general lockstep with my daily comments.

Here's what stands out to me as I look back at July and prepare for August:

- Decent start, then the blunder of the year followed by rapid EESM recovery, one more strong push, and then consolidation.
- 18 profitable days; 5 draws.
- 7 days with gains > $15K; 2 days with losses > $15K *[$15K being my approximate benchmark for a decent or atrocious day]*.
- And back to point #1, a clear lackluster performance over the past week or so.

Conclusions? I see two. First, the EESM recovery mode clearly took its toll on my trading later in the month. The intense state of focus during that week of comeback activity was just that—**intense**. You could have poured hot water on me on any day during that time and I probably wouldn't have noticed. Yet it was a necessary interval to address what happens to me once every year or two.

Second, I haven't adjusted enough to the late-summer trading pace where volumes have been limited to dog-pile in/out moves in the first and last 30 min of the session. *Got another one to close today, this time to the downside . . . 4 days and counting of extreme closing dog piles*. Oh, do I look forward to fall trading again!

What doesn't show in the chart is that about $1/3$ of my net gains for the month came from the DAX . . . which is an extremely high percentage for me. This also tells me that such trading in the early morning hours has taken its toll on my focus as the transition is made to the U.S. markets later in the day.

I share this info in part to remind myself and anyone looking over my shoulder that this business is **so much more** than simply chart patterns. Rather, it's about the whole package. When I first look at my suboptimal results over the past week, and then review the chart patterns, I scratch my head big-time. Yet when considering at how the month has unfolded, the time of the year, etc., the results come into a very clear perspective.

If you look back at my posts or published writings over the years, you should notice that I talk more about my challenges than my successes. Even now, despite topping $100K in monthly earnings for the fifth time this year, I **have** to enter August with a renewed comeback mind-set, as if I've once again just experienced a mind-numbing fall. The actual curve above shows consolidation over the past week. The key now is to mentally translate that consolidation to a serious drawdown and **believe that it really happened that way.**

Thus I begin August in a mental hole and have to start yet another comeback month. For the eighth time this year, I have to scrap and scrape to get back to even ground. I've just lost a significant portion of my capital, can feel my stomach tightening over the grotesqueness of the fall from grace, and must do everything in my power to start yet again. How could it happen? What must I do to prevent it? In other words, see the mall map and directory.

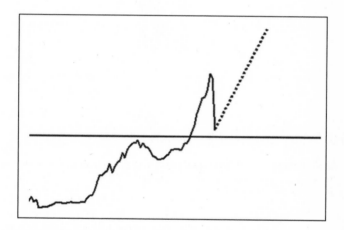

If you're looking for pats on the back, don't look here. I haven't accomplished anything. Nothing. Nada. Zilch. We're always just one Hail Mary Eli Manning–to–David Tyree Helmet catch away from ruining a year's worth of strong work in one fell swoop. The other team has just marched down the field and scored. Thankfully, we're not yet at the 2-min warning and there's time to come back. But not much.

Retrospective 2008 Race Progress Update

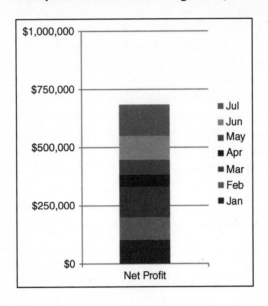

August 2008 Journal Excerpts

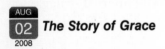

The Story of Grace

As I began final preparations for the 2008 Race and thought more about the Chinese bamboo concept, I thought back to an incident that had occurred about six months prior, during one atrocious two-day trading period. I vividly recall that it was a Monday and Tuesday after a weekend during which I had been shopping for a car to replace my 2000 Tundra pickup.

Now for the last 20 years, my car-buying strategy has consisted of buying clean vehicles that are about three years old with about 50,000 miles on them, as this is often when the warranty expires and the previous owners trade them in. *I've found it to be a great niche market where I can get great value (heck, I'm a trader).*

Anyway, I had been looking for a particular model that would likely become my main mode of transportation for the next 10 years, and I wanted to get both a comfortable car and value. The car I'd selected was a BMW 3-Series E46 that had been in production from 1998 to 2005, and it was now a matter of finding one that had all-wheel drive and was in decent shape. *And believe me, that model isn't easy to find as it's one of the most popular and highest-rated models ever produced by any firm.* And during that weekend, I'd looked at a couple that didn't quite fit the bill. BUT—and this is key in terms of a misstep—I was feeling good about ultimately making the purchase as the year was going well, life was good, and trading had been consistent at the time.

Then Monday and Tuesday "happened," which seemed to come out of nowhere. *Looking back, I know I fell into the "Gee, if I can have a great Monday, I can pay for it in one day" trap.* Then Wednesday came and I found the car I wanted listed on the Internet—a black 2003 325xi with about 46,000 miles in very good condition at an acceptable price. The problem was that given the last two days, I had a huge pit in my stomach and felt I no longer deserved it. And even though it was a used vehicle and the net purchase cost after my trade wasn't that bad (the Tundra held its value well), it was still a significant purchase in my mind. Yet I was continually bothered by the events of the previous two days and wondered whether I really deserved any car with the letters "B-M-W" in it, no matter how old.

Frankly, as I drove the 90 miles to look at the car, I was actually hoping that I wouldn't like it. Then when I saw the car and test-drove it, I thought, "Damn, this is the right one." The internal struggle was enormous. I then called my wife and told her that I really liked it but wasn't certain about taking the leap. And although she wasn't fully aware of the extent of the prior two days, she knew me well enough to know it was a tough couple of days for me. Yet when I asked for her advice, she said, "Do it. You work hard enough and deserve it." Those comments immediately put me at ease, I felt a burden lifted, and I made the leap and completed the transaction over the next hour.

Yet before I made the purchase, I had to translate what my wife told me from "You deserve it" to "You **don't** deserve it," because I didn't. We rarely deserve anything we get. Yet I bought it anyway on the leap of faith that it was still OK to treat myself to something that I would enjoy. On the way back home, I named my car "Grace" because she wasn't deserved, yet I was allowed to have her anyway. And yes, I love the car.

Grace has some years on her, and if you look closely, you'll see several nicks, scratches, and other imperfections . . . just like her driver. And I had no clue that the next day would be the day when my Bamboo Tree would finally break the ground's surface and begin its climb. Through all the years of toil and frustration, I'd frankly forgotten that I'd ever planted the seed.

 *FOMC Day*

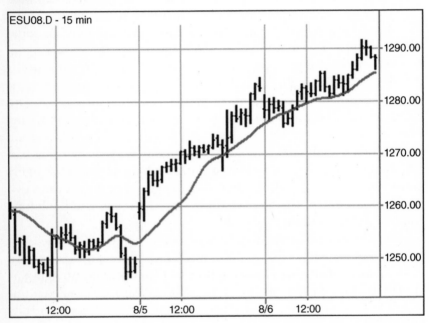

1:17pm   DAX trading recap so far: Got a full night's sleep and didn't trade. ES trading recap thus far using a few relevant poker terms: Fold, fold, fold, fold, small blind *(a small required bet that requires one to participate)*, big blind *(a larger required bet)*, fold, fold, fold. In other words, two toe-in-the pool trades today that I promptly folded after seeing the "flop." *The flop reflects three common cards dealt face-up and used by all players to join with their own two cards.* Pretty lame day as we await FOMC (Federal Open Market Committee) data in about an hour. Day pretty much following standard pre-FOMC patterns in terms of little personal trading and pathetic volatility. Passed on the early gap and run off the open since Europe had already rocketed out of the gates in its session. Was looking for early pullback long entries, yet the hands all seemed marginal at best and the prime entry continuation entry was right around 10am when the ISM (Institute for Supply Management) number was released. *Sort of like making a bet while the waitress spills a few drinks on your shoulder.*

So, it's back to the journal to stay out of boredom trades and plan the afternoon. **#1 objective of the day remains staying out of trouble.** There are 250 trading days in the year, with the next one being tomorrow! #2 objective is to fade any extreme FOMC move with small size on any absurd TICK and price spike combination and cover on the reversion toward the mean.

My general thought on FOMC days is that since I want opportunity balanced with low-to-moderate risk, I don't expect many entry opportunities, and that 10am continuation was too close to news for my liking. Yes, trends in place when nonemployment data news is released "usually" continue—*and pocket 8s are "usually" a starting strong hand*—but I frankly was willing to pass and wanted to see more hands.

Note to self heading into the announcement . . . I want a profitable P&L and not excitement. Take it if it's there, but pass if it isn't and come ready to lock and load on Wednesday with your capital intact. *Yea, it makes for a boring journal . . . so be it.*

2:00pm   Would love to see a drop to the mid-1260s on announcement . . . good support there for the moment.

2:08pm   Changing my price ladder from a one-tick interval to a three-tick interval. Buy order sitting at 66.00 just in case and will manage risk with size.

2:15pm   Missed fill on spike down by 1.00. TICK wasn't extreme enough. –541 Max . . . that was it? Such is life.

2:29pm   No woulda's/shoulda's . . . focus. What is next entry point? *Tomorrow?* Teeny volume. 15 min about the only trend in play and high percent played out on that pop. *If the market pops and few trade, does it make a noise?* Likely move now? No clue. One thing is certain . . . I won't trade the last hour.

2:36pm   Still no personal conviction and no PM trades. Looking more like a day off with each passing minute.

2:47pm First trade ES long on holding TICK and supports. A whopping 75 basis points from 7.50 to 8.25. Tight scalp taken out on the short-covering TICK extreme.

2:50pm Frankly very satisfied with management today and closing shop. Missed a stellar sequence on the drop by "that much" . . . big whoop. Two scratches and one scalp . . . pretty funny. If we run into close either way, you know the drill for the morning. 3pm witching hour approaches . . . not time to force anything.

Current-Day Note: The day subsequently ended +$0.5K.

 *Post-FOMC*

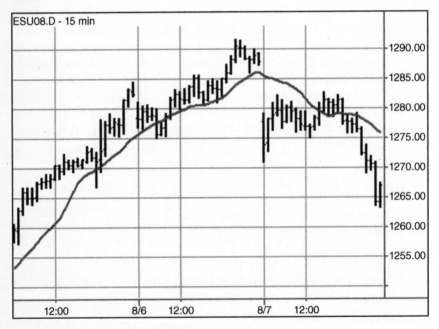

1:06pm Well, we definitely got the chop as expected, yet the pace has frankly been a bit sloppy—*even for chop if that's possible*—and well-contained within a tight range with pathetic volume with a capital "P." Been keeping size modest (*haven't yet seen a clear "all-in" entry point*) as a result and have simply been doing some light liquidity-providing scalping to keep my mind in the market.

Have traded both the DAX and ES sessions with the day-after-trend-day mentality with a bias toward the long side on dips and 1-min turns given the downtrending VIX, and the results have been acceptable but certainly not stellar. In the spirit of Yogi Berra, it seems summer trading may not go away when fall arrives. Best push back up thus far was around the lunch hour.

Not relying as much on 3LB in the oscillating market as that tends to be a lagging indicator on nontrend days. Might be a better indicator in the PM.

2:24pm Well, for some reason, I just lost my journal draft that I was typing over the last hour *(there was some good stuff there too!),* so here's a quick and dirty recap. Was getting extremely anxious in the prolonged chop—from not trading—and mentioned the tiny number of ES contracts I've traded over the last three days (1,720 Monday, 150 Tuesday, 846 through noon today, with Tuesday's likely a career low!). It was starting to drive me bonkers, and I needed to make sure I wouldn't lose focus.

I was finally biased long shortly after 2pm on the imploding VIX and holding price trends and took longs at 8375 and 8475 at 2:11pm and 2:12pm. Stop was if 1-min 3LB turned back south. Scaled out on the approach to 8800 and am mostly out now. Best exit so far 8725 and took most out at 8650. Holding small portion "just in case."

Most short-term conviction I've had in a while. Had a good read and execution as I was looking for this coiled spring to pop and felt least path of resistance was up, although I kept contract size still fairly modest. Still, best sequence in a while and managing well today, all things considered. It won't be a home run day, but finally got some decent wood on the ball with a couple of solid singles.

2:34pm Taking more out on this price and TICK pop. Best fill 8775.

2:43pm Flat at 8875 and that may be it for me.

That admittedly wasn't exactly my bread-and-butter sequence, but I suppose you have to eat off the menu presented.

Chip count up modestly on the day +$7.7K, which although lower than most days after trends, I'm OK with today's management. I'd love to see a close at new highs to set an even better stage for tomorrow and stretch this puppy some more, but an hour to go still.

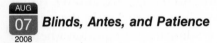

Blinds, Antes, and Patience

11:29am A bit choppy on the seas this morning as clean triggers have been few. Did OK in the Globex session but struggling a bit with the U.S. open as the best wholesale entries have fallen into what I call the "fade and wait" category, which is a blind fade on the extreme spikes and then a hold while the market takes its time to revert toward the mean or range end. Continuation triggers are tough since the market really isn't clearly trending on any decent time frame and the trigger premiums eat into much of the profit potential, and even the 1-min charts have been sloppy. Pace and feel is incredibly important to me, more so than chart patterns.

That early 8-point postopen plunge likely caught more than a few gap faders, although early and late-day summer dog piles shouldn't be a surprise by now.

11:52am   Bought a few tops and sold a few bottoms providing liquidity in this range . . . not a good strategy. Laying low for a while. Don't have the personal rhythm today so shaping up to be a draw day. Goal for the rest of the day will be to keep today's antes and blinds cost manageable.

The 10am–3pm intraday opportunities continue to be almost nonexistent as the summer gets late. September can't come soon enough. Having a hard time remembering the last time I had a 100-contract position on!

1:13pm   VIX on the fence . . . no help there.

2:16pm   Looks like a blinds and antes round today at this end. Nicked up a bit ($4K) but not too bothered with attempts . . . gotta get in the pool to swim. Tomorrow may not be much better in terms of volume and pace. Considering taking the day off if this keeps up.

2:47pm   I want this pullback short! Sitting at 7525 and 7550.

2:50pm   Took 7500 short. Cover orders in 73s. Stop on 1-min 3LB turn.

2:55pm   Added 7550. Looking for an elevator drop. Lots of size spoofing and finally a range break. Shorted into a phony-sized bid.

2:59pm   Covering on the drop. Flat at 7250.

3:03pm   Here we go again with the last hour. *Careful, Don . . . not your strength.* Not many market supports out there if this implodes. Watching.

3:10pm   Doing some wholesale scalping; Strong 1-min TICK divergence last drop. Hmmm . . . volume bars. I almost forgot what those looked like.

That might be it. Tough market when there's maybe just one or two meaty entries all day, and you have to be there and be ready to hit it hard. Could have sized larger, but tough when you've had chop all day. Very similar to yesterday in that regard.

3:22pm   VIX sneaking up. Early Friday entries may not be bad after all. Flat and watching.

3:27pm   Nice rhythm down here as the TICK has been helpful on overextensions for short covers or quickie wholesale longs.

3:33pm   Bottom falling out; VIX leading the way.

3:49pm   OK; nice scalp sequences to end the day. Decided to trade when the market said to, despite the last hour. Who'd have thunk? Kept things tight, though. Nice comeback to end slightly green.

Looking forward to the open.

Current-Day Note: The day subsequently ended +$0.9K.

 *Fool Me Once . . .*

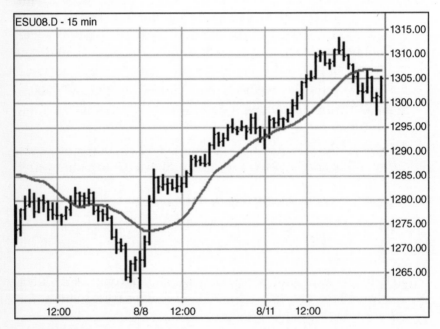

6:23am   Pretty sloppy Globex session. ES traded to 1274, but no clean shot. I suspect there may be only one shot postopen on the first sharp move either way.

10:22am   Yup . . . monkey see, monkey do. Complete carbon copy. Altered strategy again on the fly, this time thanks to a dress rehearsal. Want the first hard pullback long. 1277 area would be a gift . . . doubt we'll get it. One thing is clear: There are a ton of stuck shorts that will have to cover on the first move down.

11:13am   Not bad. Did pretty well adjusting and going with the flow. Pullbacks up here have been shallow, so been nibbling only. True to my 6:23am comment, there was another stampede 5 mins after open with very little reaction time. Yes, it would have been nice to load the boat and ride the moon shot all the way. *Then again, I'd like to win a bracelet at the World Series of Poker.* Just trying to grind away like Michael Mizrachi.

11:22am   Back in the midday summer nothing-doing mode.

12:07pm   One interesting observation is that both of the planned DAX and ES pullback shorts would have worked for decent gains, but in their respective premarket sessions (2am–3am for the DAX). The normal session simply didn't pay.

1:53pm   Finally felt like shorting on that last spike on strong 1-min TICK vs. price divergence at 1:42pm. Had been sitting on the sidelines. Averaged into short to 9475 and covered into the TICK drop to zero. Got a decent bite on that one.

2:03pm   OK; major day and week income preservation mode now. Considering the cost of early short probing and stops, I'm OK with today's performance +$7K. A bit more scrambling over the last two days than I'd like, and I'll need to take a look at that. Keeping sizes relatively small in these whipsaws has kept me out of major trouble even when wrong . . . and I've been wrong a lot this week.

Lots of work left and miles to go before we sleep. Target remains 12/31/08.

Current-Day Note: The day subsequently ended +$6.9K.

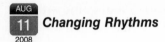

Changing Rhythms

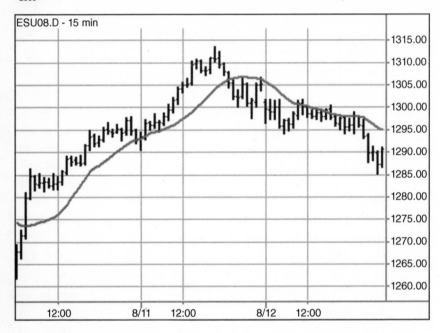

1:20pm   Admittedly, it took me a bit to get the blood pumping today on the heels of a family event from which I returned late last night. Got some of the initial pop off Friday's supports, but have been watching the rest of this climb. Finally felt confident about putting some size on this midday pullback to 5-min support. I'm currently long and will take it out into any pop with a stop on the 1-min 3LB (bottom chart) reversal. Faded into long best price 1307.50 and added on the 1-min turn. Very high probability, but as Forrest Gump would say, "Market is as market does." VIX 15-min looking to continue its downtrend . . . which also suggests price bounce.

1:25pm   Taking it out into the pop. Looking for 1310+ on final exit.

1:32pm   Flat. Nice setup and pace. Took the high-probability reaction. It can run to the moon now for all I care.

1:37pm   Yea, yea, yea, I know ES ticked 1313+ and 1310 now looking like a stupid exit. Then again, other days it would be the peak and I'd look like a genius. Neither, of course, would be right . . . I want the high probability move and don't like to gamble! Had OK size on, but could have added a bit more on the turn to take out into any extreme pop. *Steady as she goes, Don . . . step by step, day by day. Eyes on December 31 only.*

1:50pm Heading into income preservation mode. $7K on the day and a good start to the week. Gotta be a helluva pullback entry now toward 15-min support as 5-min high-probability move has already played out.

1:59pm Would love a cliff drop toward 1305 . . . might have some late-to-the-party stuck longs bailing. *But has to be a premium hand only.* Might do some light wholesale scalping on any drop as volatility picking up a tad.

3:10pm OK, earlier exits looking better . . . too funny. Scrambled a bit on the drop, which did come in all the way to the top of the AM breakout range. *ES only overshot my 1:59pm wish list by 5 points!* 3LB continuing to be a great SOOT guide as it never went long on that full retrace. Picked up a few extra $$ on the drop, but picking optimal wholesale entries a bit tough. Hate it when the whole world sees and wants the same thing!!

3:21pm Definitely got some stuck longs on that earlier blow-off top. Nice market rhythm today, though, with lots of mini-trends in play. Did OK and nudged day's chip increase up to $8.4K, but it won't be hard to find some things I didn't like about my trading today. Size management may be one, and perhaps a bit too cautious in the PM. Also been a while since I've had a five-figure day . . . need to put my finger on that. Maybe size management again.

Will need to do better.

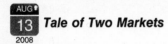

Tale of Two Markets

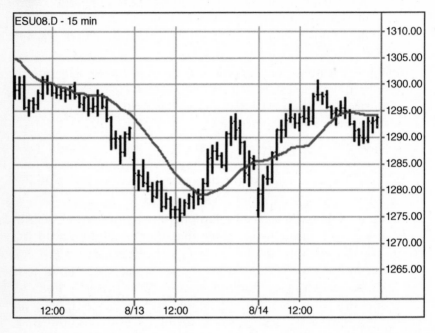

12:03pm   I don't know why, but I tend to trade better when mad. After botching an overnight opportunity in the DAX on its late-day breakdown out of consolidation prior to the U.S. open, I got ticked off and have finally got back in lockstep with the U.S. market. I guess it's how I'm wired and why the fictional draw programming works for me *(that is, when I actually believe it . . . which is becoming an issue I'm struggling with).*

15- and 30-min has initial resistance above in the mid-1280s, and I'd like to either buy the next leg down or fade a clear retracement with some size. Just a matter of the market cooperating before and after! *Not much to ask, is it?*

I almost did a late-night journal entry last night as I was thinking out loud trying to figure out if I've gotten complacent in these late dog days of summer in terms of reduced size and interest at times or if my size management has

actually done a decent job of keeping me out of trouble—
and if so, I'm simply beating myself up over nothing. I
decided to instead get a good night's sleep after figuring
that time would provide the answers . . . time in the context
of a few more trading sessions before I jumped to any
conclusions. Plus, I was tired from watching the 36 runs in
the Red Sox–Rangers game!

I sometimes think back to Herb Brooks's constant
encouragement to his team during the 1980 Miracle on
Ice run when he often chanted, "Play your game." Those
words ring very true to me any time I feel unsettled, and I'm
relying on them strongly as this summer nears an end and
days of treading water run together. My game? Chip away at
the market providing some liquidity day after day—sometimes marking time—until such time I feel that I'm locked
into an opportunity, at which point the defense comes off
the field and the offense finally lets loose. Right now, the
defense looks tired and is screaming at the coach saying that
they want to come out of the game. And the offense is taking
off their warm-ups.

12:42pm Want to begin establishing a short position if ES gets to
1283 with a preferred position closer to 1285–86. Been nibbling on the short side on this midday climb, but keeping size
light and holding time tight.

1:16pm Longs have some work to do as we're back below
Friday's breakout for now.

1:28pm Shorted partial 1282 in case that's all she wrote. Will let
it run against me; managing risk with size. Can run to the
30/60 min (1286–88) and still sustain downtrend.

1:32pm Added small 84.75.

1:48pm Right read on expected squeeze; wrong read on extent.
Did some dancing on size mgt and reentries. Flat now and
looking for possible reentry on any divergences with 30/60
min at back.

2:04pm Reestablishing short position 88.00. Prefer to see 1-min
turn now to add. Hard stop at 90.00. Will take it out on TICK
drop.

2:11pm Dive little TICK, dive.

2:12pm Flat best cover 86.25. Didn't add . . . traded what I had. Too much action to memorialize all activity, but think I captured the gist of it. **Just** missed a clean reversal long at 1:50pm as I was scratching the short sequence on the drop and had bids in below to reverse. Want a mulligan on that one. Very fertile ES scalping market on overreactions. Reassessing charts now as we have multiple time frame Ping-Pong going on.

2:25pm Quick self-assessment. Decent size management, which is a good reminder that risk can be managed by size, stops, or both. I never had full size on and had a fairly loose leash on initial short probes. Seems I ended up essentially flat on the sequences. A reminder if you're looking over my shoulder that I do fade immediate moves at times to provide liquidity . . . but have seat belts and airbags at my disposal. I prefer to trade with the 1-min trend, yet sometimes I'll put some probe bets on, expecting the market to run against me initially.

2:34pm Still kicking myself over that 1:50pm reversal pitch over the heart of the plate that I just missed. Good battle of a strong 5-min uptrend banging up against 30- and 60-min resistance. Not too interested for reentering right now as they battle it out and less interested in shorting.

3:01pm Tale of two intraday trends with equal opportunity . . . trend shorts win in the AM; trend longs early PM; overreaction longs AM; overreaction shorts and longs PM. Trader flexibility critical today as in not getting locked into changing biases. Personally, I think it's tough to clean up on both sides . . . probably better to SOOT on one. Did pretty well here on the shift at least by staying off the short-trend bias as the day went on. Potential longer-term triangle as we now bounce around a bit, but decent wholesale opportunities within the larger range with good pace. Also a good day showing why moving averages are only relevant when used in combo with momentum and strength indicators.

3:04pm Gain preservation mode.

3:45pm Clipped a couple of stretched bungee scalps to end the day. Decent comeback from the early DAX mess to end +$8.7K with a solid ES showing. Missed enough opportunities and was still wrong enough, though, to have plenty to work on tomorrow . . . not a bad combo.

140 days to go.

Trend Day

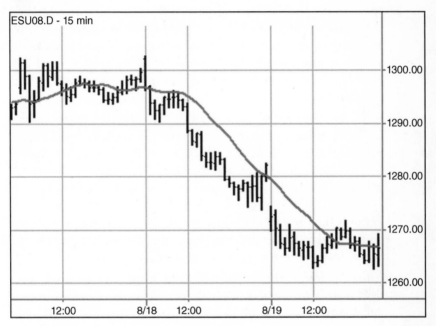

1:36pm Interesting rhythm today as it's been a spike-consolidation teeny-pullback-repeat day, which can make it difficult for both extreme spike and deep pullback wholesale entries. Doing OK so far as traded the DAX to the long side on the Europe mid-AM climb and have traded ES both long and short on the drop south, covering on the retracements back toward the mean. First trade was a 9:37am long on the early drop, which I quickly scratched for a small loss upon seeing further weakness, and then began focusing on the short side given both the early weakness and the 15-min VIX, which has been uptrending all day.

I've only traded three or four ES sequences, booking modest profits on most, and have not looked at my P&L since the U.S. open, but sense I'm reading and trading in fairly good rhythm so far. I'm not too interested in going into gain preservation mode yet given the nice market movement and potential future opportunities in the afternoon. *And I don't expect traders to be leaving early today as was the case Friday!* Market seems in no-man's-land here, but might be interested in fading the next hard move up or down.

2:58pm   A bit tricky down here as 3LB went long, then shaked and baked and hasn't been much help in the chop indicating no sustained buyers and thus no likely short squeeze in the afternoon cards (yet). Focus now turning toward the morning-after-trend setups and being cautious heading into the last hour.

3:33pm   Disappointing pace/rhythm in terms of clean entries . . . either that or I'm just not in sync. No trades since 3:03pm. Looks like the prime entries will be in the AM. Pretty typical performance for me on a trend day . . . up minimally on the day (+$3.8K, half of which was from the DAX), which is pretty irrelevant in the larger scheme of things. Call it close to a scratch day as I look toward the morning. Strong resistance in the mid-to-high 1280s for the moment and looking for day rhythm in the morning if we close down hard.

3:55pm   Watched the swimmers fight it out to the finish line and wasn't interested in participating as the goggles were a bit foggy. Pretty wild price swings toward close and am hoping they save some of those for the morning. Should be one or two solid entry points tomorrow and will have to be on my toes.

Any Green Is Good

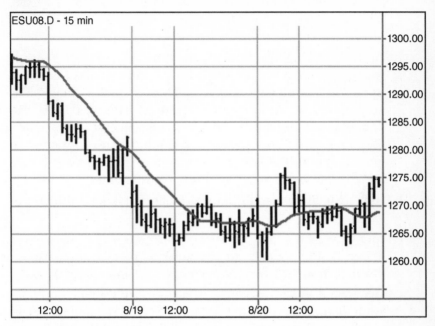

11:13am   As I suspected last night, much of the tradable post-trend oscillation action unfortunately happened in the last hour yesterday with ES climbing 8 points off its low in the last 25 mins, and thus far the optimal pullback toward key 15-min downtrend supports (my term for trend lines supporting down moves instead of "resistance") occurred at yesterday's close and again in the Globex session. As a result, I've been trading enough to keep the blood flowing, but that's about it. Tried a few longs looking for bungee snapbacks, but they never materialized and I'm essentially flat on the day with small winners offset by small scratches.

    Keeping an eye on the next consolidation break, which I sense may be down given the morning buyers' strike, uptrending VIX, and TICK that has been nowhere close to sustaining a + reading, but darn tough to short a market that's short-term oversold, and entering on trend extension signals on the day after a strong trend is typically a road to ruin. Going to let the market make the next move.

11:32am   Still no conviction at this end . . . this too shall pass. Focusing on my nonmarket obligations but keeping an occasional eye on the screen.

1:00pm   Watching the slow climb. Prefer a stronger squeeze surge to short into, although action thus far has been at a snail's pace both ways. As I've said before, market "pace" is as important to me as technical setups. This has been like watching the "Slowsky" turtles in those Comcast commercials. Been paper trading a bit on the climb, but no conviction to put capital on the line yet. *Amazing how paper trading fills are never a problem.* 15-min trend still down for now.

1:38pm   No rhythm at all to today's pace, making it difficult to enter cleanly.

1:41pm   OK, I'll bite . . . shorted 70.25 stop 71.50 going for lower high . . . small size because of past patterns (more on that thought later). Never mind . . . scratched 70.75.

1:46pm   Shaked and baked . . . that wascaly wabbit. Everyone wanted the same thing . . . hate when that happens. Next slight pop should be better entry.

1:48pm   Reentered short 1270 as that TICK pop was pathetic.

1:53pm   Best cover so far 1269 . . . heck, a point in this market is like filet mignon. Too funny. Sitting at 68.25 on remaining cover.

1:56pm   Ding, ding, ding. Flat. Might finally get a decent scalper's pace going if this keeps moving. *I don't care which way, just move!*

2:05pm   Caught some of the overextension down by grabbing a wholesale long for a few ticks. Keeping everything tight in terms of profit expectation and size for now. Longer-term "investors" not looking good now . . . lots of overhead resistance in the 1280s and charts looking worse vs. early August even at the same price.

They can, of course, bust through it, but it will take some work.

As an aside, that earlier short shake-and-bake sequence was very typical of this summer's rhythm. Traders entering anticipating lower highs or higher lows and using prior highs/lows as stops have been getting stopped right before a whipsaw turn. If you go back and look at the short-term summer ES charts, you'll see that pattern time and time again. I was aware of that pattern going into the first entry, which is why I scratched before my stop was hit sensing it might happen again . . . saved a point or so by doing that.

Not too interested in much more sardine-can trading, though, and it's lining up to be one of those days where any green is good. May take my paltry $900 (yes, that's **two** zeroes) to the bank today and let them run the market either way into the close . . . which has also been an extremely common summer pattern.

Actually feeling pretty good about not overtrading today. Tough to do much with 5–8 offsuit, and you can't bluff the market.

2:35pm   zzzzzzzz

2:42pm   5-min attempting another leg down, but no conviction in high probability entry points as larger time frames are stretched.

3:07pm   Got a small nibble shorting that last reaction up, but keeping it tight still.

3:48pm   Quite the closing spin-cycle. Closed barely green for a sandwich or two, but any green may be good on a day like this.

Current-Day Note: The day subsequently ended +$0.6K.

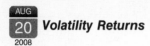

Volatility Returns

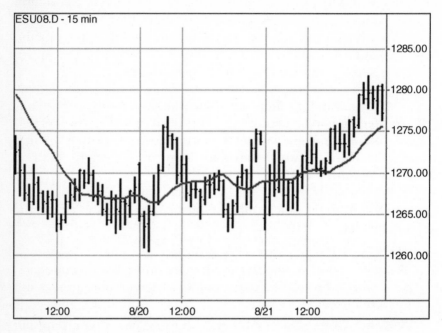

8:10am   Starting the journal early today as I'm a bit peeved that I woke at about 6:15am, right after a textbook DAX and ES retracement occurred off their overnight highs and in the area of Tuesday's resistance. *Now I need to channel that ticked-off feeling to productive action for the rest of the day.* The good news is that Tuesday's resistance seems to be intact, despite the slight overnight pop, and early focus will be on carefully establishing a core short position—ideally in the mid-to-high 1270s—assuming the market gets back there in the normal session. A nice gift would be the market trading up there, pausing, and then turning south on a 1-min time frame. Should that occur, I'll look to establish an initial position on the fade with a long leash (managing risk with size) and add to it on a turn.

My general feeling is that I should be able to let off the brake today and press the accelerator given we're now in "day-after-day-after-1st-trend-day" mode. As a result, I expect several good oscillations today, which would normally have occurred yesterday, since we're stretched even further and given the overnight action. Bottom line is I need to be sharp, make sure the gas tank is full, **and not be a wuss,** meaning that I'm willing to risk more chips given what I feel are high-probability opportunities. The market dealt Aces overnight when I was sleeping, and I expect it will deal Kings at least twice during the day.

12:20pm Wow . . . where do I even start? So, many themes . . . so little time. Well, we did get exactly as we expected—in terms of the delayed day-after-trend-day action—which because of the one-day delay resulted in even greater **and extended** intraday volatility that's still in play as of 12:20pm! *When's the last time that happened? Said another way, imagine an absolutely still pool, and then Michael Phelps jumps in. Can you say "ripples"?* The hourly downtrend also remained intact, volume increased, and the market did trade into the mid-high 1270s.

Lots of TICK vs. ES price divergences on both short-term peaks and valleys throughout the morning. *By the way, if you nailed that 11:14am spike to short, congrats. While I was expecting that same "take out the swing high stops and then whip down hard" rhythm that I mentioned yesterday has been a common theme this summer—and was ready to scale into a heavy short position on that last thrust—the bottom fell out. Apparently, the market didn't get my memo asking for a PAUSE! (See 8:10am comment.) Very tough entry with little second chance, and at the time, I felt the subsequent 1-min turn was too far off the high to enter. In hindsight, it wasn't.*

Ironically, despite my early eye on shorting, I've actually traded much more from the long side given the early plunge and then the "frustrate the hell out of everyone" 11:14am shake and bake. No matter, though, for if we can nail the rhythm, plenty of opportunities should evolve as the day develops. I've also traded smaller sizes than I expected to . . . perhaps because of the violent action . . . often scaling in and out of modest 30–40 contract sequences, and have missed a few prime entries. Yet today is another great example of where you only need to nail a few of them to carve out decent profits.

One of my huge concerns heading into today was fear that I might not be able to make an effective brake-to-accelerator transfer, especially since the foot had fallen asleep on the brake in recent lackluster market action. Kudos to an onlooker's comment to Sunday's post that helped me turn the missed Globex opportunity frustration into a call to focus and action during the regular session. His note was well timed.

There's no doubt I could have traded better, and in the words of any decent sports coach after a win, there will be plenty for me to work on for tomorrow's game, yet I'm OK with the morning $13K take in light of the relatively small sizes traded and violent early action. And although that could have easily been doubled if I'd nailed the 11:14am short *(give it up, Don!)*, my primary goal for the rest of the day is not to try to make up for lost opportunity and lean on the brake a bit as I wait for the next strong hand.

1:37pm Looks like it's back to the still pond again. ES trading right **on top of** both its 5- and 15-min 15MA moving averages.

2:04pm Going for a quickie short sequence on the attempted turn . . . looking for 1–2 points on small size. 3LB went short, and the 2-min charts trying to turn off that last high. Stop 1271ish on a 3LB turn north. Will scale into cover on any drop.

2:12pm Good . . . averaged up to 67.50 on the entry and best cover 64.75 on the drop. It ran more, but I wanted the high probability in case they jerk this back north, am getting a bit tired, and want to lock up the day shortly. Plus, we're still in a larger triangle pattern in the middle of today's range.

2:59pm Too funny . . . exit looking better now as ES turned up hard. Amazing how that happens: One minute you're the donkey on the flop, then after the turn you look like Daniel Negreanu. I want the high probability period . . . others can gamble.

3:30pm Market back to flat line . . . calling it a day. Nudged the day's take to $14.1K. Not a grand slam and definitely fouled off some pitches today, but overall a pretty high on-base percentage and touched home a few times. 133 days to go and back to work tomorrow.

Range, Range, Break

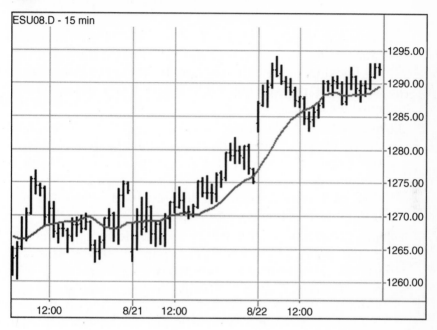

1:44pm Someday, they're going to take this market out of the current logjam range . . . and the break will be hard. That much is certain. As for the when, how (don't care), why (don't care) . . . OK, as for the "when," who knows, although it will likely be when everyone has been sufficiently lulled to sleep. Been nibbling on small 1-min attempts to bust out of the longer-term range much of the day, with one early stop, and most other sequences doing OK as I've been dumping the majority of my position as we approach the range tops and then typically cutting the rest loose on divergences or a move back down. That way, I lock in something while keeping a small position on in case "she blows" . . . even if it would just be a moral victory with a very small size.

Have only traded 360 x 2 (360 buys and 360 sells) ES and 38 x 2 DAX contracts . . . **teeny** sums for me . . . with much of ES on the 1pm–1:30pm climb and attempted range break.

Not too much to complain about here and am satisfied with the very modest $4K take, although I could have been more aggressive at the open on the early move up as I instead opted to see more cards.

2:27pm   Pop goes the weasel. Caught some of that using the same strategy, and this time the VIX pointed the way.

Looking for the first strong pullback. Might be a while if at all since I expect this pop will be strong. Range-bound traders now stuck.

3:02pm   Nice . . . nailed 78.75 entry on the retrace . . . taking it out on the pop. Clean trade and good market pace. Coin-flip shoot now . . . if they run the close, will gear up for AM after trend mode. One eye on clock and one eye on gain preservation. 3LB turned south on that last hard retrace, so not interested in riding any further wave.

3:09pm   Good decision for now . . . market down 2 points off my exit. It might hold here and gear up for another move, but it will go without me as I'm now looking to the morning. $7K now in pocket. I actually thought that pop would be stronger given the likely # of stuck range-trading shorts. There's still time, though. 5-min trend now in play for the first time in a while.

3:14pm   That's more what I expected . . . fast 3-point surge. Caught the first move . . . sat out the second. If 3LB had held, I would have considered a long on the deep retrace. Hard 2+ move back down now. Too tired here now with 40 mins to go. Calling it a day and will let others have at it. OK day, but I need to find something I didn't like about it as the week's not over yet.

Current-Day Note: The day subsequently ended +$6.9K.

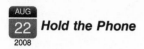

Hold the Phone

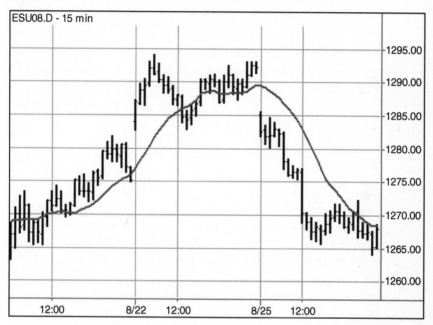

8:11am Ugh. It's shaping up to be one of those days as I got caught short on the 7:40am DAX 45-point spike on fairly decent size. Talk about an early and unwanted wake-up call. Funny thing is I sensed that the spike might happen as it was shaping up while I was providing liquidity, yet still walked right into it. *Of course, right before that I received a disturbing phone call from home (nothing major, just a nuisance). Coincidence? I think not.* The better news is that I was able to cut what could easily have been one of those "ruin the weekend" losses by a whopping 2/3 by refocusing immediately, covering on the first retrace, nailing the second spike on waning momentum, and covering on the second retrace.

OK, so the comeback mode feels "real" for the first time in a while. It was like the band was playing the waltz for much of the week and then all of sudden transitioned to the Mamba. As I mentioned yesterday, it was likely going to happen when no one expected it, and the Friday Globex session has provided the backdrop . . . at least for the time being. Immediately going into EESM mode for the rest of the day. Bernanke speaks at 10am, which might create some opportunity for the focused. Will go dark on the journal until noon.

12:31pm   Been doing some heavy ES scalping in EESM mode, but am still slightly off my game. I did let ES trade without me at open again, and this time it kept me out of early shorting trouble. Immediate goal is getting close to a scratch on the day, but the entries have to be cleaner . . . somewhat doubtful heading into a summer Friday afternoon. Got a solid week and month going, and need to keep it that way.

Note to self: Another good example of how irrelevant "daily goals" are. Let's say I had a silly $1K daily goal . . . I'm probably down $6K–$7K or so now—not sure of the exact # but I do know I'm pretty pleased with where I stand, all things considered—so I have two choices: (1) Try to find $8K from a day when I'm slightly out of rhythm and likely turn the $8K loss into –$20K or (2) pick spots and book the day's result without much attention to it and wait for Monday. Using an analogy from the current Olympics, so the French swimmer is ahead on the current relay leg. Big whoop. The wall gets touched on December 31.

1:23pm   Definite change in volatility/pace today. Some shake and bakes on the midday turn that I definitely could have traded better.

2:43pm   Finished my last scalp of the day on that last push. Was a clean entry and solid exit at 91.50 into the retail thrust. Overall, a nice comeback and we'll call the P&L a scratch at a $3.5K loss. (ES trades were actually green.) *I guess I've pulled about even with the French Olympic swimmer heading into Monday's leg . . . or maybe he's a German DAX trader.*

An interesting but OK week, with most of the chips increasing on Wednesday and Thursday.

But we know the drill though in terms of the only chart that's relevant, and there will be no problem focusing strongly after today's action.

19 weeks to go. Then we'll see what all this means.

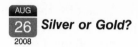

Silver or Gold?

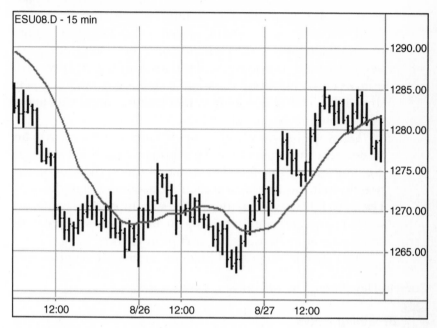

2:05am Just awoke from a nap . . . not to trade, but to try to get my head into Tuesday's potential trade. Somehow, I need to start the day feeling real pain to awake and motivate this trading soul to reach beyond what I feel has been complacent August performance. Pain to mentally translate two days of treading water into two days from hell. Pain to make that fictional draw, which has worked so well for eight months, feel real again **without actually experiencing it**.

Two days of treading water is typically a huge warning sign for me. And although I have every legitimate excuse in the book to look back at the last two days with equity-protecting "satisfaction," I can't even think of using that "s" word (rhymes with "dump")—never mind feeling its emotion—until this 2008 experiment/race/paradigm shift is over.

Perhaps said another way, I've been riding the wave of the French swimmer ahead of me in the next lane for the last half lap. What I need to do now is feel the pain of being behind and make the push when the time is right. I could coast for the rest of the month and year and easily finish with the Silver . . . 99.9 percent of people would be extremely "satisfied." I can't go there. It's nowhere close to time yet, and I want Gold.

This year isn't about greed . . . rather, it's about unparalleled personal excellence and stretching one's self beyond what he previously believed was possible . . . period. If it takes corny Olympics analogies to help make that happen, so be it. No one else is going to motivate me, and I care about one result and one result only.

Yes, we're in pre-Labor Day week, which is often when many traders take time off for the fall performance push. Yet although coasting may be fine for a few strokes—and perhaps necessary to rejuvenate me for the next required sequence of pushes—all I know is right now is that there's one swimmer ahead of me, the world-record green line is gaining on me, and my inner coach is screaming at me to time the next push right.

My coach is tough and I hate him at times. He's also right.

Current-Day Note: The day subsequently ended +$1.4K.

 Breathing Room

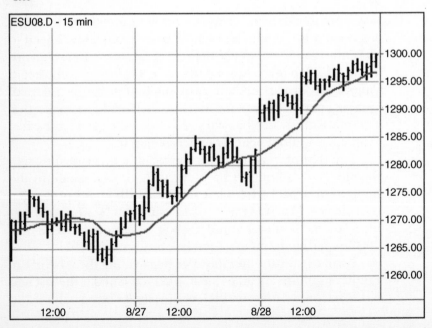

11:48am Well, I'm not quite sure if it's me or the market, but one of us has better rhythm today. I sense it's probably a bit of both. Got off to a good DAX start for once that carried over into the U.S. session. Looks like that initial personal momentum from yesterday, regardless of Tuesday's very modest score, did provide some nice inertia.

It's interesting that the DAX pretty much trended down from its open (and I traded largely from the short side) while ES traded north out of the gates (been trading it from the long side) . . . with the 8:30am economic data providing an interim turning point. That last sentence itself is highly enlightening in terms of both markets **actually trending** for more than 10 min as well as my being in sync in both sessions thus far. 5- and 15-min trend pullbacks provided good opportunity in both markets, and the VIX led the way on ES and kept me out of trying to short yesterday's highs.

So I seem to be on my game—including making the mental transition between markets better than I often do (which could have been tough given today's two completely different paths)—and have been dancing without stepping on anyone's feet. The result has been a decent $10K morning chip gain . . . a stack I don't intend on risking much, if at all, for the rest of today's summer session. Put it this way: It would have to be Trip Aces and I'm heading out for a long lunch.

12:12pm Putting lunch plans on hold. VIX plummeting and ES surging. Should be a decent overextension or pullback coming.

First card is an Ace. Looking for second card.

1:14pm Been stealing some blinds in terms of some light $0.50–$0.75 liquidity-providing scalps both ways on the climb. Pace continues to feel good. Last trade if it shows up will likely be fading a further exhaustion move north or steep retrace south. Have to be extremes though to carve out 1–2 point profit potential . . . everything else is tick scalps up here.

Trading still feeling very natural. Stroke by stroke, I seem to be gaining on the French guy. *At least the water isn't hitting me in the face now*. Keeping strokes short and swift. VIX gets the award for the indicator of the day.

Guess no lunch for me today . . . a good reminder that the market dictates breaks, vacations, etc. As Napoleon Hill once said, success means being willing to do what the vast majority of others won't do (Hill 1963).

1:32pm   Come on, one more major thrust down to shake out the late-to-the-game longs.

1:46pm   Looks like I let that bus pass. Got dealt A–J unsuited and wanted a high pair. Oh well, next deal. I did catch a piece of that first pullback for a few ticks, but wanted one more thrust for entry safety. Market a total coin flip up here now . . . lousy probability.

Heading into afternoon gain preservation mode. Day's chip count +$14K and feeling slightly better about my trading vs. recent days.

1:52pm   Hmmmm . . . this might get tempting on a further plunge. *Shhhh . . . be vewwy, vewwy quwiet. Don't do anything stupid, Don.* ES has to be in the 76–77 range for a decent low-risk long-scalp attempt.

2:00pm   Nibbled on short-side . . . noticed 3LB never went long on last climb and there's room to fall to longer-term intraday supports. Currently short from 82.25 small size, covered partial already, and holding teeny size now. Sitting at 79.75 and on free roll for the rest now.

2:04pm   Good read. Covered more 80.50. Size very small, though . . . getting tired given the early AM DAX trading and market also approaching another "on-the-fence" mode.

2:07pm   Flattened final at 81.25 and calling it a day . . . still room to drop, but clearly losing focus and stamina. Final chip count +$14.7K, with a little under $\frac{1}{3}$ coming from the DAX. I'll leave the next few relay legs to the rest of the team. At least we have some P&L breathing room for the moment. Any run into the close will set up Thursday AM.

2:14pm   Funny that ES just ticked 79.75. I guess that gives me something to improve on for tomorrow. Not a bad thing at all.

It's been an interesting dance thus far today, as I try to balance opportunity with monthly gain protection. Been keeping sizes on the light side to compromise between the two, which helped protect early profits when I gave some back fading the drop after the first hour (often a high probability move on the day after a strong trend).

So another month comes to an end, and for the eighth time this year, another hole has been filled. Conclusions? Well, it was certainly much more consistent than July with lesser volatility. The 17–3 daily gain/draw ratio is OK, but I'm a bit concerned that I had only three days of $14K+. That the largest draw was $5.2K—essentially mouse you-know-whats—seems OK, although I seriously wonder if I'm being too conservative in terms of risk/reward and position sizing. I need to think about that.

What I find extremely interesting is that both July and August arrived at about the same endpoint, albeit via two completely different paths. I also now have almost two full months of postjournal data, which gives me some indication that documenting my thoughts this way hasn't explicitly hindered my trading, with each month producing six-figure results. Again, though, it's tough to measure whether there was greater potential without exposing one's self to undue risk.

You know the drill by now. September cleans the slate once again and this all means squat. For the past—both immediate and distant—will **always** remain irrelevant. All I know is that I see four more holes ahead of me. Hand me the shovel.

AUG
30
2008
Digging to the Surface

Reviewing August's results got me thinking about taking a more detailed look at my monthly performance trends throughout this year of the grand experiment, yet doing so in a way that would **keep me out of all the dangers** of looking back in the middle of the race in progress so that I keep pushing ahead.

2008 IRA Futures Fund Performance

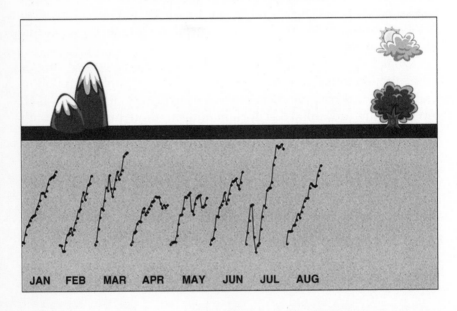

JAN   FEB   MAR   APR   MAY   JUN   JUL   AUG

So, this crazy 47-year-old mind got out his QuickBooks, Excel, and some virtual crayons to craft this monthly performance chart, which will hopefully balance a quick rear-view mirror analysis with keeping the eyes on the road ahead to avoid a possible loss of focus and crash.

If you've been following any part of this journal for very long, you'll probably be able to quickly understand why the chart appears the way it does. It's an Excel chart based on a QuickBooks download, with several adjustments, including adjusting the horizontal x-axis from zero to a level above my best performance (ground level) so that my goal remains to break through from my starting hole to above ground . . . which hasn't yet been achieved. Each sequence of lines reflects a sequence of daily performances within a single month.

Taking this larger look back does provide some interesting observations, including putting the post-journal-starting performance (last two sequences) into greater perspective. It also shows how I was apparently more aggressive in March and July, resulting in greater volatility in results—including the July miscue—**yet ranking 1st and a virtual tie for 2nd of the eight months**. Perhaps this is the most useful conclusion as I begin yet another attempt to "break ground." Maybe I need to find that lost aggression and be willing to accept the swings (sans brain cramp) that accompany the final result. *On the other hand, I'm not sure what the April and May lackluster attempts mean.*

I'm going to study this chart some more, but thought you might be interested in the approach. There are four months left, and I need to break through to that surface. I need to breathe some air.

Retrospective 2008 Race Progress Update

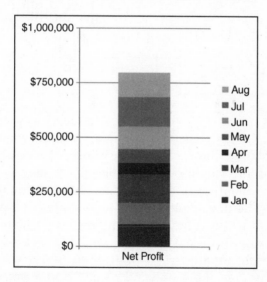

September 2008 Journal Excerpts

 *In the Zone*

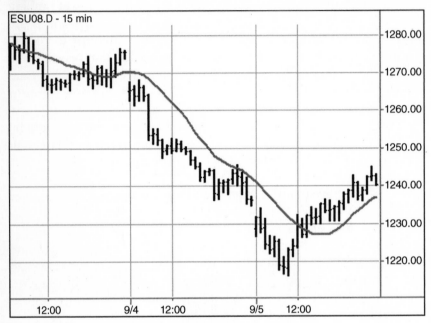

11:00am   OK, this is getting scary. Very much in rhythm today on ES and the volume is a welcome return. I have no clue what my P&L is and won't look until the next sequence is complete, which will either be a short of an approach toward 1260 or a buy of the next capitulation. Got a couple of 2-pointers with decent size thus far, especially on the 10:42am third push down where I picked up ES on sale for 52.75, took it out on the approach toward 54.75, and then repeated it again at 10:50am. picking it up at 52.25–52.75 on lesser size.

We could stay range-bound down here for a bit, but clear initial resistance at 1260 on **any** attempt back up today or tomorrow and I want that trade.

11:22pm   Long . . . best price 48.25 . . . 45 contracts. Will let it float a bit. Target exits north of 50.

11:28am   Flat all but 5 . . . took 49.75 and 50.00 on most. Sitting at 50.75 on final.

11:31am   What the heck, added at 49.00 . . . should get north of 50 easy. If we break 50, should approach 52ish. Sitting at 50.75 and 51s for exits.

11:42am   50.75 exits taken out; back to small position and final exit sitting at 51.50. *Definitely in the zone and feeling it today. Man, an approach toward 1260 would be an absolute gift short.*

11:49am   Ding, ding, ding . . . 51.50 taken out. Next entry a short on any surge north and high TICK reading.

11:54am   Shorted 52.50 small size . . . 5-min trend in play and should get one more push for 1–2 pts.

11:57am   Ding, ding, ding . . . covered final 50.75.
   EXCEPTIONAL MARKET PACE TODAY . . . BEST I'VE SEEN IN MONTHS!!
   Noontime P&L check . . . +$23K on only 681 x 2 contracts. That's a ridiculous Dustin Pedroia–type efficiency ratio. *Get over it, Don . . . plenty of day left with ample opportunity.*

12:05pm   Any strong push north from here should be shortable, but the problem is that most everyone knows that, and it could take a day or some really stupid shorts who forgot to cover in the gift plunge. ES range-bound now, but not leaving my workstation until 4:15:01!

12:22pm   Got 1260ish marked on every relevant chart I can find. Don't want to lose sight of it. Trust until broken (TUB). ES in no-man's-land, though, for now.

12:35pm   Adapting my postdraw comeback mentality to the rest of the day, I need to view the PM trade as if my morning was a large draw, which it has been for many stuck longs.
   Step up your focus, Don, and don't do any more damage by getting sloppy or forcing trades! Push yourself.

12:58pm   VIX poised for another leg up and ES another leg down. Watching only for now. No buyers in sight. Looks like September will be a bear for long-term investors . . . huge resistance to overcome.

1:42pm   Little bit of a tricky bottoming attempt . . . been dipping some toes in, scratching, reentering, etc. Holding long core position from 42.00 looking for a PM squeeze attempt.

1:56pm   Added long 43.75. 1-min 3LB is now long and this thing is stretched. Sensed exhaustion on last push down.

Stop is 41.50 or a 3LB turn south. Room to squeeze hard if we can clear 45.

2:04pm   Scratched for now 42.75.

2:06pm   No "oomph" (technical term) at all to that last lift attempt. Couldn't clear 45 to trigger panic short covering.

2:10pm   *Helluva scratch, Don.* Markets getting ugly. Dow −310.

2:15pm   Back in the "buy the panic extreme" scalp mode . . . similar to morning barf. Tried for the reversal but was no go. Scalping extremes now.

2:40pm   Tricky down here. On sidelines.

3:05pm   Not in sync down here. Tough to read. In gain-preservation mode for now.

3:50pm   No trades.

OK, only a few trades in the afternoon and nothing with size. Closing the book on a decent and highly efficient +$25.1K day. Clearly, a very painful day for investors. The key at this end is to make today feel painful for me as well.

Today is history . . . tomorrow matters.

Less-Than-Peak Performance

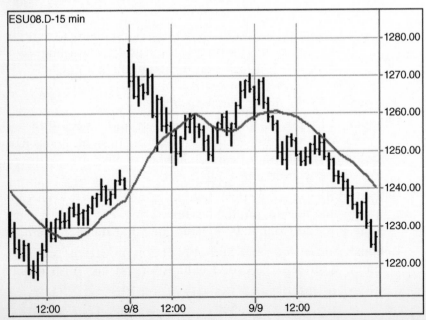

11:32pm (Sunday night.) Wow. As I write this, ES is up 37 points from Friday's close and hammering swing traders shorting the market at Friday's close worse than those with Tom Brady and the Patriots on their fantasy teams this year, after what looks like a season-ending knee injury to Tom.

And although there are times I wonder if multiday swing trading would result in less stress and fit into my toolbox as a supplemental strategy, tonight's action reinforces my personal preference to **never** hold a position overnight to limit exposure to potential catastrophic overnight events when the market isn't open. *In this case, of course, it was the federal bailout of Freddie Mac and Fannie Mae announced Sunday morning.*

Ironically, I was out most of today celebrating my 23rd wedding anniversary with my wife, was unaware of the news, and was thinking during the day about establishing a modest short position when Globex opened earlier tonight should the market open around Friday's closing 60-min resistance. When I checked to see how trades were lining up around 5:45pm today just before Globex opened for trading, imagine my surprise when I saw bids being posted in the 1260s!

So again, the game plan changes. Monday should be interesting, and it won't surprise me if I don't trade much at all until the dust settles. The smooth-running natural market rhythms of Thursday and Friday have clearly been disturbed, and it may take the market a while to regain its footing and find its new rhythm.

10:47am Grrr . . . I have to pay more attention to my own journal. Again, I should have been more aggressive in fading the first postopen move up AND adding on the 1-min turn south on an unsustainable TICK++ reading. I saw it and read it right, but it was tough being too aggressive right out of the shoot on a Monday. *No excuse, though . . . just like being dealt Kings on the first hand of the game and slow playing them!*

11:11am Jittery and rumor-driven market. UAL "files/didn't file/thought about it a few years ago" bankruptcy rumors helping whip ES around. 15-point plunge and recovery. *Reminds me of many years ago when a former vacuum cleaner salesman turned analyst came out and gave a price target on an*

Internet stock . . . and forgot to take into consideration that the stock had previously split (my best trade ever). At this rate, ES could bounce around when Tom Brady's MRI results are revealed! Like the Pats on Sunday, I'm looking for my trading defense to now rule the day and expecting a low-scoring game. My immediate goal is to have both knees intact for tomorrow as I see a lot of traders buckled over. Definitely have to stay out of the woulda-shoulda business big-time today, Don. *Yea, and if Tom had just stepped to his right.*

11:37am   Been trusting the 15-min uptrend and trading small sizes with that bias despite the chop, but the first high percent bounce already occurred on the UAL fake-out and I don't trust another test without a clear 1-min turn. A few more milliseconds on that 11:00am rumor drop **and a pause** would have been sweet, though. *Get over it, Don, and move on.*

11:55am   NQ –25 pts . . . not good for stuck longs.

12:02pm   3ES 3LB 1-min turns up; 15-min holding; not trusting longs a whole lot, though, given NQ tank and VIX turning north. If ES loses 1250, look out.

12:07pm   1-min 3LB turns down; shorted 51.75 small size . . . this should plummet.

12:11pm   Covering on the drop . . . sitting at 46.25 on final . . . still looking for a final Wile E. Coyote drop.

12:13pm   Took 47.50 on final on TICK barf. Finally finding "some" rhythm. *Then again, even Matt Cassell can throw "one" touchdown.* Still not at my sharpest, though.

12:44pm   Providing some tight-range liquidity but still not adapting well to the larger swings as I should. Initial scalp sequence entries always 0.50–0.75 too soon and trading not feeling natural. Intraday chip count check +$6K but working way too hard.

12:59pm   1260 seems again pivotal.

1:05pm   Short biased against the 1260 level and will use that as stop on any shorts.

1:14pm   Good read and sequence but backing away big time and going into income preservation mode. Today's win thus far as ugly as the Pats/Chiefs game. Some good decisions, some poor decisions, including inaction. Good is outweighing the bad, but the bad is providing huge warning signals performance-wise. Need to get my #$%& together.

1:25pm   Market somewhat on the fence now, although 1260 still looks good as short pivot, 3LB still short, and VIX trying to push back up. Long-term long button taped over for now.

1:54pm   Shorting the next pullback.

1:56pm   Short 50.50, target new intraday low with VIX on the rise.

1:59pm   Free-riding now with partial profit taken and stop at entry.

2:04pm   Very sloppy on final cover 53+. Best cover 48.25 but gave some back on final. *Reread your last post, Don . . . "stop at entry." Small contract size, but doesn't matter. Again, sloppy.*

2:08pm   That's a wrap. Not happy with performance at all. +$8.8K chip count meaningless. A on reads; C on execution and crispness.

Dreadful Start

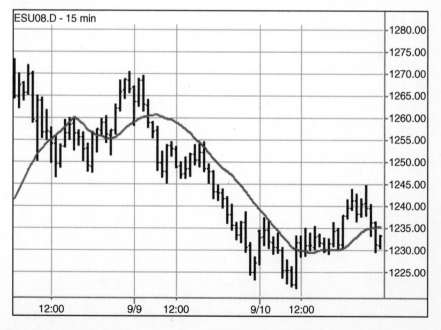

10:19am   ES was a tough read this AM as despite the strong net climb yesterday, today wasn't a clear "day-after-trend" day since ES essentially traded net flat yesterday. Still not in rhythm this week, and liquidity-providing trades are clearly unprofitable for the morning (–$11K). On top of that, I've had connection speed issues for the first time in about a year. So, the early part of the week is now net negative and I now get to trade a $3\frac{1}{2}$ day workweek. Joy.

These recent and surprising early-morning trading problems are starting to tick the heck out of me since for years it's been my strongest performance time and I can't put my finger on why I'm hesitating in this "be quick or be dead" market pace.

Will chalk the day up to a draw and simply focus on executing with small sizes going forward. Tightening up the focus and bootstraps.

10:44am   OK, got a point on a nice 5-min pullback . . . 15 teeny contracts. Good read and execution. P&L completely immaterial now. Day's goal is to get back in rhythm and restore some confidence. Call it mini EESM mode until I get it back.

10:51am   Two in a row, this time with 30 contracts buying the TICK extreme.

10:54am   Three. Maybe market (or me) finding its footing and rhythm after Sunday's "throw a wrench into last week's smooth-running BMW engine" news and Monday's bogus market bounce. *That's it. Don. Get mad. Get the blood flowing.*

11:00am   TICK can't sustain + readings. Monday's pathetic uptrend broken and 5-min in interim downtrend for first time this week. Looking to short any strong retracement and step up size slightly. Want anything near 1255; will start scaling small sizes on approach.

11:14am   Four (shorted minor pullback; out on extension).

11:17am   Five (bought extreme TICK; out on snapback). Small sizes still.

11:45am   Six, seven, eight. Scalped against deeper pullback toward 55 and took sure profits.

12:00pm   Wowzer . . . wiped out the entire morning draw . . . that's frankly hard to believe given the atrocious start. *No clue why my mid-to-late morning trading is now better than my open.*

Interesting; looking back at the early-morning chart, it was erratic, yet tradable, but like Monday, I was still early suffering from early-entryitis and couldn't get in step. Just need to get my head out of my a$$ I guess.

1:05pm No trades.

1:20pm One teeny liquidity-providing trade for $0.50. Not planning on making any others unless it's Kings or Aces. VIX and sub-1260 ES suggests more room on downside though.

1:30pm Purdy . . . nailed the pullback to 50.25 . . . covers 49.50 to 48.50. If we lose low-of-day, look out. Might get the barf some of us were looking for yesterday (the one I stopped on the final lots around 2pm).

1:34pm Shorted 1248 . . . VIX says ES going down. Keeping PM sizes small. Best cover 46.50 and trying yesterday's free-ride again for a low-of-day break.

1:44pm Added high 47s. VIX looking to pop. May need to wait for 2pm volume. *Who the heck would buy this market? Charts looking sick.* Need some ACME dynamite for the Coyote.

1:48pm **Kaboom** . . . got 42.50 on some . . . sitting at 41.25 for final. *Still keeping sizes light. I just want to stay in rhythm. Gotta love it, though, when you can't see your average entry price on the price ladder.*

1:59pm Practicing some patience on a single ES contract . . . still holding out for 41.25. *More principle than anything.*

2:05pm Be vewwy, vewwy qwwiet.

2:08pm Missed it by two ticks. Good example to recent questions on use of stops—including trailing stops . . . as in **it's only one contract!** Stop is largely irrelevant to me . . . size matters.

2:12pm Market such a tease, came within one tick. Took it out at 43 after it didn't break further. *Learned from yesterday's 2pm lesson.*

2:17pm Too cruel . . . now she blows:-). That was a nasty tease and fake-out. Still, a good read and sequence overall . . . was having fun more than anything on that last nugget. Still think we'll get the drop.

Slowing down now. ES on the fence and clear as mud down here . . . overextended short term, but bounce fakes frustrating many dip buyers.

3:34pm   Been watching most of this to see if we get a closing trend to set up a truer morning-after-trend open. Couple of small ++ scalps to keep my head in the game but not going to bookend the day with poor sessions. Tomorrow's another day.

4:00pm   Cowabunga . . . minicapitulation with volume into the close. Huge futures activity down here.

OK . . . Helluva personal intraday $17K turnaround to +$6.2K. *(For newer readers, all $$ quoted in this journal are net of transaction costs; actual gross gain is higher.)* Never thought I'd be so pleased with such a pittance. Early-morning grades: Reads C, Executions D–; rest-of-day grades: Reads A+, Executions A+, with a bonus for not trying to get cute buying late dips.

Hopefully back in rhythm for the only day that matters . . . tomorrow.

Looking forward to it.

SEP
10
2008   *Solid Performance*

3:50am Decided to rewire the brain to try and step up performance by trading a couple of NQ sequences for the first time in over a year as well as work out yesterday's "getting going" kinks in the Globex session, especially in case ES traded back toward Tuesday's rock solid resistance overnight. And lo and behold, Europe's open—and even its preopen positioning—took the DAX and ES right to the brick wall for three subsequent smack-downs.

Caught the DAX opening short and got a good chunk of its drop, although I purposely had better size and holding time on ES and caught a few of its convulsions. Toughest thing frankly was trading it on no sleep (haven't been to bed yet) . . . but the read, execution, and **conviction**—the "c" word has been missing as of late—were all there and got the "day" off on a better foot.

Heading for a nap now.

6:57am Two-hour nap . . . which means I'll be toast by 2pm. As I look at the charts—and although it was good to be around for the Globex session, I'm a bit concerned about the predictability of the normal session as ES has had no less than **four** solid short approaches to the 1240 area with the expected smack-downs overnight. Usually, such overnight action lessens the probability of similar action in the normal session . . . although it can, of course, still happen if the resistance and underlying trend is strong enough, and so I'll trust it this morning until broken.

10:42am ES indeed provided another opportunity for those sleeping through the night as we're in classic morning-after-trend mode. Ironically, the Globex pace seemed easier to trade, but I did catch a piece of the 15-min resistance short. *Still have to work on that 9:30am–9:45am crispness, though.* On sidelines here waiting for the dealer to deal the next quality hand. Long term, seems down is the way to go, but short term a coin flip.

11:48am Did some bottom fishing on the 11:30am price vs. TICK divergence, although the oversold snapback profits compensated for some foot-in-the-water long testing stops. Slowing down here and lack of sleep catching up with me. Nice extreme scalping market . . . textbook day-after-trend action with strong volatility. *Noticing I'm not as "early" as I was yesterday on fade entries . . . critical in this market and likely reflects my conviction of the expected market pace.*

ES on the fence heading into the lunch hour. Little interest here.

I mentioned earlier that I traded NQ to scramble the brain a bit. Just seemed that I needed to trade another market to clear my head a bit and think it helped. Netted a whopping $25 (that's dollars) . . . but the task served its purpose.

12:48pm   No trades. Been looking for an extreme to fade, but tight range for the most part.

1:17pm   Teeny liquidity-providing $0.75 scalp on tiny range break. Just don't see anything, though, and not interested in playing Ping-Pong in a phone booth.

1:39pm   Taking this range break attempt long. Long from 34.75, took 1 already, and will add on pullback if we get it. Free-riding rest. VIX poised to pop ES.

1:43pm   Added 34.75. This can pop toward 40 if shorts get scampering. Stop at 32.00 (about where 1-min 3LB would turn down).

1:47pm   Scratched 33.00/33.25 for loss; didn't move quickly enough. May reload if it breaks last high, but that attempt was pathetic.

1:51pm   *Good decision to scratch, Don. Nice read.* Will only take a break of 36.00 long now.

1:58pm   Nibbling on scalp short now 32.75 *(if it ain't going up!)*. Think we have stuck longs on that last pop. Small size, though, and in income preservation mode for the PM.

2:02pm   Flat; best cover 31.00. Let's see which way they take this now . . . 5-min trend flat as a pancake . . . NOT fertile conditions and a total coin flip. *Seem to be getting second wind now (me . . . not the market), but don't think it will last.* Need to see more cards now. *Don't guess, Don!*

2:13pm   Long from 35.50 and 36.00. Took 1 pt and free-riding rest. Should see approach to 40 now.

2:15pm   Pared 38.00; Sitting at 39.75 and 40.75 on rest.

2:16pm   39.75 hit. Nice. Keeping PM sizes modest. *Not sure how I'm still on my game . . . been a looooong day. Don't question it, Don; just react.*

2:18pm   40.75 hit. Sweeeeet. That may be it unless we get a short-covering capitulation spike to short. Resistance in mid-40s, but won't touch short unless it spikes toward 1250. Nice profits in hand today and **not** handing over my chips to anyone.

2:25pm   Focus fading big-time now . . . bordering on exhaustion. *Who says trading isn't a sport? **Where's the relief pitcher?** Just don't bring in Papelbon.* Getting some water.

2:36pm   Resistance zone here, but mind not clear enough to trade it . . . reflexes poor . . . watching only. 1236–1244 clear range for now. *How about a Globex-type 15-point spike to short?*

2:54pm   Shorted breakdown of 41 for a point.

2:58pm   Long off 37–38 for a point.

3:02pm   Clearly hitting diminishing returns on my trades. Also very tentative. *Where's my blankie?*

3:23pm   I'm officially toast now.

A solid +$27.4K net.

111 days to go. I might just make it.

Someone please hand me a towel.

AM Offense; PM Defense

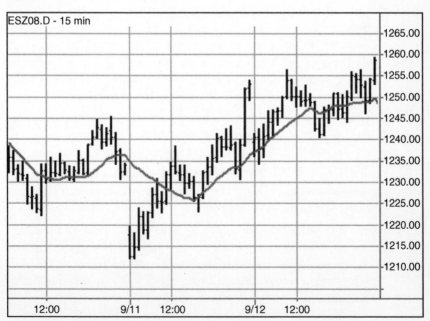

11:25am   After dreadfully suboptimizing early morning Globex trading (profitable, but not nearly enough despite a full night's sleep)—including botching the DAX's textbook retracement to 15-min resistance *(how the heck can my DAX net be negative on that sequence setup?)*—I seem to have again found my mid- to late-morning rhythm. And despite a cruel ES stop-triggering 11:04 spike into its own 15-min resistance— *which I managed around pretty well after learning my lesson with the DAX!*—the results have been OK.

11:34am   ES going for a possible short squeeze here . . . shorts may need to be careful over the coming sessions as shorting has been way too easy on pullbacks lately. *My last cover off the 15-min resistance short was 1223 . . . ES now trading at 1230!*

I'll be frank here. The minute trading seems too easy, watch out, and that's how I feel right now as I've spent chunks of the last two weeks in a ridiculous zone with the exception of Tuesday's early struggles. Even when execution has been subpar, the reads have been there. HUGE WARNING SIGNAL. And for that reason, I may back off the afternoon trading altogether unless there's some setup that's damn close to a royal straight flush.

Planning on taking a long lunch today.

11:52am   Shorts getting squeezed for lunch . . . ES at 1233 and going for Globex high. *Triple checking to make sure I'm not short.* Could see 60-min resistance here but personally passing and will reevaluate conditions after lunch. Naz outperforming ES . . . interesting and maybe another reason to be cautious with shorts. 3LB has also been long since the turn off 1223.

12:34pm   60-min resistance holding for now. Did trade a couple of small scalps, but watching most of this. Heading to lunch.

1:56pm   Back from lunch . . . doesn't look like I missed much aside from chop. Dow +0.41, S&P +0.00. All intraday ES time frames and VIX on the fence. Teeny volume bars last few hours. Will it be a quiet PM?

2:11pm   Lots of little spurts on no volume. Got some of that 2pm pop long, but keeping PM sizes very light. VIX suggests up but volume pathetic. You can see shorts getting in some trouble trying to time a turn on the 1-min chart . . . not going to make that mistake.

2:25pm   What's interesting is that I'm biased long for the moment but not really trading it much . . . more just staying out of short trouble. *Not real good at trading afternoons anyway.* Will only consider shorting a spike or clear turn from here. *This is where the journal is definitely helping my trading as I think out loud about what I'm seeing.*

2:58pm   Not in sync with late day rhythms here . . . doing light "keep head in the game" scalping yet slightly net negative. **BUT**, only trading teeny sizes (5–10 contracts vs. 30–60 earlier today) and retaining most of the morning gains. Tricky rhythms continue on almost no volume.

3:14pm   Getting a few paper cuts . . . but looking back at recent responses to comments, my win/loss today is good illustration . . . likely only around 50 percent (my guess 80 percent+ in the AM; 20 percent PM . . . feel only) but the size difference on the winners has been significant as I've been barely trading any size at all this afternoon. Thus, I've held on to most of the AM gains. Many years ago, I'd have given it all back.

3:31pm   Market definitely frustrated PM shorts. Nasty turn sequence with few solid short triggers.

4:00pm   Late Lehman Brothers buyout rumors as ES runs 20 points into the close . . . more frustration for PM shorts.

Intriguing day recap . . . traded 2 of the 3 sessions poorly by my definition (underperformed in Globex session, nice AM on good size, poor PM but on small size), but chip count up another $15.7K and held onto 95 percent of AM win. Got a bit sloppy in the PM but managed sizes well. *Definitely one of my better days in terms of size management.*

If you traded the PM well, congrats. I chose to play defense instead.

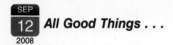

All Good Things . . .

10:52am   Well, I sensed it was coming. Being in lockstep with the market never lasts forever, and I find myself this morning definitely off my game and unable to match the market's pace as the choppy rhythm of Thursday afternoon has bled into today, due in part to traders transitioning to the December contract. And unlike other days this week, I'm not expecting to make up much ground on this Friday.

The early morning bounce off Thursday's 15-min support did eventually occur, but was choppy as heck. *(I was positioning long at the open with fairly good size, which is usually a strong percent play, and got spit out by the meat grinder.)* I've said before that market "pace" is incredibly important to me—as much as any other market aspect—and there's been little of that since noon yesterday. Looking at the charts, you can see both longs and shorts getting frustrated in a pace very similar to July and August where it looks like an interim top or bottom has been put in right before a surge out of nowhere that triggers stops.

Longer term, the climbs certainly feel like salmon swimming upstream.

So, I may simply lick my wounds today (–$10K) and call it a week. *–$10K is somewhat of a warning signal for me . . . and since I view each day as a single trade, it's my way of trying to "minimize losers."*

So the 13-day streak comes to an end and I get to start a new one on Monday. While I despise Friday draws, I supposed I can draw on several positives this week including a strong week overall and that, even today, my DAX trading was +.

12:03pm   Hmmm . . . I may have spoken too soon as ES finally finding some pace. Got a couple of good rhythm scalps on overextensions, and let's see if I can at least whittle this draw down.

12:20pm   Not trusting this climb much . . . VIX on the rise. Maybe we finally put in a right shoulder top?

12:48pm   ES breaking south on volume.

1:05pm   Shorting this pullback 44.25–44.75 (December contract) modest size.

1:09pm   Took partials and free-riding rest looking for 40.50.

1:24pm   Did OK . . . best cover 41.75. Resistance now at lower end of last break at 1248 and will reload if we get close.

1:33pm   Shorted up to 47.25 . . . covered down to 45.75 and free-riding small again.

1:37pm   Closed at 44.00 (helluva wholesale fill) **and closing down!** Incredible as I'm now **green** on the day by $0.9K, but these occasional days of poor early AM performance have got to stop.

By the way, I titled today's post before the afternoon session, but thought I'd leave it. Perhaps all good things indeed come to an end, but apparently today wasn't the day. A good week, but plenty to work on, as always.

A Market Blessing

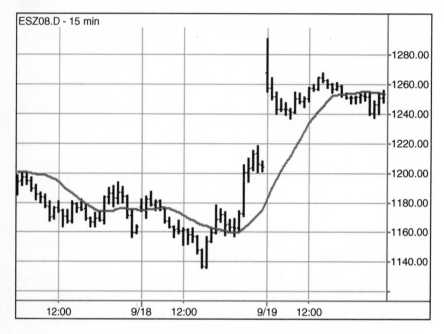

I'll be frank up front: This is going to be my toughest post ever. I'm not even sure where to start, but I'll try.

Normally, specific days don't faze me. I've said for years that each day is fairly insignificant over the course of a year or career except in aggregation with all the others. Once the trade or day is done, it has to be forgotten, as tomorrow is indeed the only day that matters. And yes, that silly blog clock counting down to December 31, 2008 is the only earnings time frame that means anything to me.

Yet today I find myself deeply moved as I've been blessed with a career trading day. *Yes, a **career** day that was pretty much over by noon.* And since I've been candid writing about my losses and miscues, I suppose I should be candid on the upside as well.

It started out innocently—and actually on the frustrated side—as I was thinking about going long last night after the market closed on the panic and also planned on getting up with the Eurex open at 3am. Well, I remained flat overnight *(that's me . . . I simply can't sleep with a position on)* and didn't wake up until around 5am, when I saw that I'd missed a couple of prime opportunities. I wasn't too pleased. Yet something told me to just sit tight and the opportunity would be there.

Perhaps it was the frustration of missing out early that sharpened the focus, but from that point on everything fell into place. *And I mean everything.* Once ES starting pulling in around 9:45am, and with my eye on the TICK expecting a much higher initial low than yesterday, I started buying and buying heavy. From then, the next few hours were frankly an unconscious dance with the market. Size, entries, and exits seemed within ticks of perfection and there was no hesitation. None. *It was like that scene near the end of Trading Places where Louis and Billy Ray were taking down the Dukes.* Perfect afternoon earnings protection (minimal trading) while adding a small icing. It was like all the experience of the last decade flooded into the moment. And I mean flooded. I just can't describe how I felt much more than that.

Exchange	Product	MMMYY	BuyQty	SellQty	NetQty	P/L (Last)
			3291	3291	0	
CME-F			3047	3047	0	
	ES		3047	3047	0	76625.00
Eurex-F			244	244	0	
	FDAX		244	244	0	-2012.50

When all was said and done, +$70.4K net was in the bank on an absurd $76.6K ES gross. 7 percent of my annual earnings target in one day. I still can't believe it and have captured the gross figures from my trading platform so I know it's real.

Oh sure, I didn't do some things well, including passing on the afternoon long (got some nice short extension clips, though) and losing on the DAX in the morning. And that will give me motivation for tomorrow. But that would be like saying you didn't like Manny's hair when the Sox finally won it all in 2004.

Those who have worked with me over the years know that I have a deep faith. I don't talk about it purposely as I try to live by example (often not doing a good job of it) rather than rant, but it's there. Today was a blessing, which is frankly hard for me to comprehend right now. Other than that, I'm at a loss for words until this sinks in.

In the meantime, I know I have to forget about it and move on. Time has shown I can come back from draws—Tuesday and

Wednesday are recent cases in point—and believing that I'm always coming back from the abyss has become my cornerstone. Now I need to find out if I can keep that same even keel and believe that the day of all days was really the draw of all draws.

There's another day left in the week, and 104 days left until this means anything. The journey must continue.

A Forgettable Week

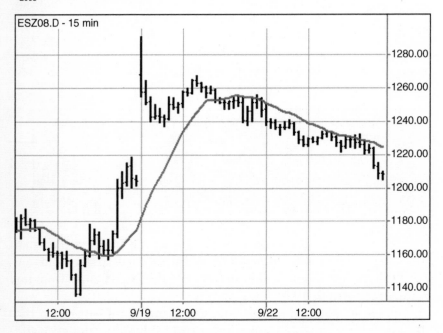

3:40pm   Well, I expected to learn something about myself after yesterday, and I indeed learned that I don't trade well after a windfall, as I delayed making my first trade for far too long and then hesitated on almost every sequence after that . . . essentially not feeling that focused fire. Actually, I had the "gimmie" premarket short all locked up heavy in the 1260s—positioning to ride it down 10–15 points—until more news broke that shot ES into a locked limit rendering stops and reentries useless. *And I wasn't sharp enough to short the DAX (while ES was locked), which was still trading and topping.* That left me scampering with the goal of minimizing damage after the open . . . a far cry from the solid profit I'd have booked if not for the limit. *Amazing how one rarely used market circuit breaker can turn +$30K into –$30K in a heartbeat.*

This is a week that will not soon be forgotten by many of us who put ourselves and our capital on the line day in and day out. Many traders were likely wiped out, and despite the net week plus at this end, I have a few bruises that will require healing.

On December 31, this week will be a distant memory. The weekly equity curve will show a decent net chip gain of essentially Thursday's trade on the week, but it simply won't show the wild swings and bruises that are at times an unavoidable element of this business. *There's simply no playing it safe in this business by being a bystander.*

I know that I trade better after pain, and today reinforced that notion. For the first time this year, I couldn't fool myself into believing the "coming back from draw" mind-set that has been the cornerstone for this year's incredible journey into an unknown land. And the results showed badly as the crispness of focus and execution simply wasn't there. Yesterday should have been energizing, but it wasn't, and two draws of more than $20K in one week is simply unacceptable. *Taking a vacation day today was also not an option as that's what weekends are for traders, and I knew that "sitting on gains" is absolutely no way to continue to grow the chip stack. Plus, the morning opportunity was there in spades.*

I'm not pleased with this week. I need to forget the week. Fully and completely.

Current-Day Note: The day subsequently ended –$25.7K.

Raising the Bar for the Final Lap

With one week to go in the quarter, I've done some deep soul-searching and decided to do two things as I prepare for the fourth and final leg of this year's race. The soul-searching was prompted by some tiredness setting in at this end as well as a peek at my daily equity chart.

First, and for the first time in nine months, I'm going to shift gears and play a bit of extended defense over the final five trading days of this 3rd quarter, essentially putting myself in major income-preservation mode for the final days of the quarter. The reason is simple: Performance over the last few days—despite getting back on track today—tells me that I'm lacking some focus and am extremely drained right now *(not a good combo with a volatile market!)* after what's been a record push this month. So, I want to lock up what's been a strong third leg and get mentally refreshed for the final push to year-end. I'm also not typically a strong end-of-month player.

So, for all my old and new friends who have been screaming at me to slow it down, stop the DAX trading, switch to the rubber hammer, etc., this stubborn type A person is finally listening. Yes, I'm tired. The journal entries show it, your comments show it, and the diminishing returns of the last few days show it. Keep talking to me as we work to strengthen one another.

In doing so, I do have one major concern, which is losing the aggression that's brought me this far. That brings up my second adjustment, which is **raising the annual bar another notch** by setting a "stretch" net income target of $1.25 million so that I keep motivated right up until the final score is tallied on December 31. "Stretch" meaning my initial goal still stands and remains my objective, but I'm viewing the "stretch" as a bonus carrot and am considering donating a portion to charity and giving back to this industry even more in some way if attained.

Three laps almost complete and then one final 3-month push to the finish line. The counter shows under 100 days to go, so the race isn't close to being over yet and a lot more work remains. I'm just momentarily coming up for air before holding my breath for the final swim.

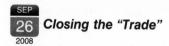

Closing the "Trade"

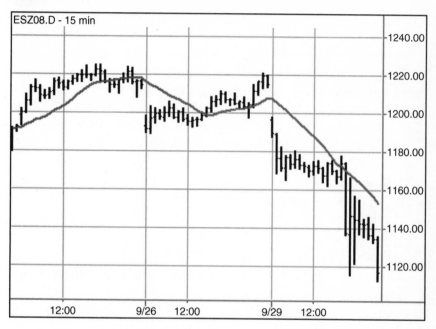

11:39am   I've continued to keep the powder dry for the most part today, although I did go long on the postopen barf TICK reading (see chart), taking it out on the move back toward zero. That's typically a pretty strong play, and I took one quick risk-protection scratch before immediately reentering. The sequence was a bit trickier than normal as Bush was about to speak, so you had to be nimble as immediately after ES made its 8-point climb off the TICK low, it gave it all back in a heartbeat before making another push. *If Bush hadn't been speaking, I may have gone heavier.* Other than that, I haven't been too interested as the market has simply been chopping back and forth reacting to any bailout news traders can get their hands on. *I'll take normal nonnews supply and demand patterns, thank you.*

The VIX remains on the rise heading into midday, and who knows what will happen in the PM as folks cover positions ahead of the weekend. Gaps of 20–30 ES points have been the rule lately *(boy is it nice to be in cash every night)*, and it would seem as if we're lining up for another one—either way—on Monday if less-than-stellar news breaks over the weekend. *As an aside, it would be nice—from a trading perspective only—if we eventually see one more bona fide capitulation as we did on the 18th, but that's just bar talk as I have no clue and just care about the next high-probability short-term pattern.*

1:34pm   Pretty decent scalp rhythm and pace on the 12:30pm –1:30pm climb. Been nibbling on the long side with the 1- and 5-min trends in play. Looking for one more sharp pullback to entry for scalp if ES pulls in toward 1203 (now trading at 1206). Certainly don't want to get too aggressive on a Friday afternoon, though—*you know how I despise Friday draws.*

1:42pm   ES climbing that wall of worry without me. Took the early scalps, but passed on the higher-risk ones. My price or nothing, and I can live with nothing. Now interested in ES near 1206.

1:59pm   OK, took 1206.50 to 1207.50.

2:04pm   Long 1204.75 for a couple; will take it out fairly quickly.

2:05pm   Took it out 1206–7.

2:25pm   Underestimated that run, but keeping it close to the vest on a Friday PM.

2:30pm   Geesh . . . not looking as dumb now.

3:02pm   Interesting afternoon in that it's a pretty fertile scalping market, but I'm keeping things tight in terms of sure profits and not trading every move. *I.e. taking 0.50–1.00 when there are often quick 2-pt moves.* The chart shows the nice 5-min-trend pullback around 2pm.

3:47pm   Quite the whip-o-matic into close as it looks like shorts definitely afraid to hold over the weekend. Did some light scalping, but nothing significant. Definitely sacrificed some gains today, and wouldn't mind having a mulligan on the 3pm temporary barf again. *(Get over it, Don.)* On the positive side, I didn't get caught in the end-of-day short cover stampede . . . that really would have ruined the weekend.

OK, on Monday I said my goal was to get back in stride after consecutive draws on Friday and Monday, even if I ended the week with a modest draw, and we'd look at the week as a single trade. Turns out the "trade" was still able to increase the chip stack by $28K—with the five "hands" playing out as −$11.1K, +$12.1K, −$0.2K, +$17.3K, +$10.0K—which all things considered including Monday's draw and deciding to scale back heading into the final days of the quarter, is an acceptable—albeit not stellar—result. Which leaves us with two trading days left in the quarter and 96 calendar days to the finish line. Snow will be here before you know it. Let's hope the bamboo can withstand the cooler weather. I'm bringing it indoors on December 31.

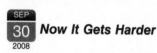

Now It Gets Harder

2008 IRA Futures Fund Performance

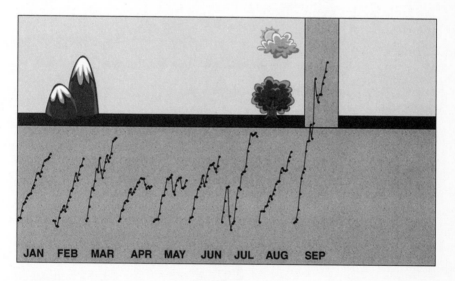

JAN   FEB   MAR   APR   MAY   JUN   JUL   AUG   SEP

Please reference the August 30 post for a description of this chart.

Now it gets harder. One lap to go and I can see the finish line. Today officially closes the books on the 3rd quarter, and now all focus must turn to a strong finishing kick over the final quarter of this incredible 2008 journey. What's past is past and now has to be forgotten, including and especially a September for the ages.

Yet we'll first take one last look at today, which I played pretty tight to the vest . . . not trading much at all in the afternoon and letting the afternoon "too early" shorts battle it out with the "too late" longs and the quarter-end window dressing fund managers. Essentially, I didn't want to give away any chips at this end for lack of clarity or tiring focus. I actually felt better pace in the Globex session (vs. the U.S. day session), where most of the day's $14K chip gain occurred on buying pullbacks.

So, I'd grade today an A for discipline and market reads, and B– for performance. We'll grade the quarter a B++. *(OK, I'm a tough grader, but there were two bonehead moves and some income suboptimization at times, so despite the equity spike, the grade will serve as a reminder.)*

And so the final leg begins. The bar has been raised and we start digging out of another hole tomorrow. 9 holes dug and 3 remain. 75 percent complete. But 75 percent is not 100 percent. 92 days left. The bogey is now $1.25 million. If I succeed, drinks will be on me on New Years' Eve and you're all invited. *I'm thinking Foxwoods.* Yet now it's time to reset the mind. I've just experienced the largest draw of my life and I'm sick to my stomach. It's comeback time. Ouch. Hand me the shovel.

Retrospective 2008 Race Progress Update

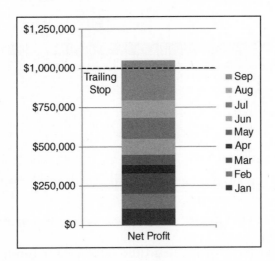

October 2008 Journal Excerpts

Current-Day Preface

Every race has that point toward the end that serves as a wall that stands between the runners and their ever-elusive goal. In the case of the Boston Marathon, it's called Heartbreak Hill, which reflects a difficult ascent about 20 miles from the start where many runners succumb to their humanity just when it seemed the goal was in sight.

In the case of my Race, early October 2008 was my Heartbreak Hill, which tried desperately to bring me to my knees just days after I'd briefly touched the $1 million mark almost a full 2 months ahead of schedule and was in the process of increasing my $1 million target to include a $250K bonus or "stretch" incentive. And then life intervened.

Here are the some of the key day-by-day journals from that month as they were recorded. And cue the Dramamine.

 *Monday Mess*

Yes, I took it hard on the chin—and cheek and neck—today. I was off my game in the morning, wasn't focused enough, got stubborn, and decided to "invest" some of my hard-earned gains by swinging for the fences in the morning, not believing that the market would give (throw) up its early low given the opening multiyear 50 VIX reading and strong 10-point thrust off the 9:31am lows.

I played it perfectly up to 9:45am, buying the initial thrust down and selling on the spike north. But then, the errors began, perhaps the most crucial being that I ignored the 3LB indicator after the initial pop and mismanaged size. *Certainly ES wouldn't lose another 40 points below its early low!* As the market tanked and the VIX climbed toward 60 . . . that's **sixty** . . . I felt like Tom Brady with a defensive lineman around his knee. And I heard the crunch.

Maybe it was looking at my year-to-date results over the weekend when I've said all year that I'd careful with that until 12/31. Maybe some invincible feeling bubbled to the surface. Maybe it was lack of sleep after the late-night Sox game last night. Maybe God decided that I needed to be humbled big-time to set up the next run, or it's His sense of humor that I should take the rest of the year off. Maybe . . . maybe . . . maybe.

Fact is, the real reason doesn't matter, so I won't analyze it to death. All I know is that it happened and I know better. I'm not a home-run hitter . . . I'm a singles and doubles liquidity provider, and all that swings like that do are tear muscles. Right now, it's critical that I focus on the good as I head into a rough evening.

- I'm wounded but not dead. Time is a great healer.
- All earnings/losses do are gain/lose time . . . so I'm a few weeks younger now.
- The afternoon session was positive.
- I just invested in continuing education for the second time this year.
- On 12/31, this will be a distant memory and the wound will have scarred over.
- Percent-wise, it's not my largest draw.
- It wasn't a triple-digit loss.
- I'll still earn my goal of $1M this year.
- And yes, believe it or not, the financial hit could have been (and was at one point) much worse.

So there it is . . . in all its ugliness. The human element rears its ugly head again.

Current-Day Note: The day subsequently ended –$93.6K.

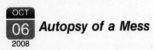 *Autopsy of a Mess*

OK, I know that I said I wouldn't overanalyze today, but looking back for a moment, I'm not feeling quite so bad. Here are a few observations.

Let's start with the TICK. First, the low was a staggering –1684. Never seen that in 10 years of trading. Second, it took about 90 mins for the TICK to come close to approaching zero from the downside. Can't ever remember the last time that happened . . . that's 90 mins of sustained selling at open without a breath.

Let's now look at the VIX, which reached a 19-year high today. My platform data doesn't even go that far back, and my oldest daughter who's now in college hadn't been born yet.

As an exchange member, one of our roles can be providing liquidity, a role that requires us to put our own capital at risk so that others can buy and sell even during panic times . . . and such infrequent days can often be painful, as was the case today. Yet in the long run, we serve a useful role and are more than adequately rewarded for that occasional sharp pain.

In this business, it's truly a case of no pain, no gain, and my eyes remain steadfast on the gains ahead.

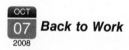

OCT 07 2008 *Back to Work*

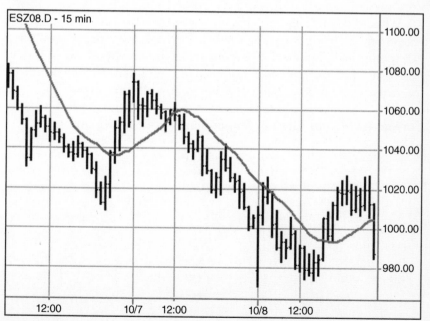

Well, as much as I was out of step with the market in yesterday's debacle, today's been pretty much error-free, and I'm going to keep it that way by shutting down for the day here with the release of the FOMC minutes.

With respect to going back to work after yesterday, I must say that although I normally have no problems going back to work after a driver's ed video day—which has been my strength over the years and formed the foundation for this year's cornerstone concept—I tossed and turned a great deal last night thinking over the day.

So, I had the following checklist coming into today:

Reduce size—Check

Don't force anything—Check

Get into EESM mode—Check

End the morning green—Check

End the day green—Check

I said recently that the market seldom does the same thing on Day 2, and that certainly held true today where liquidity-providing fades were very high probability and all worked out well.

What did surprise me, frankly, was that by 2pm, I ended up recovering a whopping 30 percent of Monday's draw and have now come back almost 70 percent from my low point on Monday. *Even I'm having a hard time believing that.* Thankfully, life is full of tomorrows . . . and we have another one, well, tomorrow.

Current-Day Note: The day subsequently ended +$25.4K.

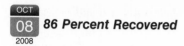

OCT 08 2008 *86 Percent Recovered*

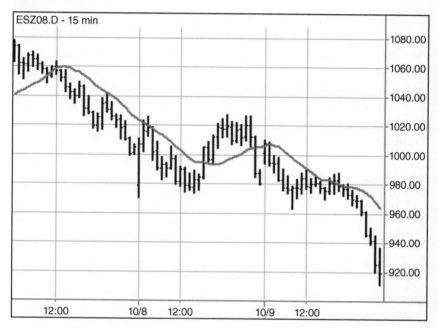

Where do I even start. How's this . . . I decided to cover my last Globex short at 6:53am to take a shower. When I got back, ES had shot from sub-1000 to 1040 on the interest rate cut. Funny thing was—and I kid you not—I was thinking in the shower that I should have some small-swing long position at the ridiculous ES Globex levels on just in case we got a cut. *Who'd have thunk buyers missing that would have had another chance in the regular session, and at even cheaper prices.*

That was about the only thing that went wrong today, and although I don't normally use the "proud" word, I'm extremely pr . . . pr . . . *(nope, still can't go there)* satisfied with my performance over the last two days, and today in particular. Perhaps my response in last night's comments says it all in terms of postdebacle EESM mode (which I've been in twice this year, "mini" modes not included), meaning that it means I step up the focus more than anything. And my brain feels it as I'm fried right now.

Suffice it to say that I had my second best day ever and was able to ramp up recovery of Monday's car crash to 86 percent in less than two full sessions. *That's like being in a real crash where your car is totaled and then waking up in the hospital two days later with a Band-Aid on your finger.* Most of the gains came on shorting the rate cut news in the 1030s, buying the open and adding as the market climbed in my favor, and then shorting the monster climb on its approach to the 15-min resistance. Talk about the monster of all day-after-trend days. Although I still don't get why the market gave up its earlier 7am interest rate cut gains and more BEFORE the open, it's not our job to figure out why . . . we'll let the talking heads figure that out. Our job is to react, period.

I won't ever be able to fully describe why I trade better and more focused after a draw. I just do. I'll be frank as always: Monday would have destroyed most. Capital, confidence . . . you name it. I got caught in a once-in-a-century tidal wave in a raft. And yes, I purposely didn't disclose the # and have only talked in percent terms over the last two days *(until today . . . more on that below)*, not to hide a darn thing but to keep my mind focused on the task ahead. It was comeback time again . . . this time for real.

Such is life. Yet by comparison, it pales compared to real-life issues. Consider these: I likely wouldn't have even been born if my parents didn't have a devastating stillbirth before I came along. I almost lost my spouse to a massively burst appendix a few years ago. As I've mentioned, my daughter was diagnosed with type 1 diabetes at the age of 10. I broke my ankle and had a massive virus just before entering 12th grade and missed our basketball team's championship run. I almost went broke when I gave up my executive career a decade ago to trade full-time.

You see, for some reason, and with all due humility, I'm used to coming back. I can be nicked, stabbed, kicked, wounded, ridiculed, challenged . . . you name it. But you can't kill me. The strength doesn't waver, it only intensifies. And I'll again be frank: My faith in God and the abilities He's honed over years of occasional hardship has a lot to do with it. Although I purposely don't choose to flaunt my faith, none of this year's bamboo tree experience would have been possible without lots of hand-holding along the way over the last 47 years.

The end-of-month and end-of-year charts will show a Monday draw of –$93.6K (or 5 percent of my capital), followed by comebacks of +$25.4K on Tuesday and +$56.2K today. Monday **shouldn't** have happened, at least not to that extent, and I'll again learn from it. Yet it did and life goes on . . . step by step. Now, less than two days later, it's essentially as if it never happened and we can start talking about the Q4 bonus again.

The wound has healed remarkably fast. It's truly a team effort . . . if you know what I mean. I just wonder where this darn Band-Aid on my finger came from.

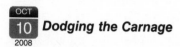 **Dodging the Carnage**

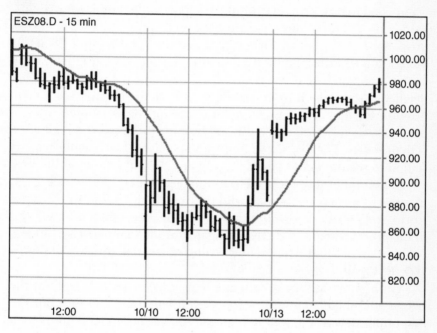

Wow. Wow, wow, wow, wow, wow.

Where the heck do I start? First, the daily chip tallies for a week that none of us will ever forget:

Monday –$93.6K

Tuesday +$25.4K

Wednesday +$56.2K

That much you already know. Then comes Thursday at –$4.8K and today at +$56.2K. But we need to dig deeper into the box score of the last two days to get a true appreciation for my attempt at riding the roller coaster.

We'll start with Thursday in which I had a solid morning and then gave back the gains on the market's late afternoon belch . . . which at the time—let me repeat that—at the time most of us thought was the final capitulation. Yea, I know I don't normally trade late afternoons. But the afternoon meltdown really felt like the big one. Suffice it to say that I escaped the day with no gain and no pain. *I still can't believe that the VIX is 73 as I'm writing this.*

Then comes today, which made Wednesday's "monster of all day-after-trend days" look like a kitten. Actually, "today" started last night when I had to pick up a relative at the airport and wanted to put a small swing position on at the close after the 600+ point/7 percent + Dow drop. So, I got to Logan Airport at about 6pm and bought ES at 908 (15 contracts) with a planned exit in the 920s on an overnight reaction back up. I watched it for a while . . . trading up to 915ish . . . but decided to simply let it cook a bit for a while (keep in mind it was a small position for me). Then we stopped to eat on the way home where I peeked at the position and it was still holding 910 or so and I felt good with the entry. Then we drove home and an hour later I sat down at my station to see the market gave it up again . . . to the tune of the 880s.

At that point, I proceeded to minimize the damage by scaling out into the moves up and actually did pretty well navigating through the storm, so to speak. Then after two brief naps overnight, I nibbled a bit in the premarket and did OK and again wanted to put a small long ES position on before the open and again saw the market give it up on a Wile E. Coyote dive.

Then (catching my breath as I write this), I go long right at the bell, see ES spike 10 points or so, take off half for 8 or 9, and buy the first pullback with the lot I'd taken off for the prior gain, after which ES decides to completely ignore the VIX and barf yet again through its opening price to the tune of 30 points ON TOP OF the gap down.

All I could do at that point was wait for the eventual pause and buy the daylights out of it . . . which I did after a few probes and stops, with the best and final price of 839.25. From there I scaled out for +10 to +20, which finally put me back in the green for the day, and more importantly FINALLY got me in rhythm with this damn thing . . . which led to several sequences of 3–6 points throughout the day and has led to the decent day's take.

I'll be clear: For most of us, this week was about survival, period. Those who survived the week (few and far between) will live to trade another day. Those who didn't will be replaced by others, some of whom will make it and most of whom won't. This business is a war of attrition, and the chips go to those who survive when others are getting slaughtered. Chips are always transferred from the large number of losing traders to the small number of consistent winners.

At this end, the weekly score will show a +$39.4K chip gain and a decent dent in the year-end $250K target bonus. But it could have been higher as the box score is another story, as I was early more often than A-Rod peaking before the playoffs *(apologies to NY sports fans)* in this market where the term *extreme* gets redefined hourly. Fortunately, I was able dodge the carnage that's lying everywhere and managed well enough to live for another week. I realize that many others aren't as fortunate and feel their pain.

I'll post a video over the weekend . . . after I recover from the motion sickness.

Current-Day Notes: And there you have it. After falling and landing flat on my face on the approach to Heartbreak Hill and bleeding all over the proverbial pavement, I somehow, some way, found some kind of a second, third, and fourth gear to claw my way to the other side. And to my glorious amazement, after wiping away the blood caused by my own stumble, downtown Boston and the Prudential Center were in sight.

OCT
15
2008   *Day Off*

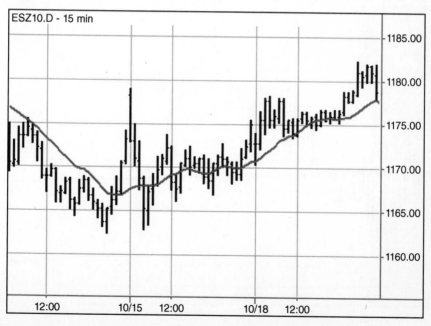

For some reason, for the second day in a row I haven't quite felt myself in terms of alertness and focus, so I chose to trade extremely lightly—only trading a handful of sequences for a very modest +$5.5K gain. Perhaps one reason was that I didn't come into the day with any opening setup conviction and never could ramp it up during the day as many time frames seemed to be in conflict with one another.

Perhaps it was for the best as I avoided potential losses that might accompany less-than-optimal focus . . . especially during the late-day decline. Call it a "day off" of sorts, which I suppose beats an "off day."

Current-Day Notes: I selected the previous entry for this book as an example to show that cumulative trading gains over time are largely compiled by hitting singles rather than the more glamorous doubles and home runs, which I'll address in greater detail in Part VII. And while we're on the topic of baseball, the next post provides one of the better glimpses as to the sacrifices I made during 2008, especially for—at that time—an ardent Red Sox fan.

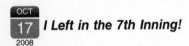

OCT
17
2008   *I Left in the 7th Inning!*

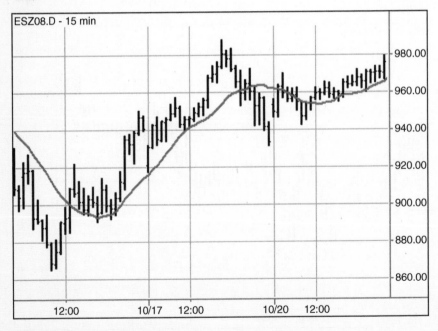

We had the best seats: a corporate sky box on the third base side angled toward the plate. The food and digs were incredible. Yet by the top of the 7th, the place was a morgue. Not just the box . . . the entire Park and city. Fenway was dead, and the Sox looked old and beaten. Papelbon gives up the double to make it 7–0 in the 7th, and we (and others) clear out of there to begin making our way to the train and then home. Someone on the train says something about it being 7–6, which we discounted. Then we get in the car about an hour later just in time to hear Drew's game winning hit . . . on the radio.

Second biggest playoff comeback ever. Largest since the early 1900s. One of the best Sox games ever. And we're sleeping on the "T" (Boston's subway) during the comeback and listened to the final hit **on the radio**. As much ribbing as my friend and I have taken, everyone has told me they would have done the same thing. Plus, we were exhausted from our respective crazy schedules. And I wanted to be alert for today. The net result? One ticked-off fan, but a solid +$26.3K Friday chip gain due in part to a decent alertness that I wouldn't have had if I hadn't left when I did.

I've said all year that this year was one of sacrifice and focus. You have to do what others can't or are unwilling to do. Last night, I made a sacrifice. It hurt. But it hurts a lot less now. I think that it's the little things in the business that mean a lot. I was tired all day. But it was a manageable tired, and exhaustion didn't set in until now as we pass the 3:30pm mark on a Friday. I didn't do anything dumb today and even traded the 2:30pm–3:30pm market whipsaw well.

Most of my trade entries were fades into trend support (including the opening 15-min support from Thursday afternoon) or unsustainable pushes, and I often clipped 1–4 points in this market, which continues to provide incredible price volatility.

At this end, the week began with a –$11.1K chip hit . . . and it ends with a +$118.5K net gain for the week. The Sox head into the bottom of the 7th losing 0–7 . . . and win 8–7.

I guess we both had them right where we wanted. When we both eventually go, it will be kicking and screaming. But you'd better do your best O.J. impression, because we don't die easily.

And so the journey continues . . . for both the Sox and me.

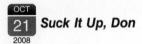

Suck It Up, Don

I felt that I needed this special post in this diary of mine to tell myself to "suck it up," in part because I traded a bit hesitantly in today's trade, clipping far too quickly at times once the market "opened up" a bit. I also feel some complacency sneaking in as I balance playing defense during earnings week with taking maximum advantage of opportunity when it presents itself.

Like poker, changing gears is important in this business, and I didn't do it very well today. For example, I felt myself coasting when stepping on the accelerator was more appropriate. The more time I've had to reflect on the day, the stronger I feel about that, especially in light of last week's strong week and the current year's score.

Perhaps my concerns are unwarranted given the decreased market volume this week. Yet today's modest results and hesitancy are bothersome enough for me to document it tonight so that I remain aware of it.

And again as in poker, the key at this end remains recognizing and feeling the frustration of many traders in the market who have been trying to unsuccessfully trade range breaks over the last two days of marginal volume . . . and using that to my advantage when the resulting setups occur.

I need to forget about the past and not get complacent. I failed today and need to get angry again. With less than 20 percent left in this year's game as of tonight, I need to find another gear.

Current-Day Note: The day subsequently ended +$9.9K.

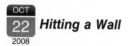 *Hitting a Wall*

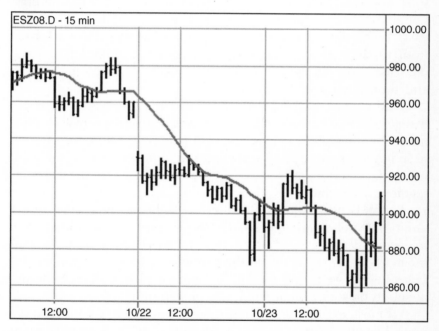

My trading has clearly hit a wall. On this October 22, 2008, after 295 days and well over the annual $1M target, I'm simply spinning wheels and treading water now . . . and am **not** happy about it. I traded the last hour horrendously after a strong morning—even in a pace for which I'm very well suited—and am now back to a scratch for the week.

It's completely unacceptable, and I have to make some clear decisions before moving forward. I'm not sharp mentally and am clearly getting extremely sloppy and complacent. I know sub-consciously that I'm letting up and coasting . . . exactly what I didn't want to happen. I need to make some tough decisions.

Current-Day Note: The day subsequently ended –$7.5K.

Role Reversal

First, thanks for the overnight comments to yesterday's "short and sour" post. Yea, I was ticked off after booting away a fine day on pure sloppiness. I was as mad as I've been all year . . . including the disaster days. And it wasn't the minor chip ding—although that's a **far** cry from where I stood at 2pm—that bugged me. Rather it was the unfocused sloppiness that had begun a few days ago and finally ended up biting me.

I did a lot of thinking last night, including reverting back to *The Tao of Poker* that had about 20 excerpts that described my late after-noon, the ones about fatigue and distractions, momentarily slipping back to rookie mode, and sometimes by thinking two steps ahead, we're one step too early. They all applied. Those and my own new segment on "stupidity."

I know better. I stink in the afternoons. I really stink after 3pm. I don't trade well when tired. *(And in this final leg of the race, I've also been finding myself tired more often lately . . . with no relay baton to pass.)* I had the market read perfectly, yet the connection between the mind and fingers was frayed. And for the first time in a long time, I allowed myself to blow past my mental trailing stop on the daily "trade."

Yet most importantly, the more I tossed and turned last night, the more I realized I've accidentally slipped in to "Ivan Drago" mode lately, including when he finally gets cut and the announcers scream *"The Russian is bleeding"* and when Duke says to Rocky, *"He's worried! You cut him! You hurt him! You see? You see? He's not a machine, he's a man!"*

You see, I'm not Ivan Drago. I'm supposed to be the other guy. The humble underdog. The comeback kid. The guy who talks funny.

I don't know what today will bring. But I've been pounding bare meat all night and we'll see if that helps.

Sincerely, Rocky

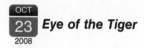

23 *Eye of the Tiger*

2008

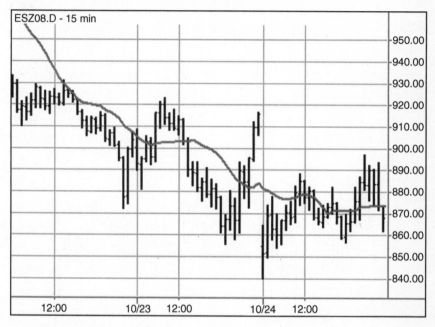

Better. Strong and sustained focus (despite a restless night for obvious reasons), recognized and successfully navigated the early 15-min oscillating diamond pattern (late yesterday overlapping with early today) within the context of the continued 60-min downtrend, nailed the post-2pm barf (both long and short), took high-probability entries and exits, "trail-stopped" my earnings all day, and most importantly, stopped trading at 3:15pm aside from a too-good-to-be-true short on the late-day spike for small size.

Result: Solid +$44.8K net chip gain on 1565 x 2 trading, including +$8.6K DAX gross on a very solid performance in the early session and +$37.7K ES gross, with **no** errors that I can recall, aside from leaving some profits on the table and passing on a few decent entries, which I can more than live with today.

I've preached for years that trading is a sport, and the last two days provide yet more evidence for those who think that trading is just about chart patterns and analytics. It may not be a physical sport, but the required mental element is no different . . . not to mention that we make and absorb punches every hour of every day.

Today again also proves that I trade better and in a more focused state when angry. I guess that's how it will always be. The only thing I can't figure out is why my hands smell like raw meat.

OCT
24
2008

A Defensive Win

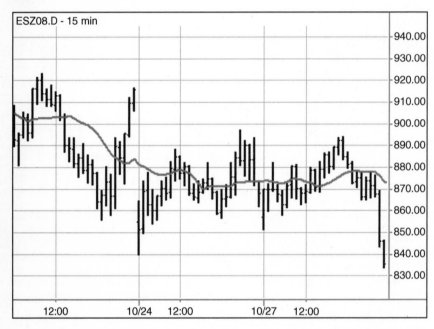

12:19pm   I've chosen to play defense much of the morning and have only traded a paltry 303 x 2 thus far for a $6.5K chip gain, with about half coming from the DAX. I actually woke up briefly around 3:30am, traded a couple of DAX shorts, and went back to sleep while Europe took ES right now to its locked limit of –60, which absolutely crippled buy-the-Thursday-close longs.

I actually got a very restful sleep last night vs. Wednesday night's toss-and-turn marathon. When I awoke and saw the lock, I decided to play it slow today and simply keep moving forward by limiting any trading to high-probability spike fades in this thin market.

Possible 5-min head and shoulders here that might take us down yet again. Nibbling on short.

12:29pm Nice. Got +4.5 on best cover (73.25 to 66.75). Only had 10 on. Not sure I'll trade much for the rest of the day as I'm now in major-week chip-preservation mode. Day chip count now slightly over $8K.

1:13pm zzzzz. I'm actually glad to see the market not moving. I imagine I'm not alone as recent daily charts are screaming trader exhaustion. 5-min ADX under 9, though on no volume, and we might still get an afternoon push.

1:20pm Here we go . . . market trying to break upward.

1:32pm Well, that didn't last, nibbled on pullback but scratched when no further thrust. Might be a fake and elevator drop to continue the hourly downtrend. *Frankly, it will shock me after that if ES closes on its highs.*

1:39pm Caught short scalp using the "If it ain't going up" theory.

1:50pm And again (65.50 on pullback to 61.00). Keeping sizes **extremely** light (5–10 contracts) to balance protecting gains with taking advantage of opportunity. Plus, this market remains as thin as wax paper.

1:55pm And again (65.00 to 62.75). Shorting every pullback and taking it out on the drops. Chip gain up to +11K on only 356×2 contracts. Efficient.

2:02pm Trend remains down, but the trade remains very thin. Going back into watch mode.

2:18pm OK, the market is officially chopping and I'm not going to do anything stupid, so that's an official wrap on the day and week.

All in all, pretty decent judgment over the last two days, and the week's daily chip counts end up –$1.1K, +$9.9K, –$7.5K, +$44.8K, +12.0K for a respectable +$58.1K. Yet there remains **plenty** of room for improvement, especially when you drill down into Wednesday's box score of sloppiness and frustration. That still doesn't sit well with me, and as long as it doesn't, that's a good thing for my trading. To beat a dead horse, complacency is the killer in this business, whether it sneaks in during a trade, day, week, or month. And the killer must be avoided at all costs.

This leaves one week to go in October, then two short months (especially considering the holidays) to the finish line, which is beginning to come into view. The Q4 bonus tally will be updated to reflect 97 percent shortly, which depending on where that stands next Friday could set up the final two months of digging as free-roll on top of free-roll. *It also means that I may have again underestimated the extent of this year's bamboo growth and may have to raise the bar yet again.*

But let's not get ahead of ourselves. Five more days of digging and a **lot** of work remain before we can close the month and head for the final two turns. And there will likely be more earnings landmines to dodge next week.

And so another two days off before the journey continues. This amazing, indescribable, frustrating, wonderful, get-punched-in-the-face, get-back-up, tiring, rejuvenating race of the century.

What's done cannot be undone, and all eyes are on the road ahead. The dealer returns on Monday, and the chips had better be ready.

OCT
28 *Dodging Landmines*
2008

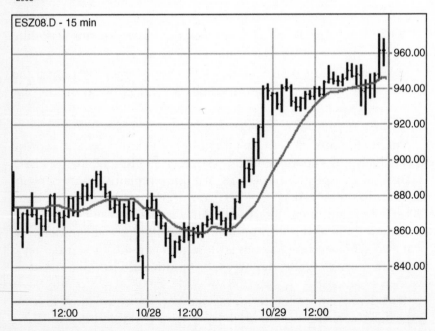

1:35pm   After a rather adventurous overnight Globex session in which Japan—and then Europe—took the U.S. back out of the Monday PM abyss **and through its late-day range-break low**, ES is again trying to form an inside day heading into the late-afternoon session. At this end, I traded portions of the overnight session, focusing on shorting approaches toward Monday's late-day resistance, and took some losses in the form of repeated stops until it was clear that ES wasn't going to give it up overnight. The good news is that I recognized what was happening, kept sizes fairly light (I think I took 4–5 probe entries), and kept the loss at that time to under –$7K (heeding my lessons from earlier in the month).

From there, I didn't do much until the U.S. day session and have continued to focus on short-term contratrend scalps, keeping sizes and holding times extremely light in light of continued decreasing intraday ranges and trends . . . the late-day 30-min barfs notwithstanding. I've had a moderate degree of success thus far, having turned the –$7K chip loss into just under a $10K chip gain.

As I write this, the 15-min ADX is down near 10 and pretty much flatlined with no trend in play. Even the 5-min hasn't seen much of a trend over the past few days, which leaves 1-min trends and fading extreme TICK spikes are the main games until the winds again change.

2:27pm   ES again trying to break to the upside. One of these days—who knows when—it's going to stick for one of the all-time short squeezes. Watching for now. VIX also trying to turn down.

I'm admittedly running a bit on empty heading into the PM session given the long night session with only a few naps, so the thought process at this end is to stay out of trouble.

2:51pm   Shorts getting squeezed. Still cautious here as I'm not particularly focused and need to find another gear if I'm to trade this aggressively.

4:15pm   Not a big surprise (note 2:27pm comment). Considering how tired I was and the huge potential for liquidity-providing locals to get killed on the squeeze, this extremely tough grader is going to give himself a rare A++ for both market read and staying out of trouble throughout the day . . . and especially on the late PM climb. I actually even managed to grow the chip count a bit more by scalping clear extension and pullback extremes to end +$14.1K on the day.

For those new to the journal, I don't typically make much profit on strong trends, which is often the case for liquidity-providing exchange members. The morning-after the trend is typically when we do well, and I'll need to be on my toes tomorrow, especially with the FOMC decision looming. For me, today was about avoiding potential land-mines—both during the Globex and regular sessions—and not about profit maximization. The modest chip gain was a bonus.

OCT 29 2008

A Step Slow

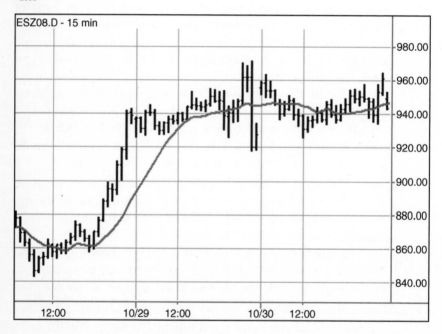

1:48pm   It's often been said that 99 percent of work is simply just showing up. Yet every so often, you have one of those days where you're simply not at your station during the prime entry times. Such has been the case for much of today at this end as sleep, restroom breaks, and nonmarket priorities kept me away at key turning moments . . . especially during the pre-6AM gift of an ES pullback to sub-920 once the DAX finally lifted off a prolonged consolidation phase. *And actually, most of the solid action came in the overnight session as the early post-U.S. open oscillations were much shallower.*

And as is often the case under such circumstances, I found myself scrambling and pressing a bit trying to capture pieces of the textbook morning-after-trend oscillations, and the result of missing the prime entries has resulted in a subpar +$5K performance heading into the FOMC decision.

I also think that the month's efforts are catching up with me, as I continue to note a lack of keen focus and concentration over recent days and a poor transition from defense to offense when needed. And we all know that trying to trade FOMC action with a lack of full concentration can be deadly.

3:37pm Not much better in the afternoon, although I stayed out of trouble and nudged the pathetic chip gain to just over +$6.2K by catching some of the post-3pm consolidation break and extension.

Clearly not one of my better days, but a win is a win and tomorrow is another day.

Welcome to My Final Table

OK, so the final table for the 2008 World Series of Poker (WSOP), which will take place on November 9 and which ESPN will telecast on November 11, is now set. All nine players are guaranteed $1 million. (OK, the first guy out gets "only" $900K, but that's splitting hairs as everyone else gets more than $1.2M with the winner getting $9M.)

The battle has been grueling and minefields abundant as players have had to battle lost sleep and lapses in concentration resulting from the constant stress of having to make decision after decision as thousands of hands are played—not to mention bad beats from 2 percent probability river drownings.

And yes, those left standing have also been lucky. They've escaped jams, sometimes as the result of their skill, but often as a result of simply being in the right place at the right time. Sound familiar?

Those who have been following this journal know what's next, and I'll apologize up front for what may seem like an overdone analogy.

Yet I can't help it as it's extremely relevant and timely as we get ready to enter the "final table" of November and December. *Plus, this remains my diary, so anything goes.*

You see, for some reason I've been put in a position similar to those who will battle it out on November 9. On Monday, I'll be entering my version of this year's 2008 "final table," essentially playing with the house's money.

Yes, I've been on a mission this year. For the first time in my trading career, I decided to suck it up big-time for 366 days and make sacrifice after sacrifice to push myself harder than I ever had. In doing so, I sacrificed hundreds of hours of sleep, plenty of personal time, nontrading business income, and some of my sanity . . . not to mention the 7th–9th innings of the second greatest baseball playoff comeback ever. The goal was simple: personal peak performance. And like the WSOP, the game isn't over yet.

Of all the players at this year's WSOP final table, I can most relate to Dennis Phillips, who will be the oldest player at the table at 53 . . . just six years older than me. And yes, I'm rooting for him to prove that there's something to be said for decades of life experience. Yet my favorite player (not at the final table) remains Barry Greenstein, whose silent stealth play over his career has put him in a financial and psychological position to donate his time and funds to greater causes. And I can also relate to Michael Mizrachi, a fellow "grinder," albeit in a different industry.

I'm well aware of the landmines. The story of Archie Karas will always serve as a reminder. And as this year's televised WSOP hands have again validated, it only takes a single mental slip to undo thousands of hands of a well-played game and to hand the entire chip stack over to someone else. I need to remain aware of both of those lessons before I can close the book on this year's tournament on December 31.

Tomorrow night, we'll take a final peek at October result, which will, of course, mean nothing when the new dealer shows up in November. And I anticipate that the next two months will be among the toughest trading months of my career and that I'll be on the defensive much of the time. One reason is that the rhythm of the last few months—now that we've grown accustomed to it—will likely change yet again.

So, the goal at this end is now fairly simple—incremental gains balanced with chip protection. I won't raise the bar again or risk

10 months of sweat and hard work. For unlike the WSOP, I get to keep whatever chips I have on December 31.

But it should be fun. Welcome to my final table.

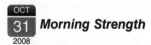

OCT 31 2008   *Morning Strength*

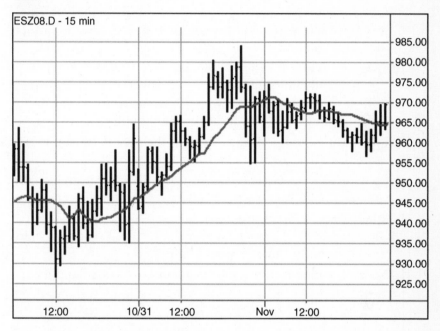

12:00pm   I almost forgot what it felt like to trade an uptrend. Yet with the TICK spending most of its time above zero this morning and the VIX downtrending, I've been biased to the long side in the U.S. session, buying pullbacks, especially once 3LB broke to the north and we broke the early-morning range. The charts tell the story, along with the VIX which remains in a 15-minute downtrend as I type this, albeit stretched to the south a bit. From here though, it's a coin flip *(thus the journal typing)*, as ES still hasn't broken its late Wednesday high just north of 970, and I've thus been exiting on each extension.

And although the decreased volatility should have me ramping the sizes upward, I'm keeping it light because

(1) I need to get the feel of a less volatile market again, and (2) it's a Friday and last day of the month . . . and I'm in major chip-gain preservation-mode today.

The brain cramp of the day so far was shorting the DAX too soon on its consolidation break, which has limited my net chip gain to only +$7K. It was stupid and cost me some tuition, yet I recognized it, quickly moved on, got some better wholesale shorts, and used those mental notes to be alert for a possible repeat in the U.S. session, which has been helpful.

1:21pm   ES trying for the 970 break.

Been nibbling small sizes long on this last push, but keeping things very tight on a Friday. VIX remains in a downtrend and has extended from its late-morning pullback.

1:25pm   Ding, ding, ding . . . think the whole world wasn't watching that? 7–point extension.

1:28pm   Nice . . . shorted 76.25 and exited/reversed on the pullback. Still keeping sizes small.

1:38pm   Took FESX short on that last ES extension . . . 2632 down to 2626 . . . practicing for the future. Emotion is emotion . . . doesn't matter what country.

1:45pm   Looking for an ES pullback toward 5-min support.

1:53pm   Got it . . . best entry 73.25 and exited on the pop. *I'll let others go for the riskier further extension.* Getting close to shutting it down here. Maybe one more long if we drop toward 70.00.

1:56pm   Nice . . . best entry 72.00 and out on the pop. That was a gift. Going into major income-preservation mode. Chip gain now + $12K (trailing stop +$10K), market depth thinning out, and I don't do Friday afternoons well. I'm also losing focus a bit, so that might be a wrap regardless of what the market does now.

2:17pm   Passed on that last extension as the 15-minute chart got pretty stretched. Sellers hitting bids now.

2:22pm   Nice read . . . nibbled some long on the sub-70 emotional barf. You can just feel the emotional excesses in the trades. Sometimes I feel like tipping them . . . especially since I'm sometimes on the wrong end as well!

As long as the VIX continues its downtrend, pullbacks remain buyable and shorts are scalps only on emotional price extensions for those nimble wholesalers. See the posted VIX chart for the "wind at your back" chart of the day.

2:47pm   ES resistance at 980 for now. Only a 10-point thrust so far . . . hmmm. Path of least resistance still up, though.

2:56pm   Still doing light nibbling for long scalps on retracements. 980 resistance yet again. I might consider a small long on a trade at 981. Shorts must be getting tired as price keeps holding.

3:03pm   Come on, giddy up.

3:04pm   Sweet . . . out. Actually chose entry from earlier pullback vs. the 981 in case the momentum died *(second range break of the day a lesser percent)*. Best exit 983 and that's a wrap for today, the week, and the month before I do something stupid. Locking in slightly more than +$15K.

3:06pm   Wow . . . 9-point Wile E. Coyote drop. Damn good decision.

Current-Day Note: The day subsequently ended +$16.9K.

 *October Wrap*

Before I begin, I have to stress for myself and those looking over my shoulder that the moment I click post, this all has to be forgotten. It's history, and that's all it is. There's a reason I have the "complacency" comment prominently displayed in the blog, as that's what prevents the vast majority of traders, poker players, and others—including me in prior years—from achieving greatness in terms of sustained equity growth.

I also expect that the market's conditions will revert back to more traditional rhythms, which will lessen the opportunity for monster moves and P&L impacts—especially for those of us who fade emotional moves—but that, of course, remains to be seen.

2008 IRA Futures Fund Performance

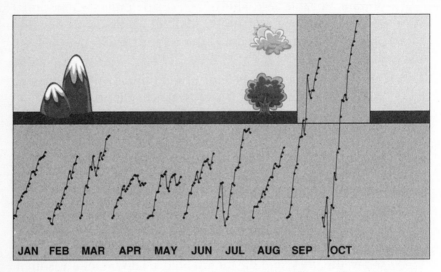

JAN FEB MAR APR MAY JUN JUL AUG SEP OCT

I really don't know where to begin to describe this month. Yet it's probably safe to say that I'll never see another month like this as long as I live. Never. It was a career record month in many respects, including my largest single-day draw *(before I got used to the "new market")*, most number of days > +$20K (nine), and largest total net of $318K. There's also probably a record in there somewhere for the most hours of sleep lost, but I don't track that.

And the truth is, I made a **lot** of mistakes—two significant ones come to mind—and those errors are the **only** elements of October that I'm going to take with me into November. *By the way, if you're looking over my shoulder, there can't be stronger evidence that this business and life are about overcoming mistakes. Make a mistake? Get over it and **keep moving** (yes, I'm shouting). There's a reason we've been given a world of tomorrows. For despite the industry hype to the contrary, profitable traders make plenty of mistakes, and if making that point is the only purpose sharing this journal serves, it will have been worth the effort.*

I'm not sure what else to say. All I know is that October is officially history, no longer matters, and the new game starts on Monday. The 2008 final table.

Two more months of tunneling to the surface before this year's game ends and countless opportunities for continual self-improvement. *The self-improvement game will, of course, never stop . . . even after December 31.*

So, we're once again back to square one with the only chart that matters:

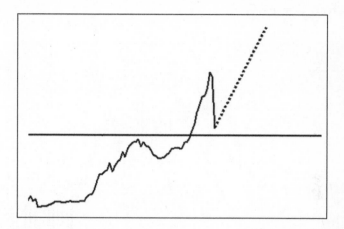

My "coach" tells me that October was an awful, gut-wrenching, sick-to-my-stomach draw and that I need to get back to focused recovery mode. He says that I have two days off before I have to get back to work. I think I'll need a new shovel, though . . . the one in my hands is so worn it looks like a spoon. Have a peaceful weekend.

Retrospective 2008 Race Progress Update

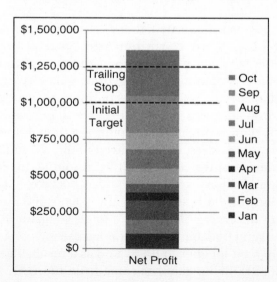

November 2008 Journal Excerpts

 *A New Game?*

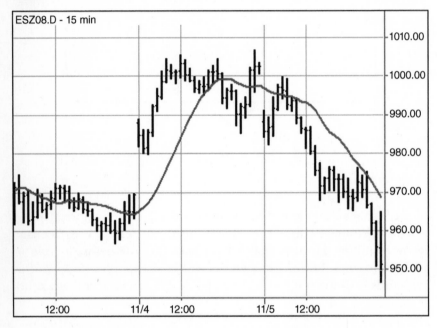

1:47pm   Just as we expected, there's a new game in town for the moment in terms of rhythm, pace, and price action. It's admittedly taking my eye some getting used to as the days of minute-by-minute emotional price spikes have subsided for the time being. Yet the VIX continues to provide a strong backdrop in terms of rhythm expectations, and I've done fairly well in seeing it and adapting—although I need to keep an eye on my sizes, which I haven't adjusted much from the past few months and which is resulting in some profit suboptimization.

Many of the best patterns and pace came in the Europe session in terms of breaking Monday's logjam to the north, with several tradable pullbacks along the way. I found the U.S. gap up a bit tougher to trade, and as a result, about $\frac{1}{2}$ of the day's +$12K chip gain has come from the DAX and FESX.

2:04pm   VIX trying to cross up on the 15-min, and we're also stretched on the 60-min chart, so anything goes heading into the afternoon and there's the possibility this respite was short-lived, but time will tell.

2:19pm   That's a bit more like it in terms of my preferred rhythm. Gotta love it when that 15-min VIX crosses to the north. Picked up a few extreme emotional scalps. *(If only I could read other poker players as well.)* Chip count now approaching +$13K. Approaching my witching hour in terms of less-than-stellar results (much like my late-night poker performance), so am going into major gain preservation mode for the rest of the day.

2:29pm   992ish holding as interim support . . . scalped a few longs off that. Got some Ping-Pong trade patterns here as short-term trends (1 and 5) are down and long-term trends (30 and 60) are up, so anything other than scalps questionable. Chip count now over $15K, and given the trend conflicts, that may be it for me.

3:00pm   Calling it a day. I don't care to flip a coin heading into the last hour. Any run should set up the morning trade.

Current-Day Note: The day subsequently ended +$15.9K.

Fighting It

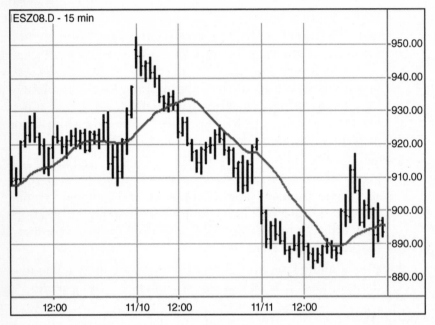

What is it about Mondays? I was definitely fighting it a bit all day, starting with a rough Europe session where I probed for long breakouts (I hate those patterns) and was generally off my game, after which I spent most of the U.S. session clipping and clawing to get back to even. We'll call it a scratch on the day with the chip stack pretty much holding steady at +$2K.

I still never felt particularly on my game throughout the day, though, and my trading was a lot worse than the score indicates. And although I don't track trade specific win/loss percent, my feel is that it was probably under 20 percent. The modest green on the day is largely the result of decent size management, though, as I kept lot sizes small most of the day and only put size on twice when ES was setting up for a couple of high-probability midday downtrend extension entries . . . both of which paid off.

That's where poker has definitely impacted my trading for the good this year in terms of paying the necessary blinds and antes throughout the day (you don't win if you don't play), while betting stronger when the hand and pace of the game dictate. Still, I'll need to suck it up a bit tomorrow to put in a better performance.

Complacency and coasting: They're killers, and I feel them slipping back into my trading. That notion was reinforced in spades while watching tonight's Celtics game vs. Toronto, as the Celts—the better team—sleepwalked through three quarters before getting serious and coming from 15 points down to win. Sure, they played last night and were tired. Big deal. Toronto was in the same situation and played highly motivated, aggressive ball for 3+ quarters.

Sounds too familiar, and I need to do something about it. October is history and irrelevant. The market is my opponent, and I need to prove that I'm the better team in November. I need to feel some pain before it becomes real. I'm 15 points down, and it's time to get serious.

Current-Day Note: The day subsequently ended +$2.1K.

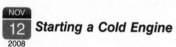 **Starting a Cold Engine**

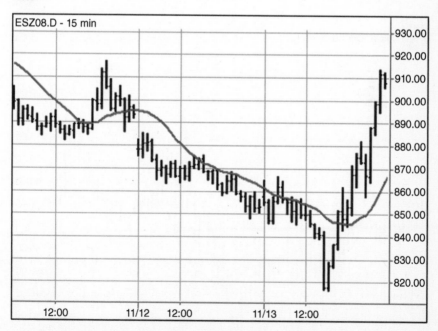

Once, just once, I'd like to begin the day in rhythm and not have to fight my way through some early struggles. Such was the case again today as I could never find the Europe rhythm on the textbook lower high (vs. yesterday's unsustainable squeezeroo) and it wasn't until midday in the U.S. session where I finally got it in gear. *I know, I know . . . some will tell me to stop trading Europe. I won't give it up . . . yet . . . and I don't like to lose.*

Actually, I spent a lot of time—and some tuition in the form of scratches and commissions—today trading FESX fairly heavily to see if I could get a feel for that sucker. And based on today's results, it will definitely take some time. Yet today may not have been the greatest test as pace in the Europe session was horrendous. And as I've said before, pace is more important to me than any other market attribute. More than charts, setups, etc. One thing was certain: I wasn't very patient with it today, and FESX definitely has its own unique rhythm unlike ES and DAX.

Actually, I didn't find the ES pace to be much better today . . . or maybe it was just me being out of rhythm in both markets. Nevertheless, the score will read a very modest +$7.1K chip gain on the day, and although that's mouse you-know-whats, I'm considering much of the day an investment in the future.

NOV 13 2008 *Jack Be Nimble*

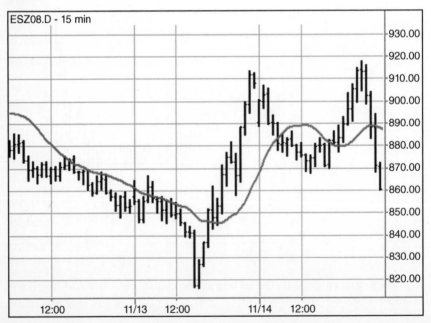

2:16pm–3:10pm   *(Various posts while not trading.)* Where do I start? First, I got a good night's sleep (after a bad poker beat last night . . . more on that later) and woke up naturally around 5:30am completely forgetting that today should be setting up as "morning-after-trend day." Nevertheless, both the market and I got immediately in decent oscillation-mode rhythm, and I started off the day in the plus, trading FESX well.

Then the U.S. market picked up where Europe left off and had its own series of textbook oscillations with some beautiful wide price swings. Shorting the first spike up and buying the first spike down—exiting on the snapbacks—both worked well. *After the first oscillations play out, it's then typically a wait-and-see mode as all bets are off, and I stayed out of trouble once the ripples stopped.*

Fast-forward to lunchtime when I almost made the mistake of leaving my station but thought that we might get a break one way or the other, so I hung around with some hunger pangs. And, of course, just before 1pm, the ES bottom fell out and smashed through its October and multiyear lows. I caught a couple of barf entries, including buying 818.25–819.50 hard on the pause, which turned out to be the trade of the day that I took out into the climb.

Then it got really tricky as after ES had its initial postpanic strong reaction back up, it had minimal action back down before blowing back up north catching **a lot** of shorts. I definitely gave up some of the earlier profits shorting down-trend retracement moves, but thankfully I realized what was going on, took the stops, and then shorted the next post-short-covering exhaustion spike after the pass back though the 1pm break line and covered on the snapback.

From then, I scaled sizes back drastically and simply faded a few more emotional extremes into about 3:10pm with very modest success, at which point I shut down for the day.

The charts clearly show stuck longs on the way down and shorts on the way back up, with both stuck groups getting hurt hard. I can see where one could easily misgauge both, and it took an extremely clear head to be nimble enough to adjust and not be one of the "squeezees." Fortunately at this end, the head stayed clear enough to grow today's chip stack by +$46.9K. *There's no doubt the day-after-trend day continues to be my favorite. The key, of course, is executing. As with golf, the weather on the course can be great, but you have to hit the shots.*

3:56pm   Wowzer. Shorts getting absolutely crucified on the climb. **You have to be flexible in this business . . . those who aren't won't only not thrive, they'll get slaughtered. Jack be nimble or Jack be dead**. You also have to always be aware of multiple time frames, as the 120-min chart was clearly stretched on the early afternoon drop.

Back to the comment about last night's bad beat. I came in 4th in a tournament despite having played my best poker in some time, but taking a bad beat on the river. Here's how it played out: I had pocket Qs, and the flop came 4–5–9. I successfully trapped the guy holding Ace–9, got him to bet strong (putting me all-in, which, of course, I didn't mind one bit), called him, and then lost to an Ace on the river. The good news was that it cut my night short, allowed me get a "full" six hours sleep (yes, in this business, that's "full"), and allowed me to stay focused much of today.

NOV
15
2008

The Power of Momentum

A snowball at the top of a mountain turns into an avalanche that destroys a city. An out-of-control speeding driver skids on black ice and can't stop as he slams into the car stopped in front of him. Through 63 percent of the 2001 regular season, the New England Patriots were an average team with a 5–5 record before going on to win their last nine games to win the 2001 Super Bowl. The Dow crashes 778 points in one day, which sets off a wave of worldwide panic that takes months to repair.

Momentum. It's powerful and often unpredictable. Merriam-Webster defines it as the "strength or force gained by motion or through the development of events," and it can propel one to new heights or new depths. And although it's still not yet time to reflect on the past $10\frac{1}{2}$ months, it's hard not to speak to the tsunami in which I'm currently caught. You see, I really hadn't planned on doing much in November and December as the holidays began to approach and market volatility returned to more "normal" levels . . . however that's defined these days.

But then the market that keeps on giving gave again on Tuesday. And again on Thursday. Emotions continue to run rampant, which continues to provide the market with highly fertile soil in which this year's Chinese bamboo is rooted.

Perhaps Thursday was the market's final blast. One enormous clap of thunder before the storm moves on. Or maybe it was just the eye in a larger storm that is only half over. Who knows. All I know is that our job is simply to react to what is happening now and continue rotake the other side of emotion. When others are panicking, we're there with catchers' mitts. When others "have" to cover to stop the pain *(been there)*, we're on the other side. When others are too caught in the emotion of a short-term time frame and as a result panic out on pullbacks in larger uptrends or downtrends *(been there, too)*, we're again there to take their trade.

And emotion is **all** that successful traders see when they look at charts. Forget the algorithms, spinning doji whichamacallits, and cute trade setup labels, the charts show the actions of people and their state of mind . . . and nothing more. When I'm on my game I see it. When I'm not, I don't. Pure and simple.

Unfortunately, the only way many traders finally "get it" is having been on the painful side time after time. And yes, I lived in that neighborhood years ago and still visit it from time to time. Yet if you can make that first turnaround, you may find momentum as powerful on your side as it seemed when it was against you. Personally, I'd love to see a forest of bamboos being planted and cultivated in some small part through the seeds of this journal, with many trees higher than mine. When I look back, that would be the greatest reward of this entire journey.

NOV 20 2008   *Managing with My "B" Game*

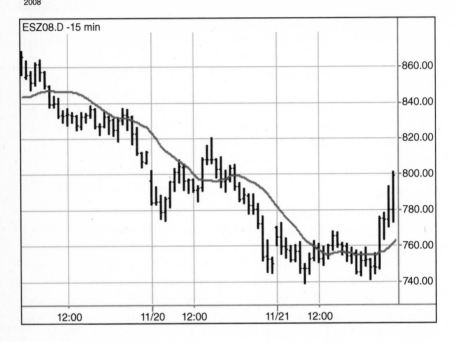

1:33pm   For some reason, I've been a bit hesitant today on yet **another** morning-after-closing trend day, where I normally do well. *That particular pattern just keeps coming and coming. This fall has simply provided tremendous closing trends to fuel the high-probability next-morning trade.* The result has been my scratching and reentering a number of trades, and although I often do that to some extent every day for risk management, I feel that I've done so much more than normal today, and as a result my transaction (commission) costs have eaten into the day's chip gain, which currently stands at a rather modest +$14K. Another area where I'll grade myself rather poorly today is holding time, as my entries—or should I say reentries—have been OK, but I've definitely been a bit too quick on my exits.

Which leaves me heading into the afternoon a bit frustrated, yet extremely cautious not to do anything stupid heading into the late afternoon—*a.k.a. my weaker period*—

especially since I apparently didn't bring my "A" game today. *Yea, I know it's impossible to bring our "A" game to every one of the 250+ trading days we have each year, but knowing that still doesn't make it any less frustrating.*

    I'll be surprised if we get another sustained uptrend in the afternoon as (1) some of the midday juice was supplied by the automaker off-again/on-again bailout news, and (2) we're still in a strong 60-min downtrend. If so, the salmon will definitely be swimming upstream.

2:05pm   Feels weak. Shorted ES 797.50 small size on a 1-min turn; stop 800.

2:08pm   Added small at 795.75.

2:10pm   Nice . . . covered most—best cover so far 792.75—holding small on free-roll for fun.

2:19pm   Flattened 788.00 into extreme negative TICK. Not bad. Kept size very modest, took early sure profit, and free-rolled rest. That might be it for the day. Nudged chip gain to +$17K.

2:22pm   ES now 4 pts up from final cover. Amazing how some markets make you look like a genius while others (hard trends) make you look so lame. In this case, 1-min 3LB was short at the time, and we were in the hourly downtrend. There might be more on the downside as the 5-min is trying to join the 60, but I'll take the high-probability move and leave the longer-term intraday swing trading to others. Nevertheless, the long-term trend definitely remains down, and if the 5 min continues, there might be another higher-probability pullback opportunity.

2:32pm   My personal witching hour approaches. Still sensing I've had my "B" game today and at times during parts of the week, so sticking to defense for the rest of the day. VIX turning back up and TICK looking pathetic again, but ES trading in the middle of the morning range.

2:40pm   Getting tired and ES chopping around. Not a good combo. *Careful, Don . . . keep the sizes small.*

2:44pm   Considered shorting this 5-min pullback but execution not sharp. It was nice entry for those who got it.

2:47pm   No second chances so far on that one. Right read, tired fingers. Should get one more pullback try, though . . . sitting at 785 to 786.

2:55pm Not bad . . . got my fills and took one scratch and reentry (yes, again), but got some of the drop with best cover 781.25. Chip gain now +$18K. Trend is down but pace sporadic. ES still trading above the morning low, which is another reason I'm clipping quickly.

3:02pm ES 10-point pop. From fool to genius in 2 mins . . . amazing.

We'll close it down here to make sure I don't go back to "fool." Banking the day's gain and going to search for my "A" game tonight.

Any closing trend sets up—well, you get the idea by now.

Current-Day Note: The day subsequently ended +17.6K.

 *No Style Points*

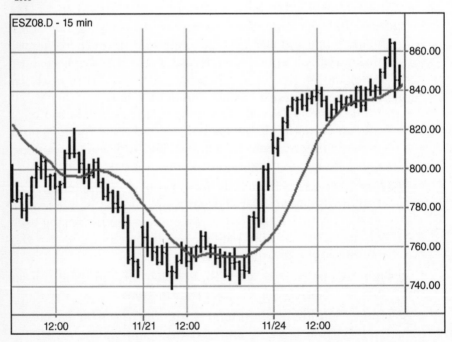

Well, week 47 certainly wasn't my best effort of the year, as I felt slightly out of tune much of the time, including portions of today, which was essentially a scratch until I eked out a +$6.7K win on the late-day short squeeze (more on that later). Yet as was the case with Tuesday's comment on Monday's trade, I could easily rank the week's net trade fairly high on my 2008 list in terms of—to use a pitcher's analogy—getting a "W" when I clearly didn't have my best stuff.

So, somehow and in some unexplained way, I managed to grind it out and scrape together enough good performance to offset the bad for a 19th consecutive weekly chip gain. The score sheet will show +$62.6K with the daily box scores of –$6.5K, +$21.1K, +$23.7K, +$17.6K, +$6.7K, but again, my "stuff" wasn't all that great at times, and that should keep me far away from any hint of overconfidence heading into the final $5\frac{1}{2}$ weeks. *Good thing the market doesn't grade us on style points.*

In terms of today, I felt that the overnight Europe and early ES action was a bit rough despite a somewhat textbook ES overnight pullback toward its 15-min short-trend support, with the clearest morning 1-min trigger of the day coming on the 11am ES range break and pullback that finally helped push my day's chip gain into the green.

On the other hand, a similar 2pm breakdown attempt didn't have the same follow-through, which I also took and stopped. At that point I stopped looking for short-trend trades as it was clear there wasn't enough volume or interest to push the market lower.

That data—and cost of the stop—ended up being useful later, when stuck shorts got squeezed after 3pm and I was able to avoid the wrong side (and nibble on the right side) of it. *In fact, the post-3pm trade was about the best pace of the day with decent volume as the market had been coiling hard for the previous few hours.*

This was also a good example of where I often feel it's easier to feel a market current if you're "swimming" in the river vs. watching it from the shore, as no one can feel a possible squeeze better than a trader who took a strong short entry that stopped.

As noted in the chart, ES certainly didn't like trading below 750, which led to the path of least resistance being up.

One of the areas I need to watch heading into next week is that I seem to have been forcing things a bit when the volatility dies down—e.g., suspect breakout and pullback attempts—as well as clipping too quickly on solid entries. *Essentially, I was playing CME market maker for much of the week . . . not a bad thing, of course, yet when there's room to run, the leash can be lengthened.* So, we'll work on the old patience meter over the weekend, perhaps by sitting at a cash poker game for 12 hours folding 95 percent of the hands until that perfect trapping hand comes to take the monster pot.

And so it's onto a short trading week next week, followed by the final December push to the finish. In 40 days we'll finally measure the full bamboo height, and the yardstick and ladder will be ready. Until then, much more cultivating remains.

Brutal Pace

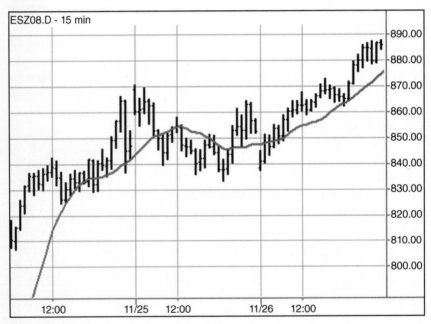

Some days you're the bug, others the windshield. Today was a bit of both for me as it took me forever to get used to a market pace that I can only define as brutal. It wasn't until late afternoon where I finally hit some resemblance of a stride, and only after looking back at my trading over the last 2½ days and getting really ticked off. *I was actually wondering when I'd feel that fire again, which had been noticeably absent since midweek last week.*

The result was essentially a –$0.8K scratch on the day (not even worth mentioning), but it was a helluva rebound from an early –$18K deficit due in part to some of the worst trading I've done in a while in the Europe and early U.S. session *(yea, I know, I know . . . no need to say anything)*, where I kept misfiring.

It's unfortunate that the best morning-after-trend-day action actually occurred before Monday's close with the large whipsaws. Nevertheless, there were a few decent early oscillations today, although I again couldn't seem to align myself with the pace.

Hopefully, it's a good sign that I finally got peeved about my performance over the last few days. I can't put my finger on the reason for the subpar performance, but as I said above, I just haven't felt the "fire" in the belly and may need to get creative again to light the fuse.

NOV 26 2008 *A TICK Tutorial*

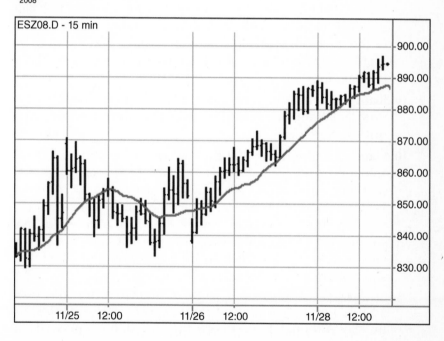

10:15am   Going to do some in-depth intraday note-taking today to try to maintain a sharper focus throughout the day. Not looking for a home-run chip-gain day on this preholiday trade, but **do** want an "A" grade on focus by the end of the day.

Got a decent night's sleep and nibbled on Europe's 7:30am breakdown via short pullbacks. The U.S. open has been tricky as there have been no clear patterns, and I've been highly reluctant to short for anything other than quick brief-resistance scalps given that the VIX is downtrending and have been taking sure, tight clips on any entries thus far to try to get a rhythm going.

10:26am   TICK strong so far . . . spending more time above zero than below and stronger pushes to the upside. Clean long entries a bit tough, although staying away from shorts has been smart . . . *so far, that is*. ES been clearly rejecting lower prices since early Friday afternoon and I have to respect that. We're also trading completely within Friday's late-afternoon range, so all trades are scalps only.

I'd really like just one or two clean shots if the market can get its juices flowing either way today and simply sit out the rest of the time in a highly focused state. Simply put, I want to be highly selective today, and volume could slow to a crawl later heading into the holiday.

10:36am   Shaping out to be one of the grind-it-out days. Apparently not many "stuck" traders on either side to fuel a fire one way or the other.

10:44am   Imagining I'm sitting at the cash poker game . . . fold, fold, fold, fold. *Starting to wonder if there's even a face card in the deck*. Both 5-min and 15-min ADXs exactly at 12.11 . . . gotta be some kind of numerical oddity. Certainly no help there.

Very much a range trade, which is clearly not my strength. Even 1st pullbacks on attempted 1- or 5-min trends are somewhat risky. *Of course the longer we coil, the harder the eventual break.*

One thing is certain. If I can get the day's chip gain over +$10K, I'm putting a major trailing earnings stop in place for the day. Although I don't normally care to focus on the day's #s like that, it seems appropriate today for a number of reasons.

10:54am   7-point ES surge out of the flat line. Buying the next TICK pullback.

10:56am   Nice, caught 855.25 . . . best exit 857.75 and took it out into the climb. Small size.

10:58am   Ditto 856.00 to 857.75. Microscalping with small sizes . . . not much market depth right now. Path of least resistance up for now but taking high-probability clips. Still inside Tuesday afternoon's range, but 5-min giving it a try. Just doesn't seem like there's enough volume for a strong push, though. Europe did something similar after its open and then imploded after catching long breakout traders on the wrong side.

11:04am   ES 5-point plunge . . . good reads and decisions. 5-min could still extend, but we're still within a larger range, and if it does, there should either be another pullback on a higher time frame or extreme price to scalp short again.

11:11am   ES next thrust up approaching top of Tuesday afternoon's range. TICK pullbacks remaining the best entry points so far. 1-min 3LB also long for now. Have to continue to respect the market microstrength *(in this day and age, we'll define "strength" as lack of weakness!)* as well as the current range. Still not interested in longer-term shorts.

11:18am   ES still not able to break its Tuesday PM high of 864.25.

11:21am   Until now . . . by a single tick. Lower TICK reading on that last surge, though. That might be it.

11:24am   TICK reading lower again on this push and stretched from 5-min support . . . scalp shorted for 0.75 but expecting a deeper retracement. Will buy any push toward 856 . . . the closer to 856 the better.

11:30am   ES pulling down . . . 4 points off high. Been purposely leaving some meat on the table, as I'm going for prime center cuts only. *I'll let the other players at the "table" gamble.*

11:49am   TICK pullbacks still the prime entries and TICK holding solidly above zero. Doing light scalping and scratching as I get a bit more active. 5-min ADX back over 20. *Granting my first national interview in almost four years at noon, so I'll need to step away for about 30 mins . . . more on that at a later time. Hopefully, it won't be the kiss of death.*

12:55pm   Back. Slow grind up, but don't think I'd have entered anyway. Volatility slow grind down. No trader emotional extremes to benefit from and definitely a preholiday nonexistent pace so far.

1:10pm   Trend mode up off open so far . . . one of those days where on the surface, pros taking sure profits look foolish as reentries are tough. Such is life.

1:51pm   There's an old trader adage . . . if you have to squint, pass. I'm squinting. You can't get blood from a stone. Volume dying as expected.

2:00pm   zzzzzzzzzzz. Let's see if the 2pm express shows up.

2:17pm   Market still rejecting lower-price probes. Strength still there.

2:20pm   Long 868.25 on TICK pullback after last break up . . . should pop.

2:22pm   Sweet . . . took it out into +1230 TICK toward 871.00. Similar sequence to earlier in day.

2:30pm   And again . . . 870.00 to 872.00. TICK gets the indicator of the day award, with an assist from the VIX.

2:33pm   Nice pop through high of day. Shorts getting squeezed. Might be one more good pullback. Finally some emotion in the charts. *(Just takes one group to be hurting, and 'twas the shorts this time.)* We have pace!

2:37pm   Sitting at 872.50.

2:39pm   Took small at 874.00 already out on pop. Want to buy any further thrust down harder. *Here kitty, kitty.* Trailing stop on day-chip gain now in effect.

2:45pm   You're sometimes damned if you do, damned if you don't on waiting for deeper retracement entries. Might still get one more, though . . . day's not done yet. *Will respect the day's trailing stop, though, and **not** get caught in any last 30-min whipsaws, which has often been the norm.*

3:02pm   TICK still a horse. In watch mode.

3:11pm   VIX still sustaining a 15-min downtrend and now "down" to 55. *Almost a 30-point drop in four days.* Shorts the ones now feeling some pain, although 2008 longs have more than a few legs up on them in that department.

3:27pm   No trades but fervently watching.

3:35pm   Tried teeny short probe on possible double-top and scratched almost immediately for –0.50. Small size and still respecting the trailing stop.

3:47pm   OK, that's a wrap. Stuck a few toes in toward the end, but pretty much watched the close. Locking in the gain at +$10.3K.

As expected, a very modest P&L day by recent standards and sizing was perhaps too light (will have to watch that if volatility continues to implode), but grading an A for solid focus and market reads, for not looking to short on this preholiday strength trade, and for the discipline in respecting the trailing stop during the late trade. *Trend days from start to finish are always tough for frequent traders as reentries can be few and far between, but I'm not going to complain.* We'll give this day to the swing longs and investors.

Warning Signs

2008 IRA Futures Fund Performance

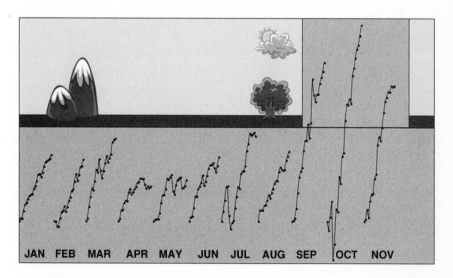

| JAN | FEB | MAR | APR | MAY | JUN | JUL | AUG | SEP | OCT | NOV |

Well, this week may go down as the 20th consecutive winner (marginally at +$18.1K with daily chip scores of +$8.9K, –$0.7K, +$10.3K, –$1.9K, +$1.5K). **However,** there are glaring warning signs heading into the final month that I need to address if I'm to finish this race the way I intended to. Two must-address items that come to mind are (1) intensity that I'd grade a 2 on a scale of 1 to 10 (10 being the strongest) and (2) hesitancy such that for the first time all year, I'd frankly describe my trading as "playing not to lose."

Now part of this may reflect a slow holiday trading week, exacerbated by the reduced volatility to which I'm still getting accustomed. Yet there are clearly many symptoms of something larger going on, including too many scratched trades on good entries that simply take more time to develop, losing focus during "lull before the storm" periods, "sleeping in" until well after the Europe open, trading sizes as if I had 10 percent the capital I do, and taking lower-probability second entries rather than pouncing on the first.

It's frankly the largest struggle I've had with myself all year, including those few days of large draws *(at least I was aggressive during those times . . . and this type of treading-water trading bothers me more than any real financial loss)*. Sure, the rhythm has changed and I may be trying to dance the waltz with a mamba beat. But our job is to continually recognize the conditions and adjust accordingly, and I haven't done that very well.

I'm not even going to address the monthly equity chart, except to note the topping pattern at the end of November, which is similar to the closes of March, April, and July.

Part of what's happening may very well be psychological, as word has apparently spread of what I'm on pace to accomplish this year. I suppose this was one risk of doing the live journal play by play. And it's not the pressure, as I've been in the public eye over much of the last decade and typically thrive under increased scrutiny. Rather, it's trying to block out everything that's happened this year and simply focus on the here and now.

The point is that January through November is now **irrelevant**, and December is the only month that matters. One month. 22 daily hands to be dealt. And then and only then will it be time to officially end the race and look at the score. *And even after that, I'll still just be one trader whose only mission this year was to get closer to reaching his fullest potential as I figure out what to do in 2009.*

We all know what happened to the Patriots in last year's Super Bowl. All it took was one brief loss of defensive focus and a Hail Mary helmet catch to go from 18–0 to a roadkill footnote. We also know the story of Archie Karas, who went from +$40 million to nothing due to sheer greed and a downward spiral that began so innocently yet from which he could never recover. Most of the temporary Internet bubble-stock millionaires lost all their gains, with many losing much more as they continued to double down at perceived "bargain prices" on the way down to zero. The list is long.

And so the job isn't yet done. For the **final** time this year, it's time to dig out of one last hole, and if I keep making the same recent mistakes, I'll find I'm throwing dirt back on myself.

We're close. But close only counts in horseshoes and hand grenades. Monday begins the sprint to the finish.

Finish-Line Adjustments

I continue to give a great deal of thought to the coming month, especially on the heels of yesterday's initial reflections of how November ended. And frankly, I'm feeling differently about things as the sun rose this morning, and here's why I've long preached that I view each day, week, month, quarter, and year as single "trades," with most emphasis on the monthly time frames and above. So, here we are at the end of the most important trading time frame—the year— which in the overall scheme of things is the **only** one that matters.

As such, the more I look back at my trading towards the end of November, the more I believe that my inner clock may have taken over in terms of activating an internal defensive mechanism similar to that which often kicks in for me during the last hour of the day's "trade," the last day of the month's "trade," and the last week of a quarter's "trade."

The best analogy I can provide is that I feel that it's 3:30pm at the end of the day's trade. Most of the work is over, the day's mission was accomplished, my focus is drained, and I'm not looking to press my capital during a time when my focus and interest may not be at their best. And as a result, I often scale sizes back and play defense. When I don't—and this journal is littered with last-hour subpar performances—it's reflected in the P&L.

Well, it's now 3:30pm of the "year." Most of the work is over, the year's mission was accomplished, my focus is drained, and I'm not looking to press my capital during a time when my focus and interest may not be at their best *(yes, that's the exact same sentence except for one word)*.

Yes, this is a major shift for me. Yet I've pushed myself harder than I ever have for 334 days and it's now showing. The focus and energy level aren't there . . . that's crystal clear in the posts and results of the last couple of weeks. As a result, I believe that there's strong risk of losing focus at a critical time and even stronger risk that I won't have the needed energy or the time for another comeback should it happen.

You may recall that as the 3rd quarter drew to a close two months ago, I chose to raise the bar beyond the initial $1 million target to $1.25 million. Then October provided seasoned traders with a gift of historic volatility during which time I was able to floor the accelerator. The result was a **month** that exceeded many previous **annual** tallies, which also made the setting of any further targets a futile exercise. And finally, November had just enough carryover momentum from October—both in terms of the market's volatility and performance at this end—to shoot the bamboo even higher.

So, there it is. Most of the work has been completed. Most of the remaining work—to the extent that I choose to participate—will definitely be over by Christmas. It's very possible that over the next month I'll sacrifice some profit potential as I often do at the end of the day. Yet as is the case during those times, I know that the next day will be here soon enough and we get to start all over again with a renewed focus and plan.

It's 3:30pm and time to act accordingly.

Retrospective 2008 Race Progress Update

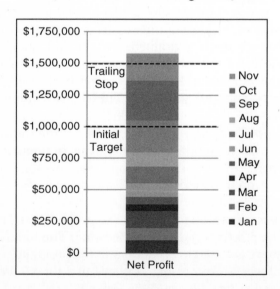

December 2008 Journal Excerpts

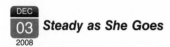
DEC 03 2008 *Steady as She Goes*

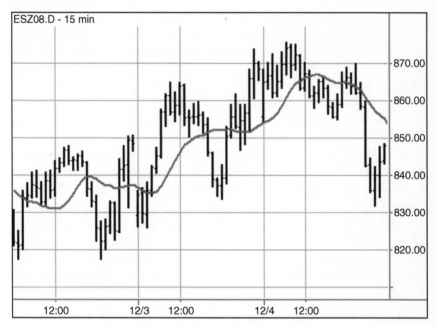

Quite the choppy and highly illiquid late afternoon as ES frustrated many PM breakout traders before the VIX finally got off the fence and helped push ES up into the close. At this end, I gave back some of the AM profits as getting a solid afternoon entry was like trying to catch a greased pig. *I just missed a prime late-day entry, but rarely ever chase and let it go.* Nevertheless, I still managed to retain about 80 percent of earlier-day gains and end with a respectable, albeit not spectacular +$15.4K on 1,248 x 2 trading. *Suffice it to say that it's unlikely I'll ever be a strong trader in the last hour!*

In terms of today's earlier action and charts, first pullbacks remain the highest—and sometimes only paying trend entries as the market plays out its current range game, and the shorter the time frame the better. 850 seemed to be pivotal several times in today's ES trade as it went back and forth between resistance and support several times during the session. In the meantime, the ADX on all major trends, including 15-, 30-, and 60-min, continue to drop.

It will certainly be interesting to see how this month ends from a personal performance perspective, in part because I'm really taking somewhat of a mental break in terms of not trading Europe aggressively (if at all on many days) while continuing to trade ES rather modestly during the U.S. session.

As I mentioned last week and in the video over the weekend, the "fire in the belly" just isn't what it was 1 . . . 2 . . . 11 months ago as we approach the end of this 365-day marathon. And although I can certainly ramp up both the intraday interest and focus when needed for particular sequences (*I took an excellent stop on the post–Beige Book short-covering rally back through 850*), I'm finding that I just can't keep it up for prolonged periods as I could for much of the last 11 months, and especially the last 3. *I suppose such are the temporary scars of "going for it" when the market shifted into its Sept.–Nov. overdrive for traders.* As a result, I'm trading far fewer liquidity-providing wholesale trades and passing on scalp opportunities that I might have taken when the market was more fertile.

I have no doubt that my prolonged bouts of sharpness will recover, yet in the meantime I continue to play a rather protective game throughout the month as I continue to consider any December gains a performance bonus of sorts or, perhaps more appropriately, final leaves on the Chinese bamboo, to keep our year-long analogy intact.

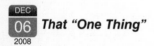

That "One Thing"

There's a great scene from the classic movie *City Slickers* where Curly holds up his finger and references the one thing in life that is up to each of us to find out. Well, as this year's journey nears a historic end, my "one thing" seems to be coming into clearer focus . . . at least the trading "thing" . . . although like many trading elements, it seems to be spilling over into personal life as well.

And although it starts with the comeback concept that I first discussed in July and that formed the cornerstone for subsequent performance momentum that is now apparently catching international attention, I now realize that there was much iceberg below that initial tip. Throughout the journal, I've long said that the power behind the comeback mentality was that it required that I ramp up my focus by visualizing the mental state in which I've typically excelled.

And that certainly remains true. Yet I've now realized that there's a second element to that concept that reaches even deeper, and that's the humbling effect that a drawdown—real or perceived—has on one's mind-set.

Why is it that many who make it to the top also come crashing down? I would argue two major reasons are pride and arrogance. And as this race nears a close, it's become clear that the greatest power behind the fictional draw chart is that it instills an ongoing inner circuit breaker that minimizes the chance of pride and arrogance seeping in. Essentially, it mandates humility, and humility trumps arrogance every day. And for my trading, humility has clearly become my "one thing."

And so I enter next week mentally reversing the sign before last week's chip gain. I've taken a humbling –$72K hit, there's certainly no reason to get a big head, and I need to go back to work to get it back. The more I believe that—and by Monday I'll think that it really happened that way—the more powerful the results are . . . in trading and in life.

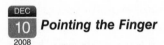

Pointing the Finger

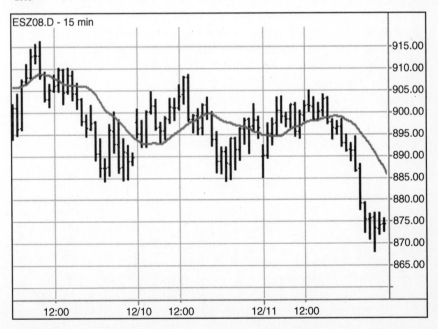

It's been quite some time since I've had close to a five-figure draw and have been really ticked off with my trading, but I did and I am. Despite the overall larger range (breakout traders have been getting absolutely hammered), today's ES market was extremely tradable, and yet I again for some ridiculous and unknown reason was pressing just enough to be out of tune enough on a day where precision was absolutely mandatory.

Sure, I'm not a great range trader, but bluntly, I stunk . . . and I can't blame the market action that currently has little conviction/emotion and that's reacting to every on-again off-again bail-out rumor. *In fact, the market action can never be blamed. It's our job to adapt, and the accusatory finger always points backward as this game is solely about competing against oneself.* The only impact the current market rhythms have on my trading is that it simply requires more precision.

As I've preached for years and throughout this diary, trading is a mental sport . . . period . . . and I'm not sharp. Oh, there were hints of strong performance, but it was spotty at best. And believe me, the –$9.0K draw doesn't bother me as the only number that matters is the one unveiled on December 31 . . . it's the performance that does. *I frankly don't care if I'm +$20K on the day. If the performance isn't there, it would still be an atrocious day.*

If there's any good news, it's that I've avoided significant damage and am in that megafrustrated mode that often proceeds the next strong run. Yet that will **only** happen if I quickly get my s∗∗∗ together and right the ship.

Order Restored

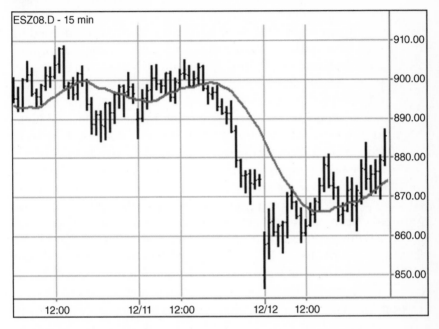

12:57pm Shortly after 11:30am, I wrote the following ADX figures down: 60-min 14.10; 30-min 11.36; 15-min 8.83; 5-min 9.30. Can you say range bound? ES continues to be completely trendless on all key time frames in what could be the tightest and longest-lasting range trade of the year.

The goal for today is simple: Be sharp, patient, and make damn sure you book a gain at the end of the day. *And although this might seem a stark contrast from my "I don't care about the daily score" mantra, it's a required circuit breaker at this end whose intent is simply to prevent daily performance momentum from building up on the downside. So far, I don't recall a 3-day consecutive draw this year.*

The day started with two successful scalp sequences shortly before 4am on an unsustainable FESX cliff drop (going long the extension and then shorting the first pullback to the 5-min), before going back to bed. *Ironically, I simply "woke up" at about 3:45am after not sleeping well (I wonder why), saw the opportunity, and took it.* Then at the U.S. normal session open, I chose to take it slow in light of the Dec.-to-Mar. contract rollover that often creates an early chopfest, although ES clearly held the 885 area yet again and continues to trade north of it, albeit in the tight range.

So, as we get ready to head into the afternoon, I'm holding on to just under a slight +$6K chip gain, having traded only 240 FESX and 490 ES (total buys and sells), and am relying on journaling to keep it north of +$5K that by the end of the day's trade.

Perhaps the best way to describe the market is "You First" as many are simply waiting for the breakout-attempt pawns to stop getting captured before moving their rooks and knights into battle. *(OK, it's been a long while since I played chess, but I think I've got the terminology right.)*

The VIX still suggests upward is possible, although so far it's been more of "no further downward movement" than anything and has kept me away from shorting any perceived short-term break to the south. In any event, this can't last forever, although clearly we're not in Kansas (Sept.–Nov.) anymore Auntie Em.

1:08pm   Yet another feeble attempt at breaking to the north. This is starting to get very old. *Tapping the right side of my monitor to see if that will help.* Of course, once that last frustrated trader gives it up, the break will occur.

1:23pm   That might be it for the upside attempts, looking for PM short bias on pullbacks. Sticking short toe in water 895.50 small size (15 lot). *Would be a helluva lot easier if the pace and volume picked up!* Could be air pocket to the south if momentum builds. Will stop on a sustained trade over 897 . . . also the 1-min 3LB turn price.

1:30pm   Added 896.50; avg price 896.00 30 contracts. Not going any heavier in this pace.

1:38pm   Scratched ½ on nonmovement and 1-min 3LB turn; back to 15 lot.

1:39pm   Scratched rest; *can always reenter.* Slight negative on sequence, but irrelevant aside from making sure today's "circuit breaker" stays in place. Thought we might get a plunge similar to yesterday's—*which I butchered at the time*—but was probably too apparent.

Pace poor and market depth thin as can be. 15-min ADX 8.18. That's sick. *Maybe we rolled to the June 1909 contract and I didn't know it!*

1:51pm   zzzzzzzzzzzz. Will the 2pm express show up today?

1:56pm   ES air pocket down . . . hard not to laugh. Right idea, but didn't want my capital in the market with no movement. Looking to short next pullback.

2:10pm   Better; got back short in 893–894; out most on the drop. *Missed the express, but got the local.*

2:17pm   Added small on drop and took it off, flattened on approach to 890 and low TICK.

2:20pm   2-point ES pop; good decision.

2:28pm   Man, this pace is terrible. No flow to me is riskier as we can air pocket up or down at any time. Next high percent short a pullback to the 5-min now. Sitting in 893s.

2:38pm   Nice . . . shorted 893s to 890–892 . . . best cover 890.25. Small sizes still. The 5-min bias is there, but it's choppy.

2:44pm   Not going to stew over profits left on table today. Also not too interested in fading this drop yet in case the range finally gives way, as it could get ugly when it finally blows.

2:47pm   Short 886.75 on TICK pop for small change. Respecting 885ish still on covers until broken.

2:54pm   Shorted 884.75 to 881.00 on last push. Took most out for 1–2 pts and covered final 881.00. Strong read for someone who stinks on breakouts, but I just "felt" it. VIX also supportive of shorts on the 15-min cross up.

2:57pm   This could get ugly . . . bye-bye long supports. Will watch for a while. Market finally finding some rhythm. See if I can remember how to match it, but will be conservative. NOT giving away day's gains in the last hour.

3:06pm   Might consider fading a further barf or shorting a sharp pullback, but the entry has to be pocket Jacks or higher. Day's initial objective remains very clear. Also already thinking to possible morning setups if the trend holds.

3:28pm   Been doing some very light probe scalping with 15 lots, but not getting cute. Only entry I want for size is shorting an approach toward the former 885ish support. Unlikely we'll get there today as there has to be a ton of stuck longs now bailing on any upticks, but you never know.

3:35pm   Passed on that last short attempt as I wanted something closer to 880.

Decent reads today and nudged the modest chip gain up to +$10.4K on a fairly low and efficient 815 x 2 contract trading. Essentially, a grind-it-out day.

3:55pm   Shutting it down. Did pretty much what I had to today to restore order and will plan for the morning.

One last note is that I purposely stepped up the journal notes in the afternoon so as not to lose sight of what was happening. There's the clear benefit of the journal and activating Dr. Brett's Internal Observer.

DEC
12
2008
The Week That Was

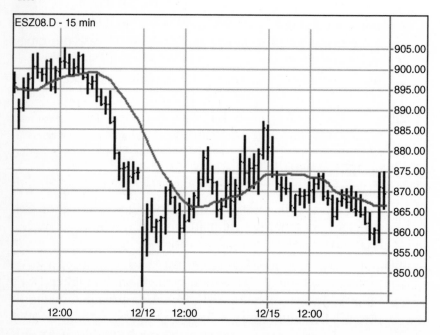

Well, no streak lasts forever, and the consecutive weeks of chip gains ended today at 21 due largely to an aggressive overnight position right before the no-bailout news hit that had bids completely disappearing and futures dropping another 20+ points from immediate overnight support and 40+ points from yesterday's closing barf. *Shades of my early October sequence, although I have no problem with the entry . . . not much you can do when bids disappear and one has to somehow find a way to manage a stop on large size (was probably around 5–6 pts or so . . . still beats the full 20 points, though).* On the comical side, I was only 12 hours early with a rock-solid entry.

From there, it was on to some very aggressive intraday scalping (8000+ contracts) on the expected "morning-after-trend" oscillations, which I traded OK but not great, to end the day at –$22.1K.

And so we put the cap on an interesting week that in my view was full of difficult rhythms, patterns, and—most importantly—market pace given the lengthy market indecision at times and cross currents with respect to the on-again off-again bailout news. Add to that a week that I frankly didn't trade very well (*I'd undoubtedly rate it my poorest week of the year from a skill-performance perspective, and that's all this business will ever be about*), and I'm scratching my head wondering how I ended down only –$10K for the week. *Then again, it goes to show that the scorecard often doesn't reflect one's performance.*

And so ends the week that was. It's now history and irrelevant. On Monday, all focus is on the week that is. 19 days to go.

DEC
15
2008
Empty Tank

Dear Diary,

As I sit here tonight pondering the remaining few weeks of 2008, and although up until about a week ago I had planned on "running through the tape" right to the 12/31 finish—or at least during this last full week of 2008 trading as I mentioned in this weekend's video—I now seriously wonder if I've simply emptied the tank dry.

I say this not because of the lack of market action or recent performance, but because for the first time all year, I can honestly say that the "disinterested" gremlin has now joined its "mentally fatigued" brother. And such a combination can be a recipe for disaster. Sure, the market's lack of recent action is likely contributing to my feeling, but I believe that it goes far deeper than that on a personal level. *And I'm also finding it hard to get ticked off at my trading, which is usually the cure for complacency.*

As I've stated all year, this year's journey was in part a test to see if I could take one year of my life and rededicate myself to trading in such a way that I'd learn what the results could be if I truly "left it all out on the field." All out, no looking back, no regrets . . . pick your mantra. It's something I'd always wanted to do, and so I decided at the ripening age of 47 that 2008 would be that year.

Looking back at September through November, aside from one large hit in early October, I seemed to be dancing with the market cheek-to-cheek, often matching its violent moves as if we knew each other's intentions ahead of time. I felt as if I were in my 20s again and my mind seemed sharper than ever.

And although I'll never use the sl∗∗∗ word (rhymes with "dump"), I'm clearly in a funk right now. My interest isn't there, which is resulting in hesitation and a flat to declining equity curve over the last several trading days. And it's now been a week since I had back-to-back positive days, which is almost unheard of for me. Frankly, I'll take a couple of modest +$5K days right now in a row. *Heck, I'll take two strong trade sequences in a row.*

I mentioned the other day that I need to find that finishing Olympic swim kick. But the arms are heavy. I can see the finishing wall, but can't feel my arms. I look to my right and left and they're still there, but I can't feel them. Somehow, they're moving, but it's a struggle. *I honestly feel like Michael Phelps in one of his last races when his goggles filled with water and he simply completed the last half of the race without seeing a thing. Except that he continued straight, while I'm starting to zigzag.*

If those looking over my shoulder are wondering if I'm over-dramatizing this, I'm not. This year has purposely been my mental Olympic race to end all races. A year in which I'd learn more about myself than any other year of my life. A year in which I'd put my decade of market "training" to the harshest test possible. A year to put up or shut up. A year of pure endurance.

It's quite possible, though, that the tank has now run dry. Although the early fall's performance momentum seemed to carry me in the first week of December, that wave seems over and I'm truly looking to a greater strength to carry me over the finish line. The needle reads E and the fuel light is on. The final outcome is now out of my hands. Maybe the true lesson is that it was never there in the first place.

 *Two Strokes Remaining*

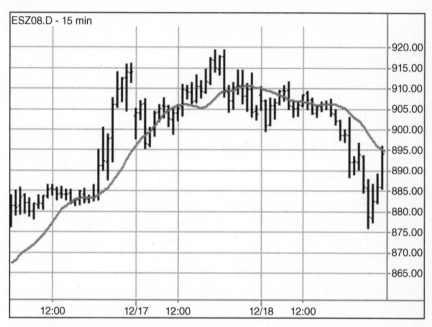

OK, first I'll address the –$16.2K day, which for important psychological reasons I'm going to break into two sessions: Europe (stopped on early break of long support), although heavy, was a bit anxious and didn't trade particularly well for a loss of more than $20K; and then a modestly profitable U.S. session, when I finally got my pulse aligned with the market's for the first time in a while, had a good afternoon "feel," and was extremely disciplined, especially in the last hour.

So, mentally heading into Thursday I actually feel that I've finally regained a sense of rhythm. *By the way, today was another example of the day's +/– results not meaning squat except in aggregation over the course of the year. I care more about my confidence and how I'm trading than any "number."*

Nevertheless, I have some decisions to make as I'm now right at a mental trailing stop on the year's earnings that I intend **not** to break. I'm not going to disclose the figure yet, but it's essentially a protective control I've put in place to ensure that I don't drop below retaining

97.5 percent of my equity high. It also allows me to bank a profitable December—even if modest—to keep me in a decent frame of mind for whatever January brings.

I view this Friday as pretty much my last trading day of the year. And so perhaps it's fitting that the trailing stop is coming into play right as this marathon race is coming to an end and at a time when the outstanding market rhythms of the fall have given way to lower volumes, poorer pace *(for my style that takes advantage of extreme emotion)*, and sporadic opportunities where it's too easy to try to force things. *And yup, I'm forcing things.*

I'd be lying if I didn't say that I'm disappointed in my performance of the last two weeks. Yet if I remove myself from the immediate moment, I'm frankly stunned that it didn't happen more along the way of this incredible 2008 journey. 49 weeks is a long time to go without an extended funk. And if this simply means my trailing earnings stop gets hit right as the race is about to end, it's more than acceptable. *Who knows, perhaps it's someone's funny way of keeping me humble for 2009.*

And although the ticker says 14 days to go before performance can be measured—which remains true—on Friday I'll disclose for the first time all year the annual tally, equity balance, and trailing stop . . . and will each day until the ball drops so as not to lose sight of this critical objective. Before, it was inappropriate to do so. Now, it's imperative.

Back to our year-long swimming analogy, I'm now only two strokes from the wall and am getting ready to grab a towel. And as long as I finish above my trailing stop, I'll indeed finish ahead of Alain Bernard to my right!

The journey has been long, we're almost there, and I'm not about to drive the car through the garage door. It's almost time to cut down the bamboo.

It Is Time

> "The race is not to the swift, nor the battle to the strong, nor does food come to the wise or wealth to the brilliant or favor to the learned, but time and chance happen to them all."
>
> **Ecclesiastes 9:12, New International Version**

I dedicate the following to my wife, Debra, and my family, who lived through my craziness over the past decade and whose faith in me never wavered; Dr. Brett Steenbarger, who will never truly know how powerful his seeds of thought in his first book were; and most importantly, to God, who gave me strength when I was weak, patience when I was impatient, and was the true gardener of this year's miraculous bamboo tree. And so it is time. Time to measure the bamboo. Time to rest and reflect. Time to lock in and protect $1.62 million on the year with a tighter-than-tight trailing stop that only allows for a less than $10,000 loss between now and December 31.

My only disappointment has been the last two weeks of subpar performance. Yet I clearly realize that's like saying that the Celtics beat the Lakers in six games last year instead of four. Fatigue finally took its toll in December via lack of focus and interest, as if to keep my humility in check for the future.

At the same time, I can see how easily Archie Karas and poker amateurs (and even a few pros at times) can begin down a slippery slope of eventually giving back all one's gains from even dizzying heights. Recognizing my mental state and having the self-control to hit the brakes after modestly donating to the market over the last few weeks and not trying to "win it back" has by far been my **most** difficult task of the year. Such is why I must now implement the tight trailing earnings stop.

$1.62 million. 97.5 percent of my chip stack high. Plus more than 200 percent return in the most volatile year in market history. Ever. Back to our ongoing poker analogy, it's comparable to seventh place in this year's World Series of Poker and fourth place in the 2007 event. And there's no profit sharing as it's my own private fund. It's still just a blur and hasn't sunk in.

Right now, my only memories are the hurts and pains. For now, I don't remember the wins. None. Perhaps that's because the fictional draw concept is so ingrained in my mind and I think that they're always ahead of me.

I now know how Michael Phelps's mental state felt near the end— emotionally drained and spent—and understand why he didn't set foot in a pool for a few months after the Olympics. At the moment, I just want to lie on a warm beach for a month (*although the market would have to be closed*). In trading, there are no off-seasons, just fast and slow seasons. We have to create our own off-season. That too, will be hard. Usually, the market or our performance dictates the off-season.

Yes, it's real, unlike the *The Bob Newhart Show* finale when Bob wakes up next to Emily after nine years at the Vermont inn and Newhart realizes it's all a dream. *At least I'd better not wake up in 1999 tomorrow . . . that would be sick.*

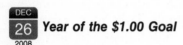

Year of the $1.00 Goal

What now? This is the question heading into 2009. As many know, this journal was a personal experiment. An experiment to determine what the effect of using a detailed trading journal—a public version open to those who stumbled across it and complete with real "chip-gain" commentary—might have on this trader's results. An experiment that took on interesting characteristics as the market decided to take the industry on a wild ride never before seen in the world's history and I tried my best to document my personal struggle to keep up with it. An experiment that evolved into a unique dialogue as the numbers of those watching grew daily.

In five days, the 2008 journey and experiment will be over. Based on both personal results and onlooker feedback, the experiment was a success. Which brings us to 2009. As I was writing yesterday's post about trading income simply buying "time," it dawned on me that I should take advantage of some of that "time" before the number of gray hairs begin to outweigh the brown. So, I'm going to take a different journey in 2009, one that seeks to increase the "fun" factor. *OK, yes trading to me is fun, but we're talking about a different kind of fun.*

Said another way, if 2008 was the year of pressing myself harder than I ever had, 2009 will be the year of getting eight hours of sleep a night, trading far less frequently, and spending more time with my wife and nonmarket priorities. There will be no pressure, no daily reference to chip gain or loss, and I'll actually even spend a portion of any trading profits realized in 2009. And if I end the year with $1.00 in profits (that's one dollar, as was the infamous bet in *Trading Places*), the year will have been a tremendous success as long as I met my enjoyment goals.

I'll be interested in how the change alters my views on trading during the new year, if at all. For example, I may find that the competitive drive is mandatory for me to do well. I may also find that taking it easier does even better (highly doubtful, though). On the other hand, I may find that I instead want to simply move on to another life challenge.

I actually thought briefly about fully retiring from competitive trading. Why consider going out near the top of one's game? Perhaps it's some boredom after accomplishment of one's goals. Many far better than me in their own fields have done it, including Annika Sorenstam, Justine Henin, Barry Sanders, Ken Dryden, Sandy Koufax, Bjorn Borg, and Michael Jordan (especially when he first "retired" in 1993 when he was only 30) to name just a few.

Yes, I know the physical demands of athletes are different and lead to shorter careers vs. traders who could sit in front of a terminal into their 60s and beyond. Yet the mental demands are no different and perhaps even more intensive given there's really no trading "off-season." *After all, how many 250+ game seasons are there in professional sports?*

And so next week I'll begin 2009. We'll go from the year of the $1 million goal to the year of the $1 goal. Regardless of what happens, it should be "fun."

2008 Year-End Grades

Time to hand out year-end self-grades for this trader.

2008 Report Card

Student: D. Miller

Grade: 10th Year

Age: 47

Major: Short-Term Market Trading

Patience: C

Student occasionally enters too soon and doesn't hold strong entries long enough. He also seems a bit overeager at times to get started in the Europe and Globex sessions when his success clearly has historically been accomplished in the U.S. day session.

Focus: B

Student is sometimes distracted by nonmarket obligations that, although they can't be eliminated, can be managed better at times. Also, twice during 2008 he should have canceled nonmarket activities for markets that were primed to move strongly, and as a result he incurred significant market opportunity cost. At other times, his focus was intense as was the case during much of Sept.–Nov., especially after initially getting knocked around. His focus certainly did drop after the first week in December, yet I can't fault him too much, and he did well to avoid major damage by scaling back.

Dedication and Commitment: A

Student showed strong dedication throughout the year, intensifying efforts even further in July with the launch of his blog, which helped him keep his mind focused on the 2008 task at hand. He ate, drank, and slept with the market in 2008. This is the highest grade I've given him in this category since I've known him.

Adaptability: B

For the most part, student adapted well to changing markets and his own rhythms, although sometimes at some high initial cost, which prevented me from grading him higher.

Tenacity: A

Student never gives up. Ever. When he finally goes, he'll definitely go kicking and screaming. This was probably the greatest reason for his 2008 results.

Plays Well with Others: B

Student did well to openly share his ongoing struggles and successes throughout the year with the public. And although I would have graded him higher if he didn't babble so much about the dark side of the industry, I have a strong feeling he'd rather accept the B.

Overall Potential—Incomplete

Tough to say. Student seems to have some potential, but he has to learn to stay out of his own way at times. He definitely still needs some work.

Suggestions for 2009:

Have some fun in 2009 and don't take life so seriously at times. The market will still be here in 2010 if you want to run another race. Also, don't take yourself so seriously all the time . . . no one else does.

DEC
31
2008

A Night to Dance

And so it is over. My personal 366-day inner journey to try to discover my true trading potential has finally ended, with the final tally reading: +$1,630,097, +214 percent.

Tomorrow, a new day will dawn, a new year will be born, and we'll get to start over. 2009 won't care about 2008 just like today didn't care about yesterday and tomorrow won't care about today. We'll all get a do-over . . . a mulligan . . . another chance to wipe the slate clean and make fewer mistakes than yesteryear. At this end, I've ended this particular journey and will trade largely for enjoyment as the year begins.

Yet for one night, we'll dance. We'll freeze this ever-so-brief moment as long as we can and dance away tonight like tomorrow will never come. We'll stand in awe of the magic of a fully matured bamboo, which will forever remain a testament to one's ongoing battle with patience, fortitude, and endurance.

About this time last year, more than a few people thought my million dollar mission for 2008 was impossible. "Foolish," "absurd," and "too old to compete against lightning-fast program traders" come to mind. As the year went on, some even wanted to see me fail . . . badly. Then, as the tally began to grow and initial targets surpassed, a few questioned whether the results were real, while a small minority tried to take away my spirit in various creative ways.

Then even the market seemed to get angry as it tried its darnedest to shake us all to our very foundation in the fall. It bucked and screamed like some monster straight from hell, even trying to kill my personal spirit with a $94K flesh wound that momentarily knocked me below my target. It spit in my face. The market then tempted me to push hard in December when I was physically and emotionally spent while at the same time drastically changing its own rhythm to try to trip me up. It was trying to put me on tilt to give up the hard-earned gains. Another spit. It was getting intensely personal.

Yet I owe all of them my deepest thanks. For they simply strengthened my resolve, which when combined with the tremendous outpouring of blog support over the last six months, simply made losing a nonoption. And although the market can't ever truly be defeated, like Rocky in his final movie, I somehow managed to stand toe to toe with the champ until the final bell. I'm leaving the ring standing, thanks in part to my decision to slow down in mid-December, which in hindsight was 100 percent correct.

And I had help. Big help. For I've seen and intensely felt God's hand this year, both during the good times and the struggles. *For those turned off by talk of faith or religion, all I can say is that this 2008 story simply wouldn't be complete without the full and accurate picture.* I doubt a lot of things in life. I don't doubt this.

Regardless of what happens in 2009 and beyond, no one will ever be able to take 2008 away from me. Ever. Like other far more important life milestones, the year will find its own place in a corner of my heart that I'll be able to tap whenever I question my ability to conquer a challenge in front of me. The funds will be well-protected and socked away, and a new game—in whatever form it takes—will begin.

And if you haven't figured it out by now, this journal goes far beyond my trading race. It's about life's race. Trading is a game, nothing more. It pales in comparison to life's true priorities and simply provides us with the analogy of all analogies, and parable of all parables. It provides us with a unique practice field on which we can learn and then try to apply the principles to life. The better we trade, the better we live, and the better we live, the better we seem to trade. For me, the $1.6M score will mean nothing unless I can now apply the learned principles going forward, especially to life.

If you're reading this, you're still breathing and I congratulate you. I don't have to tell you that life is sometimes hard. 2008 has punched many in the gut, and a lot of blood has been spilled in the form of lost jobs, foreclosed homes, and industry corruption at every turn. My punches just happen to come in earlier years and only infrequently in 2008 as fully chronicled for all to see in this deeply personal diary.

Tonight, we all dance. In part, we'll dance for the joy of personal victory, but for all, the survival of 2008 and the possibilities of 2009. And at midnight tonight, I'll drink a toast to all who have joined me on this year's journey—even if you're simply a silent onlooker or one of the small minority who may have initially questioned my motives and integrity—and to all who made it through the year, even if kicking and screaming or temporarily wounded. **You made it**. And you're a year smarter.

I encourage you to consider printing this and putting it someplace safe that you can reference if you ever get down or if someone ever tells you "You can't." Because they're dead wrong. If you're breathing, you can **and you will**. Regardless of what the pundits say or how much the temporary pain may sting, don't ever let anyone take away your spirit and joy for life. Who knows? 2009 may very well be your personal bamboo year. And if you still need a hand, contact me.

So long 2008. Welcome 2009.

Current-Day Notes: In sports terms, 2008 was clearly that "breakout year" during which multiple years of unfulfilled potential were utterly and completely vaporized, and I'll always refer to that year as my personal bamboo year as it removed any doubts in my mind as to how far my trading skill had evolved. And although the market volatility in 2008 provided an unusually fertile backdrop for traders given the extent of short-term price movement and profit potential, volatility is the epitome of a double-edged sword in the trading world, as it greatly magnifies the impact of both skill **and** weakness. Said another way, volatility tends to expose any and all shortcomings, as it did for me at times as we take one last look at 2008 by month as well as compare my total 2008 futures trading earnings to that achieved during the previous seven years.

2008 IRA Futures Fund Performance

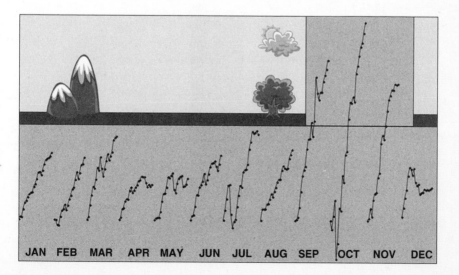

| JAN | FEB | MAR | APR | MAY | JUN | JUL | AUG | SEP | OCT | NOV | DEC |

Futures Account Performance (All Accounts) 2001-2008

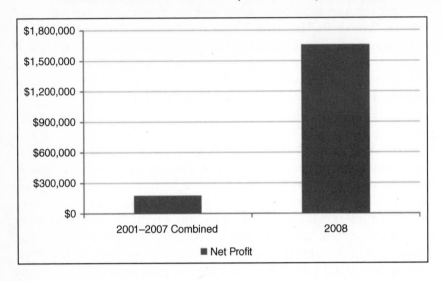

The 2008 "Race" Final Result

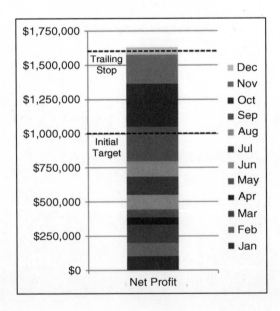

At the time, I was also more than curious how such performance that exceeded a 200 percent return would ultimately stack up against the top managed futures fund performances for that year, for no purpose other than internal personal benchmarking. I would later discover that the results compared favorably to the top 2008 CTA (Commodity Trading Advisor) program returns for funds managing less than $10 million as published by *Futures* magazine, exceeding the top performing fund, which achieved a 171 percent return. And although we must exercise caution whenever comparing single-year rates of return given the relatively short time frame and potential differences in fund intent, benchmarking to such publicly available data was nevertheless a useful exercise for me as it helped shed additional insight in terms of relative performance.

My final thought on 2008 is that it brought new meaning to the phrase "Past performance is not necessarily indicative of future performance." Although such words are often meant to temper enthusiasm by reminding us that strong performance in one period may not continue into the future, 2008 also provided clear personal evidence that **suboptimal** results—even if over an extended period of time—may also not be indicative of future potential. For such will remain true in **all** life aspects, as long as bamboos and time coexist.

PART

III

Beyond the Race: Best of the 2009 Journal Excerpts

As the first quarter of 2009 dawned, it soon became apparent that although I had planned on initially trading lightly for "fun" and with no self-imposed pressure, sufficient positive momentum remained that couldn't be ignored. Further, I felt that I might be able to improve on December's lackluster performance by eliminating some sloppiness that had crept into my trading. As such, I created the scorecard shown in Figure 3.1 as a way to identify, manage, and track how I responded to the market environment of the day.

The top section of the scorecard, titled Trading Environment, was designed to grade the day's opportunity and my preparation using color-coded shading ranging from red (poor) to dark green (stellar), whereas the lower Performance section was designed to grade how I traded given the level of perceived opportunity as defined in the top section.

Each week's scorecard became a recurring reference in my journal during the early part of 2009, and its use indeed helped correct some of December's sloppiness to such an extent that the first quarter of 2009 resulted in one of my most consistent quarters ever. I'd go on to record profits in 58 of 61 days and net another $350K+. One example of how I used the scorecard to effectively make course corrections appears in the following post.

	Mon	Tue	Wed	Thu	Fri	Total
Trading Environment						
Ability to Monitor the Market						
Focus and Energy Level						
Presession Planning						
Trade "Desire"						
Pattern Conviction						
Pace Conviction						
Volatility						
Performance						
Trade Management:						
Perceived Opportunity						
Matched Aggression						
Entries						
Adding to Winners						
Exits						
Patience						
Adjust to Changing Expectations						
Avoiding Trouble (SOOT)						
"No Regrets"						
Emotional Control						
Personal Achillies' Heel "Traps"						
9:00am – 9:30am						
Late PM						
Eurex						
Key Trade Sequences:						
Type A						
Type B						
Type C						
Bottom Line	Irrelevant					

FIGURE 3.1   Performance Scorecard

Roller-Coaster Day

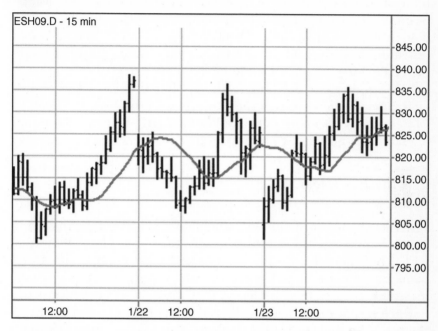

Years ago, I attended a driver's ed course that included a training simulation where you were driving through a parking lot and everything was thrown at you. First, a car backs out in front of you. Then a loose baby carriage. **Then** the baby's mother running after the carriage.

Today felt a lot like that. First, as many were likely positioning long preopen on the gap down toward Wednesday's supports (I sure was), Microsoft comes out with poor earnings. Then at open the market teases us with holding supports and climbing before it fails and trends down. Then the market breaks midday consolidation and looks as if it will trend strong into the close—even holding its first pullback— before doing a Wile E. Coyote cliff dive.

Trading can be a funny business. Yesterday, I was ticked that I didn't maximize what I felt was available potential. Today, on the other hand, I came close to squeezing everything I could out of a roller-coaster day where change was the word of the day and as a result colored much of the performance grid at least bright green. I was especially satisfied with how I reacted to the continual change in market conditions.

As is sometimes the case, most of my prime sequences today were 1st pullback types, where I entered on the first pullback and took the trade off as the market made its first thrust. The afternoon was a good example where I nailed both the 5- and 10-min pullbacks and took the high-probability scalp into the next push of retail buying before retreating to cash. And in both cases, that's all the market gave, as the S&Ps traded completely within yesterday's range.

On strong trend days, such a strategy looks foolish *(although if the market does run, there's usually a high percent contratrend trade or 1st pullback on the next larger time frame)*. On days like today, it looks incredibly smart.

It's really neither. It's simply trading.

 The Jazz Trader

Yesterday, I had the pleasure of attending a concert of the state's top high school musicians, of which my daughter who plays violin was a part. The concert participants consisted of a chorus, jazz band, symphony orchestra, and concert band. And the music was simply incredible, especially considering that those involved had just two practice sessions together, although they'd, of course, each individually practiced their pieces for a month or so leading up to the event.

Yet when the jazz band took over, I couldn't help my mind drifting back to trading throughout much of the 20-min session. I saw similarity after similarity between the players, each of whom took a turn to step out of the band to do an improvisational solo, and futures traders. And here's why.

Throughout the performance, there was an underlying rhythm—a pace that was kept by the director subtly through simple finger snaps—as well as sheet music, which was used as a guide for the players. Yet when it was time for the improvisation pieces, up stepped each player to the front where he or she performed without sheet music, playing the tune as he or she saw fit from the heart. And while the underlying beat provided by the director and rest of the band remained in the background, the inspiring improv solo performances clearly reflected each player's soul, vision, and individuality, and they combined for a truly outstanding performance.

And here's where I segue into trading. Those of us who take up the "instrument" of trading and are "students" of the market are indeed those improv soloists, where the market provides the beat and we are free to trade as we interpret the piece. As I've often said, there's no right way to trade *(except, I suppose, for ultimately making sure net purchase prices are less than net sales prices after expenses like any business)*, just as there's no right way for a jazz saxophonist to play his or her piece.

I'm sure there were a few missed notes, momentary loss of the underlying rhythm, and some performance stress during yesterday's jazz band set, *which also happens to describe almost every day of my trading career.* Yet I certainly didn't notice them as they were buried in the net performance, which was all that mattered.

There may very well be as many ways to trade as there are ways to interpret one's musical soul: speculating, providing liquidity, hedging, swing trading, scalp trading, range trading, breakout trading, trend trading, 5-min chart trading, 60-min chart trading, emotional extreme contratrend wholesaling . . . not to mention the thousands of trading "instruments" out there. There's simply no "holy grail" or "right way."

Someone asked me last night why I didn't short into the shallow 30-sec chart pullbacks on Friday's opening cliff drop. My response was essentially that I wanted to short, but personally rarely take shallow pullbacks on market spikes as I prefer lower-risk deeper retracements, which may appear as the first pullback on a larger time frame *(my eventual short was the first pullback and bear flag on the 5-min chart)*. And as I'm waiting, I may very well test the waters and provide some liquidity to those bailing on pure emotion, which eventually snaps back at some point . . . often hard..

And although the question was completely appropriate, perhaps my response should have been more along the lines of yesterday's soloists in that it's probably as irrelevant for me to look back on how I played a given pattern as it would be for me to ask why the horn player chose to pass on the screeching high-C climax and instead took a momentary breath to rejoin the band's rhythm. Neither was right, yet both were right.

I suppose we are all market "players" in the truest sense of the word. We must learn the underlying market beat, of course, yet the best players seem to play their own tune that reflects their individual strengths, heart, and soul. The sheet music will always remain unwritten until we step out of the band and up to the mike to write it.

The takeaway? Don't be afraid to step out of the crowd and up to the mike in trading—**or life**—and play your soul, and don't be afraid to write your **own** music. I suspect that some of the greatest tunes ever contemplated were never heard because they remained on the composer's desk or in the soloist's heart. And perhaps some of the best trades ever considered were never made because they remained in a trader's mind for fear of doing something unique or against popular convention.

Have a great and inspiring week.

Current-Day Notes: The above "Jazz Trader" post was subsequently selected by MoneyShow.com for syndication and appeared on its website a short time later. As the first quarter of 2009 would progress and ultimately result in one of my most consistent quarters ever, I selected the following three journal entries for this book—one of which describes my only large loss of the period, whereas another describes a lost opportunity—to again share that perfection will always remain ever elusive and that it's how we **respond** to our imperfections that matters and keeps us moving forever forward. Said another way, we can never win if we can't accept the accompanying and necessary defeats.

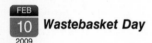

Wastebasket Day

FEB
10
2009

I'll keep today's diary entry brief as I got distracted during the midmorning drop with size and bungled my way to a major wastebasket day . . . as in, today as –$34.5k goes immediately in the trash can and is already forgotten. The score sheet will show more red than a bed of roses and will accurately reflect a day when I simply didn't have anything close to my game face on.

If you're new to this trek, welcome to the human element, and I hope this puts to rest once and for all the notion that I can forever escape the pain that will always be part of this business. I've always said that I'll share the good, bad, and ugly, and today was a capital "U." Today was also strong reinforcement that this business is so much more than about technical analysis. Trading is a mental sport—nothing more, nothing less—and is primarily about the execution. The charts today were clear. Very clear. Crystal clear. My head, on the other hand, was simply elsewhere.

I've often said that trading results do one of two things: buy or sell time. So, I'm a couple of weeks younger today. The 30-day streak is officially over, yet tomorrow is a new day and the ticker says we have 324 days before the score matters. Have a pleasant evening.

FEB
11 *The Sun Came Up*
2009

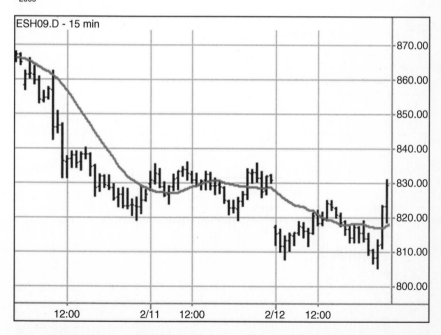

An amazing thing happened today: The sun came up after all. And yes, I'm posting early as I've closed the day to avoid the potential "screw the whole day up in 30 minutes" pitfall after recovering around 40 per-cent (+$14.1K) of yesterday's mess thanks to the classic morning-after-trend-day oscillations and a renewed commitment to focus.

Actually, I'm working on only three hours' sleep as I intended on trading both the Europe and U.S. opens, and both cooperated nicely by providing strong fade opportunities on the first retracement back towards Tuesday's resistance points. So, fade, cover, and repeat was the name of the early game as both opens chopped around, which as we all know is the expected—albeit not guaranteed—rhythm after a monster trend.

Perhaps I needed yesterday to finally stop treading on eggshells and move forward to more intense trading. *Case in point: Last time I had a major bonehead day, it provided the foundation for the $700K Oct.–Dec. 2008 run.* Maybe I needed that major butt kicking to make the fictional draw feel real again. Who knows. All I know is I that always trade my best after a draw, both because large draws are usually based on significant market moves that rarely repeat on consecutive days and because it essentially coaches me into getting my act back together.

It's amazing that it often takes one large step back to move several steps forward. But the sun feels nice. Hand me the sunglasses.

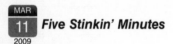

MAR
11
2009

Five Stinkin' Minutes

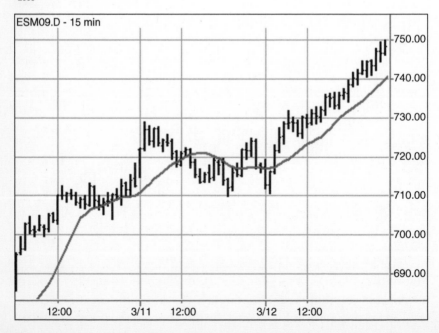

ESM09.D - 15 min

I'll be frank, as always. I was as aggravated with my trading today as I've been with any day in the last several years and for that reason am heading into the isolation tank this evening.

Suffice it to say that I lost a major chance at buying the hell out of the initial postopen retracement (my all-time favorite sequence) because I couldn't be at my trading station until 9:45am after ES had popped 8 points off the first pullback. Anything under 720 on the first TICK retracement was a high-probability GIFT, and the sequence was very similar to the $70K+ day I had in 2008 when I loaded up on the first bungee support. And while I was ready for it, especially after watching the Globex trade since 5am, I had a commitment I didn't reschedule, thinking I could be back by 9:30am. Yet I should have, as there are times in this business you should cancel **anything** short of a wedding or funeral to open the door upon which opportunity knocks, and today's open was one of them.

It was frankly all I could do to reign in the emotions and try to make something out of far lower probability sequences after that "gimmie" played out. And it was a major struggle all day to scrape together the ridiculously teeny +$4.7K chip gain I ended with—knowing I should have easily earned 1–2 week's pay today—as my emotions kept returning to the morning opportunity loss. I was teetering on tilt big-time and am still aggravated as I write this.

You plan, and then life happens. On top of that, I'm heading out of town Thurs. PM and Friday and will need to rely heavily on my laptop . . . assuming I haven't thrown it through the door by then.

And while I realize I've only had one net loss in the last 49 trading days, this missed opportunity hurts badly and is not a good way to start my 49th year on the day after my birthday.

 *Upon Further Review*

Important epilogue to today's earlier post: Although I obviously use this diary to vent, which I did today, I feel that I should more fully explain today's comments to those new to looking over my shoulder.

For those new to this journey, today's missed opportunity and reference to last year's home run **wasn't** about greed, which couldn't be farther from the truth. Instead, it was about what drives the long-term P&L in this business . . . and that is many small (and a few large) losses that **must be** offset by those occasional home-run gains—in addition to the steady modest daily keep—to drive a significant long-term bottom line. And this point is precisely what many scratch traders miss and is often the missing link that separates them and part-time hobby traders from the tiny minority that make *significant* long-term income from trading.

Of course, the concept is similar to (1) my trading day, where much of the day's income is made from a few trades amidst the 20–30 sequences; as well as (2) poker, where cash players make their keep from those rare large hands or tournament players make their keep from the small # of high-placing tournament results. The rest is usually offsetting chop.

Said another way, you **have** to be like Tom Cruise in the 1992 movie *A Few Good Men,* who went for the jugular when Jack Nicholson was on the stand when he sensed everything lined up and the time was right. Who could ever forget the exchange between Colonel Jessep (Nicholson) and Lt. Daniel Kaffee (Cruise). If you recall, while Kaffee had prepared to push the issue and get Jessep to admit that he ordered the Code Red, he was **only** going to push it hard if he sensed that he had Jessep on the ropes. And so it is in this business as well. You had to recognize heading into Wednesday's open there was a world of stuck shorts after Tuesday's action who HAD to cover on any initial drop . . . which was also clearly evident during the overnight Globex trade. And that is why the morning after a monster trend often provides such high-probability opportunities, especially if the first move is toward the most recent trend support. *As with poker, it's **not** about your hand . . . it's about the other guy's.* 100 percent probability? There's no such thing. Yet it was darn high and like being dealt pocket Aces and seeing A–A–K hit the flop. You **had** to be at the table to get dealt the dang Aces and **had** to go for the jugular when the probability was right.

So, today's earlier post wasn't about greed. Not at all. It was about **not** falling into the trap of a scratch trader and instead driving the long-term bottom line. It's about "handling the truth."

Life After 40

This one is for those onlookers in their 20s and 30s, as well as to those beyond 40 who I suspect will quietly nod and grin. I was watching clips

from the current PGA tour stop yesterday when I heard a com-
mentator mention that Tommy Armour III was a model of tour
perseverance in that he finally broke through the $1 million annual
winning mark last year, shattering his former glass ceiling by earning
$1.5 million. His age? 48. Of course, that struck an immediate chord
with this 48-year-old trader, given an eerily similar situation with my
2008 trading results. And although Armour turned pro at the age of
20 versus my beginning serious pursuit of trading in my late 30s, the
analogy remains valid.

In *Think and Grow Rich*, Napoleon Hill mentions that the average
man reaches the period of his greatest capacity to achieve between 40
and 60. In my view, Hill nailed this concept, as he goes on to cite many
famous individuals that hit their stride well after 40.

As many know, last year was my personal bamboo year, which we
all saw grow quite publicly before our eyes as momentum begat
momentum, which begat even more momentum. Frankly, when I
look back at last fall, I don't know how I did it, just as I don't quite
know what to make of this year thus far, where I'm waiting for
the inevitable multiday slump to set in or when I again momentarily let down my guard in February 10th fashion. Oh, it **will**
happen, and when it does, all energies will be directed at minimizing its damage.

So, for those onlookers under 40, I say with conviction that the
best is yet to come. For those in their 50s and 60s, I suspect that you'll
probably tell me it gets even better. *Talk to me on that one gang, if it's not,
I'll be extremely bummed.*

At this end, I find myself at a very interesting point in my life as I
contemplate how to spend the next decade while in the midst of what
will arguably be the most productive 10–20 years in one's life. One
example is that after next year, our youngest daughter will be off to
college and we'll be in our official empty-nest years.

And while I won't bore you with the questions I'm asking myself
at this point in my life, they include where trading and blogging
fit in as I move ahead. Frankly, as it relates to portions of this blog,
I'm not sure how much more I can say that hasn't already been said.
Yet for now, this ongoing glimpse into what is traditionally an
intensely private world of a trader continues, and I suppose as
with most things in life, time will provide the ultimate road sign.
I just hope the sign looks like a futures chart so that I can try to
interpret it.

Where It All Began

Today, I'm visiting my mother and father at their home "where it all began" for me, a small town in southeastern Massachusetts a couple of hours from where I live now.

What's a bit surprising, for a guy who hates to "look back" *(you can't drive forward by looking at the rearview mirror)*, is that some interesting memories always accompany me when I return, including the garage door against which I hurled the tennis ball at the age of 10, pretending to pitch that perfect game of called strikes using the middle four panels of the door, before "starting over" after any ball or wild pitch with a clean slate and trying again. *Hmmm . . . where have I heard that "do-over" concept before?*

I seldom talk about trading with my parents or my close friends, after learning years ago that most people will never understand the concept due to mass media inaccuracies, personal opinion, or lack of full understanding. So, I've instead purposely chosen to create a clear mental wall between my trading and personal lives. Frankly, aside from my wife, my family is unaware of the degree of my early heart-aches and later successes over the years. I simply don't talk about it, much like a plumber probably doesn't talk about the copper pipes he solders together hour after hour, day after day, or the bumps his knuckles receive by crawling around basements and managing around joists and rafters.

You see, for me, this is a job . . . a serious one along with my other nonmarket business that also requires attention to provide that solid bill-paying foundation that frees the soul to dance with the market. And since we know how boring it is to hear about someone else's job, I just don't talk about it.

Oh, except for this diary of course . . . lol. Yet most of my family and friends don't even know this exists; as to them, I'm like that plumber toiling away in a field with which they're not quite familiar. So, we instead talk about old times, grandkids (theirs, **not** mine . . . yet), sports, home improvement, health, and other nonmarket topics. For me, it's a very healthy mental separation and helps keep me grounded.

Yet I **am** going to try to find a tennis ball today to throw one last pitch for old—and new—times' sake. And if I miss, I'll chase it down and hurl it again. The next trading "do-over" will have to wait until Monday.

The Missing Inches

I need to step out of the moment to do some serious reflection as we get ready to wrap up May and approach the one-year mark of this public diary. After tomorrow, five months of this 2009 journey will be in the books. And it remains clear that in 2009 and my worst monthly performance in quite a while at only a little over +$40K after today I haven't been willing to fight for the inches. And if you read between the lines of yesterday's journal entry, it was evident as there was money (inches) lying all over the place in the classic morning, and I was simply willing to settle for a very modest day after sleeping past the Europe open and then leaving some money on the table early in the U.S. session before getting a bit sloppy in the afternoon. Today's trade also didn't go particularly well until the afternoon session, but as always, it's not about the day . . . it's about the year and the overall monthly earnings curve that's beginning to flatten.

And without dwelling on the past, it's clear that last year I fought for **every** inch. 365 days less the late-December pause. Many nights with fewer than 4 hours sleep . . . a few with none. Trading Europe and the U.S. sessions. Fighting not only for every inch, but every 1/16th.

There's a reason for the record run that seems to be losing steam. And that has been the living, sleeping, and breathing the market 24–7, journaling moment-by-moment thoughts, and essentially putting myself in a zombie-like zone for much of 2008 and parts of 2009 while riding the confidence and performance momentum and trading day after day, week after week, until it finally dried up.

Last year, I clawed for every inch. And at the end of the year, the fingernails were stubs and bleeding. That's simply what champions do. They do what others can't or won't. They do what **I'm not** doing this year *(not by design certainly)*—and I won't list excuses—as many of my sequences have been off by an inch. Too many. **And the missing inches have clearly added up.**

In the big picture, despite a poor May, I shouldn't complain about sleepwalking to a year-to-date $400K+ income on top of last year's bounty. *(By the way, that's **not** a boast, rather a significant* *criticism.*) And regardless of what I decide to do from this point forward, it's been one helluva run for this 48-year-old who wanted to find his true potential. The real question is, Who's willing to go after the missing inches? This year, I seem to be sitting on the yardstick. *Now that's a great visual.*

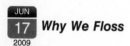

Why We Floss

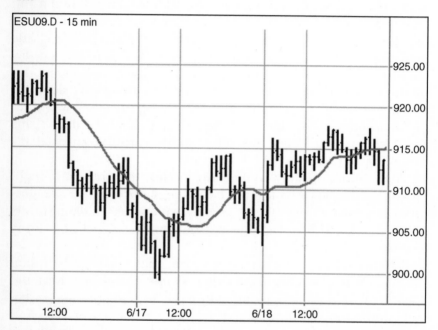

I know I've stretched the limit on crazy trading analogies since this trek began last year, yet be forewarned that this may be the most extreme. Here's the setup: a classic oscillation morning expected given two down days in a bull market, right? You know the drill: fade TICK extremes expecting oscillations, cover, repeat, etc. etc., right? It's my favorite setup, which feels like a comfortable slipper and often accounts for more than half my monthly profits.

There was only one problem today. I'm terrible about flossing and thus paid dearly today as I spent the early morning in the dentist's chair, which ruined any chance I had to dance cheek-to-cheek (pun intended) with the market's expected morning gyrations. And so the too-often 2009 personal theme continues, which at this rate I'm about to title *Life Interruptus* given this year's many personal nuisances.

As many know, last year I postponed about every personal obligation for 365 days to see what the result would be. And we learned the answer in the form of a record bounty. This year, I've decided to live a more "normal" life, which time has been telling us can be very costly from a trading perspective when the market dictates the opportunity . . . **not** your schedule.

And so for the first time since I can remember, I had a surprising draw on my favorite kind of day, which experience has shown would normally have been a very-high-probability five-figure gain. And while I thought about canceling at the last moment and rescheduling last night when it became clear that this morning would provide a high-percentage play, I didn't, out of respect for my dentist friend who also needs to make a living. Plus, it's tough to schedule dentist appointments.

And although not canceling was the right thing to do from an ethical perspective, it was admittedly a very costly appointment in terms of modest draw and—more importantly—opportunity cost as I provided liquidity for much of the rest of the day with my B– game on.

Yet as letting it get to me won't do any good, the only way to forget it is to stay focused on the road ahead, and one date and result only . . . December 31. That's why traders **must** have a nonexistent short-term memory. *My wife continues to say that a poor short-term memory is one of my strengths.*

Nevertheless, if today doesn't teach our kids—and me!—to floss, nothing will. Yet I need to remind myself that it was just another day of thousands in the career and need to move on.

Current-Day Note: The day subsequently ended –$15.3K.

JUN
25
2009
How I'll Spend My Summer Vacation

Headline: This decade-long trader who breached the single-year million dollar mark last year will likely not make any money in June 2009. A bit shocking? Yes. Planned? Heck, no. Yet as they say, it is what it is.

So, this has caused me to take great pause to consider what the heck has been going on over the last month—in fact, last two months as May was pretty poor—to see if I've "lost it." As such, here's my list of takeaways:

Key Negatives

- Have often missed prime opportunities due either to non-market commitments (especially back and neck tests) or my own indifference, which led to . . .
- Forced opportunities during marginal "hands" and a bit of "trying to make up for lost time" by pressing at the wrong/worst time.
- Diminished "feel" for the market as the result of missing key times and trying to start the engine midstream, as well as lower volatility (although it's still "me," **not** the market).
- My confidence is an issue.

Key Positives

- I'm still swinging the bat.
- I had a number of solid trades (they were simply offset by the other crap and transaction costs).
- As of now, the June P&L after costs is still positive (albeit barely).
- I'll still bank +$400K for the 1st six months (of course, most of it was earned in Q1!)

I could go on, but those are the highlights. Yes, I bleed red just like everyone else. Reminds me again of that scene in *Rocky IV* when Ivan Drago finally gets cut, after which Duke turns to Rocky and reminds him Drago wasn't a machine.

As most should know by now, I view trading as a competitive mental sport, where performance momentum begets momentum. We saw that in spades last year with an avalanche of profit day after day and month after month. And right now, I'm trying like heck to hold back the rolling snowball so that it **doesn't become** an avalanche in the other direction.

OK, so what am I going to do about it? Essentially, nothing. I'm the same person I was in 2008 and am simply going to keep breathing and swinging, knowing that at some point the performance momentum will again turn in my favor, at which point I plan to again floor the accelerator.

So, that's going to be how I spend my summer vacation . . . one step at a time.

Current-Day Notes: As much as the latter part of 2007 provided a solid foundation for 2008 and foretold of possibilities to come, the second quarter of 2009 in retrospect seemed to foretell the end of this particular chapter in my life. For although June ended slightly profitable and I'd increased my 18-month take from January 2008 to June 2009 to more than $2,050,000, my passion, energy, and desire to continue flooring the accelerator day after day was clearly diminishing, especially since I'd more than met all three objectives that I'd set at the beginning of this most recent journey. Nest egg established? Check. Learn how far I'd evolved my trading skills? Check. Generate concrete evidence to dispel the myth that successful trading is implausible or impossible over the long term? Checkmate.

Final Tally Jan 2008–Jun 2009

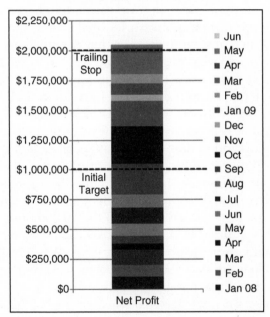

Interestingly, it was around this time that I had a long phone conversation with one journal onlooker who continued to challenge the notion that any of this was real and who was convinced that trading was gambling and that whatever I or other successful traders may have reaped in the markets was due solely to luck. Even after an hour of discussing trading as a business similar to that of a grocery wholesaler, offering account statements, discussing my Q1 2009 58–3 win/loss performance, and referencing enormous data sampling sizes approaching 400 trading days, 10,000 trade sequences, and a million contracts, he still wasn't convinced that it was anything more than luck. Finally, after some head-shaking at my end, I simply said that I must be the luckiest person on the planet and wished him well.

The discussion also reminded me of the important role that education plays in this world, for without it, we're simply ignorant as to current truths and future potential. For example, since I haven't been schooled in the physics and psychology of air travel, I still don't understand how a 400-ton airplane can get off the ground, nor will I likely ever be able to pilot a plane given my fear of heights. Similarly, I imagine that most people who pursue flight or other skill-based careers such as professional sports also fail to achieve those particular goals. Yet thousands of flights led by highly skilled pilots occur daily without incident, and we have enough successful partic-ipants in the professional sports world to fill dozens of networks on a daily basis. As such, just because some may not fully understand how successful traders do what they do or haven't developed the required skill set, there remain many traders who have worked years to hone their craft and rise above the majority to do quite well.

And speaking of work, Malcolm Gladwell suggests in his 2008 book *Outliers* that one key to finding extraordinary success in any field is a combination of time and work—specifically, 10,000 hours—and goes on to list several highly successful people where the math indeed adds up. Interestingly, I recall doing my own math when this statistic was first brought to my attention a few years ago and deter-mined that I likely would have reached the 10,000-hour mark of the futures "learning curve" in the fall of 2007, assuming seven hours of daily screen time over the course of six years. Was it a fluke that my personal 10,000-hour mark seemed to coincide with the equivalent of a trading bamboo-breaking ground? I think not.

Nevertheless, since my personal objectives had all been more than met, I was finding that the effectiveness of the fictional draw concept was beginning to diminish, as was my ability to create that required "chip on the shoulder" mentality. As such, and as I would tell a few dozen traders who gathered at my home in June 2009 at what we dubbed the Boston Bamboo cookout, I felt that I needed to find a new spark and mission. Later that year, I would also write a post called "Catching the Rabbit" that referenced the mechanical rabbit that racing dogs pursue that can't ever be caught. Except there was one key difference at my end: I caught it. As a result, the next few years would result in a great deal of soul-searching effort as I tried to decide what to do with it.

PART IV

Birth of the Jellyfish

The Genesis

As 2009 evolved, on the heels of having exhausted much of my immediate passion, I initially turned down many requests to reenter the world of formal trader education for several reasons not unlike those for initially shunning opportunities to author a book. After all, I'd been highly critical of the lack of quality trader training programs in the industry, and the last thing I wanted to do was to be perceived as wanting to "cash in" on my most recent successes, even though I had previously been a profitable equity trader and trading instructor in prior years. In fact, I had actually halted an earlier educational offering a few years earlier due to what I believed was excessive marketing over which I had little control.

Yet as we reviewed in Part I, one problem with this perspective is that the records show that my early on-the-job-training years of trading futures between 2001 and 2003, although resulting in gains prior to commissions, actually resulted in a six-figure net **loss** due largely to an inappropriate retail cost structure that few understood how to correct. Plus, there were all the other mistakes that, although they can never be completely eliminated, could have at least been reduced. As has often been said, *"If I only knew then what I know now."* As such, I thought that perhaps a unique program, if properly designed and done right—and it would **have** to be done right—could make a small difference in the world of trader education and development.

Yet two major objections remained in my mind. First, "doing it right" would require a series of integrally woven components that would effectively combine formal lecture, my own trading, and extended participant live screen time over an extended period via the Internet. Clearly, putting together such an effort would be no small task. The second objection I had was somehow coming to grips with the high failure rate associated with the trading industry, meaning that even if we were successful in developing a highly effective program, a degree of student failure would remain given the nature of a performance-based field where the minority prevail.

The latter challenge had often weighed on my mind, including during earlier times when I was asked to write a daily trading column, develop trading simulations, and instruct emerging traders. Yet ultimately, I looked to my family of life-long educators as role models, as I was reminded that future student success that begins in any formal educational setting, whether it be a full four-year college program or an adult training course, is ultimately dependent on the student's ability, motivation, and discipline to **apply** the instructed skill. In other words, inherent failure shouldn't be a roadblock for the development of an educational program. On the contrary, inherent failure should actually **increase** one's motivation in the context of doing one's best to try to make a difference and reduce the high rate of failure. Even so, I'll never be one to take defeat lightly, whether it be my own or that of a peer or student.

And so, after consulting with a number of industry leaders whom I held in high regard, and after someone all but screamed at me, "If not you, then who?" I decided that the right thing to do would be to move forward, but under several conditions. First, I'd initially work with a "beta" team of traders from a variety of backgrounds who would provide feedback throughout the effort and thus help refine the program for future participants. In return, I'd give them twice as much time with me as I had initially planned, increasing the course program from one to two months. Second, as I mentioned previously, the program would have to reflect a mix of formal lecture and extended live screen time ("extended" meaning long enough to ensure that we'd be able to monitor every type of market rhythm). Third, we'd emphasize opportunities with protective confirmation triggers. Fourth, despite strong interest numbering in the hundreds, the team would have to be small—under 25—such as not to dilute the program's instruction or intent. Fifth, the value of the service would have to far outweigh participant tuition, which ultimately resulted in my deriving a simple formula of dividing whatever the consensus of participant tuition was by two. Sixth, each and every member of the beta team would have an opportunity for a full refund if after beginning the effort they didn't feel it to be personally worthwhile. And finally, I insisted that some of the proceeds go to charity, which led to an alliance with the American Diabetes Association.

As such, in July 2009, and with the intent on creating one of the most intensive group trading experiments and educational efforts ever experienced, we launched a new breed of trader instruction whose participants we coined "Jellies." The term "Jellie" is short for jellyfish, those mystical creatures that must adapt to the ocean's current to survive as well as "sting or be stung." And what better creature could describe an effective trader, who must identify and feed off evolving market conditions of which we have no control. *I can't overemphasize the importance of continually adapting one's methodology to evolving market conditions, a concept that varies significantly from a single-style approach that may only work in some markets and at some times.* The term was also selected as the team identity because of its spiritual connotations as described by Phil Vischer—creator of the Christian animated videos, "Veggie Tales"—as described in his 2006 book *Me, Myself, and Bob,* which chronicles the rise and fall of his company, Big Idea Productions.

Selecting the Team

So, during the summer of 2009 and after reviewing hundreds of applications after an extensive interview and selection process, we selected a team of 21 participants. The individuals selected were chosen based on their general maturity and professionalism as demonstrated by previous accomplishments, an intense and balanced desire to improve both oneself and the surrounding team, and the ability to provide a unique skill or perspective that would complement that of other Jellies to help increase the probability that the team would indeed be stronger than its individual parts. Jellie occupations included a sports broadcaster and former NFL quarterback, professional tennis player, software developer, real estate broker, engineer, photographer, information systems executive, accountant, aerospace manager, telecom executive, grain trader, floor trader, proprietary trading business owner, and a small business retailer.

We agreed to work together for eight weeks, including a two-hour preparatory Sunday evening session to lay the necessary groundwork and discuss my trading approach and setups in great detail, 40 intensive eight-hour days monitoring and trading the market, and 8 two-hour lecture and recap sessions each Monday evening. Ironically, it was almost an afterthought that I decided to record the preparatory and weekly reinforcement sessions so as to provide those who weren't selected to the initial team an opportunity to passively participate, and subsequent feedback has indicated that the resulting 16 hours of video and audio content have become one of the better received educational products in the industry.

The Jellies Speak

For those outside the "tank," as we called it, it's extremely difficult to put this time into words. And although I thought about not including the following two posts in these pages given a few positive references to their "navigator" *(the posts were penned by Jellies as the effort unfolded in the spirit of giving me a brief blogging respite)*, I chose to include them, as well as my final post of the beta effort, as they best highlight some of the participants' most critical "light bulb" discoveries during those 336 hours.

Jellie Trader Journal Entry 1

 *No Country for Old Men*

I enjoyed the Coen brother's critically acclaimed movie *No Country for Old Men* for its realistic depiction of human life and experience. If you are familiar with the Coens, they are not known for warm and fuzzy happy endings. They like to present to you in various forms what we go to the movies to forget: that life is hard. Toward the end of this twisted crime drama, sheriff Tom Bell (played by Tommy Lee Jones) visits a former colleague's isolated home on a plain somewhere in Texas. After greeting each other and forcing a couple of pleasantries, the colleague looks up from his wheelchair and says, "This country's hard on people."

Trading is hard. This is part of the appeal, part of the joy at reaching a milestone, and part of the challenge. In his 1989 boo, *The 7 Habits of Highly Successful People,* Stephen Covey states that life is difficult and that the sooner we recognize and accept this, the sooner we are able to deal with things much more effectively. This is true for trading as well. After 12 days in the Jellie tank, I can tell you that there are no magic setups, no Don Miller secrets that have not been revealed in the blog, and no easy profits (though there have been profits!). However, 21 people signed up for this effort and 21 people remain. We could have left during the first week and gotten most of our money back. Nobody did.

This is a testament to Don Miller and a testament to my brothers in the tank. I'll just go ahead and say it and he might edit it out, but these last few weeks have been hard on Don. First let me say that I personally trade 2–4 ES contracts at a time and do 5–10 trades in a day. That's anywhere from 10–40 contracts per day. Don traded 550 contracts yesterday, which was a light day for him. He's done this everyday with 21 of us questioning him about entries, telling him what we are thinking, and doing stupid things that he has to correct. This is all in addition to the webinar preparations, questions at night from the Jellies, and blog updates. At dinner last night, my wife said to me, "How does he trade that much and deal with everybody at the same time?" I told her that I didn't know.

I think a lot of the Jellies wonder what Don will do after these eight weeks. Deep down, we all hope that he continues to keep the trading room open and even possibly trades with us "for the rest of our lives," as he says on a recent blog video. I have my own opinion that I'll keep to myself for now (hint, hint: it doesn't include trader education). I accidentally came across a blog discussion on a Google search last night where a guy was saying that Don was a "sell-out" for doing trader education. I chuckled to myself, thinking how foolish people can be. Twenty-one guys could have gotten most of their money back after a week and nobody did. That's my only response to any questions about Don's integrity or the quality of his efforts.

No Country for Old Men ends with Sheriff Bell and his wife at the breakfast table on his first day of retirement. He recounts a dream he had the night before, and there has been much discussion on what this final scene meant. I think that Bell is just tired, that he doesn't want to go into those "dark woods" up ahead that he speaks of in the dream, which are surely symbolic of the escalating violence he has witnessed in his formerly quiet town. He's 20 years older than his father ever was and is tired. Hence the title of the movie.

Don is young by most yardsticks, but maybe "old" in trading years. He's certainly and admittedly tired from his miraculous journey in 2008. Trading is hard on people. But in the end, as much as he loves his wife, I just don't see Don Miller ever having that "first day of retirement morning breakfast" with his wife. Make of that what you will.

Jellie Trader Journal Entry 2

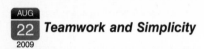 *Teamwork and Simplicity*

The great discovery of the 1950s: "You cannot understand the system by the analysis of its parts." What does this mean? And what does it have to do with trading?

The idea here is that you cannot and will not know what an engine capability is by analyzing the pistons, the rods, the crankshaft . . . you get the idea. I would go as far as saying that you would not know what the car can do until you put it all together and run it. You see, a system is all the parts together, and the system performance only shows up when they all work as designed. "As designed" means that they all work well together, we can pick the best parts from every car in the world, and with the best parts of all the cars in the world we cannot make the best car in the world. Why? Because the best parts from each car in the world are not designed to "work together"; they are designed to work for a particular car.

So, what does this have to do with trading? I think everything. As traders, we are always looking for the latest and greatest indicator that will "tell us" what to do "at this moment" or interpret the news event that will shake the market. Since 99 percent of all indicators are lagging indicators, they are always late in telling us this and we keep searching; in addition, by the time you interpret the news, the market is gone. Indicators are like the "parts" in a car. None of them can tell you what the car can do for mainly one reason: The car is you, and fuel for this car is a price chart.

The essence of the Jellies training is exactly that: "What kind of trader am I, and what can I do?" Don Miller's daily drill has been "feel the market," "feel the pace," based on this, "have a bias," then "sense, trust, and act." I have known this fact, the discovery of the 50s, for almost my entire previous career, but it hit me like a ton of bricks yesterday. It took Don's two weeks of drilling for me to go through this paradigm shift. I integrate all the data, "garbage in–garbage out." The more I put in my head, the slower I perform. This kind of learning only comes through deep immersion, lots of deprogramming and reprogramming going on. It is intense with moments of emotion only felt because there is commitment all around. I told Don at the beginning that I was committed to this effort and told him the story of the chicken and the pig for breakfast, the chicken contributes, the pig is committed.

Enter Don, as transparent a trader I will ever meet: What you see is what you get. If he is having a good day or a bad day, we all know it, because he tells us. He is his worst critic; he makes self-observations that are valuable to me as a trader. I learn from these examples and they help me create a baseline for myself. Don drills, what I mean by "drills," there is lots of repetition and correction, everyday. For example, "have a bias, but make sure to trade what you see, not what you think"; "the ups and downs, manage them, but stay in the game, you have to be present to win"; "the minute the sequence ends, look for the next one, mentally delete old sequences, only look forward." The team loves it, because we all know where the bottleneck of the system is: US! So, I am the limiting factor to become a self-sufficient trader. I can only get better if I am "coachable," open-minded and receptive to new ways of thinking, and if I have enough repetition.

Don is a great believer of simplicity. "Give me a price chart and a TICK chart, and I can make money." I love simplicity, but it is very difficult to achieve, you know why? You have to burn all your crutches, and this makes us insecure. In a 1989 *Harvard Business Review* interview, Jack Welch said that for a large company to be effective, it must be simple, and this works for traders as well.

I looked for the keys to the kingdom all over the place, and come to find out, in the trading world, that key is me and my fuel is a price chart. The only way to achieve self-sufficiency is to find the right people to help you; use your intuition about the people you choose and work only with the best. What an awesome team concept.

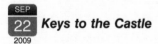

Keys to the Castle

Last night, we completed the eighth and final formal Jellie study session, where I presented top lessons learned by the Jellies to a packed house. The lessons were authored by each Jellie and reflected each trader's top three lessons learned over the last two months of full immersion.

In my view, it was a final test of sorts to see if the things I firmly believe form the cornerstone of highly profitable trading, which I had beat to death day after day in terms of both running commentary and my own trades.

And when I saw several members of the team last night comment on the critical roles that (1) market bias and (2) "outliers" play in this business, I sat back and grinned as I knew then that some of the most important concepts—those that separate losing traders from profitable traders and profitable traders from million dollar traders—were taking root. Specifically, here are comments from two members of the team as presented last night with respect to those two critical concepts:

Market Bias Is King: This was the most important lesson overall as just this one little concept can turn your whole trading career around and make consistent profitability possible. Prior to the Jellie effort, I had been sitting here with my sister showing her a strategy and it happened to enter a trade automatically. It went in my favor to start and then immediately did an about-face and ran right through my stop. I wasn't mad that the trade lost, I was upset—scratch that, beyond upset! My sister saw the look in my face and wondered why I was so upset if the loss wasn't really that large. I told her, "It's just so damn frustrating that after all the countless hours I've spent researching, reading, writing code, and studying chart patterns over the last two years, that it still feels like a coin flip every time I enter a trade." The tank changed that for me by allowing me to see a bias in the market that I hadn't given any credence to before, and by following that bias I could stay on the right side of the trade and I could make this work.

Outliers Are Critical: In poker, it's usually best to play conservatively until you get a hand where the probabilities are strongly in your favor. When trading, it's usually the same. You need to wait until the odds are strongly in your favor and then go in heavy. Unfortunately, those conditions may exist only two to three times per day and only in windows of a few seconds when you can get in at the right odds.

Outliers Are the Keys to the Castle: You add to your winners. **Try to turn each and every trade that goes in your favor into an outlier**. Get as much out of each trade as you can. Inverse applies to trades going against you. Limit your losses to the best of your ability by knowing that you're wrong and scratching before the market proves that you're wrong. At the end of the day, one or two outlier trades can make up for every missed opportunity or good trade gone bad. And those become outlier days. And those lead to outlier weeks. Pretty soon, you don't have to worry about being right 70+ percent of the time. You take all that stress of "being right" off your shoulders and that in turn makes it easier to scratch a trade that's lost its premise. I no longer think that it "may come back, so I don't have to take the loss" or "just try to get out here on this limit!" Who cares, scratch it. Next bus is coming. It's a heck of a lot easier to come back from a 200.00 loss versus a 2000.00 loss.

Yes, market bias is critical, which is why we beat it in minute after minute, hour after hour, and day after day until people were sick of me discussing it. And double yes, outliers are **absolutely** the keys to the castle, which most traders can't or won't pursue . . . often under the completely wrong guise of "worsening" average cost and ignoring the concept of incremental income or adding at the wrong times, such as in range markets.

As I've mentioned from time to time, top traders—like top poker players—push hard and add to their bets when provided with market information that confirms their initial bias read. The profits that I've earned over the last few years are the direct result of doing just that. Simply put, you have to know when to floor the accelerator and when to back off or coast, whether it be during a given trade sequence, day, week, month, or year. Like Tom Cruise in *A Few Good Men*, you simply have to know when to go for it. And experienced traders do just that.

The record, of course, shows that I sensed the kill over the last two years and thus pushed it hard. And we're talking about no-sleep, nonstop, health-affecting, hard . . . in such a way that every single penny of the millions earned in recent years came at a price few would ever think of paying. Last fall and even into this spring, I essentially floored the accelerator right through the pavement until the engine—**my** engine— ran out of fuel and was burning oil. So, this summer, it was time to open the hood, let the engine breathe, and get a mind and body tune-up.

By the way, in hindsight, my 2007–early 2009 decisions to go for it, as well as the 2009 summer decision to pause to open the hood, were both 100 percent correct. Simply put, you have to push when you sense the kill, and you—and only you—need to make the decision as to when to do so. And don't **ever** let anyone critique your trading decisions, style, or self-imposed breaks in this business.

And now the engine has been rebuilt, I've teamed with a pit crew and am now picking up the speed once again and racing around the track . . . with a "car" that's much more lightweight and nimble and a mind that's sharper than ever.

Yes, outliers are **indeed** the keys to the castle. And keys to the race car. It's one thing when I say it, yet it means so much more when it comes directly from the traders. And some day, I hope to be watching them join me in the victory lane, at which point I'd simply be content to help change their tires or dine at their castle.

Current-Day Notes: My closing thought on the beta and continuing educational efforts is that, as with life itself, the Jellie concept isn't perfect. Yet as I look back, participant feedback indicates that there really isn't much that I'd do differently, and I subsequently made additional tweaks that were the direct result of participant feedback from the beta team. My guess is that if you were to ask the participants of the beta team, the many live teams that followed, and those who continue to obtain and watch via the video series whether it was worth their time and effort and whether we began to make inroads in the context of taking trader education to a newer, deeper level, I believe that the general consensus would be that we were successful. I also believe that if I had engaged in similar training during the "apprentice" portion of my trading career, I would have been able to avoid many of my missteps.

There is also little doubt as to the significant relevance of the Jellie concept in terms of the need for **every** trader—regardless of preferred market, technical indicator, timeframe, or style—to emulate those sea creatures by identifying and adapting to ever-changing market rhythms in order to the maximize the probability of success in **all** market rhythms. And while such an objective isn't necessarily "new", naming the concept in the way we did rightly increased trader awareness of the critical and often-forgotten trading principle of flexibility.

And although I'll again emphasize that there is no magic pill or easy road to success, I do look back at that program incubation period with a sense that we developed a very unique experience and tool that can further round out the trader's toolkit. *A complete syllabus of the recorded video sessions and available discounts can be found at www .donmillereducation.com.*

PART V

Beyond the Tank: Best of the 2010–2012 Journal Excerpts

I 've selected the next several journal entries for inclusion primarily because they reinforce that ever-important notion of accepting trader imperfection and mistakes and the need to just "keep on keeping on." And although I again subsequently recovered from each instance cited—whether the mistakes resulted in real, opportunity, or perceived loss—my purpose in highlighting these particular posts is to again emphasize that it's often during our times of weakness when we find the source of our greatest strength.

JAN 08 2010 *Poker, Trading, and Focus*

It's **all** about focus. In fact, it's **only** about focus. Let's start with last night's odd series of events.

After about going through the roof early in last night's poker tourney as the result of getting called on an all-in where my opponent was chasing a **single #$%&#$ card in the deck** *(the most ticked off I've ever been playing cards)* and, of course, **catching** it, I was able to somehow come back after that hand knocked me from $8K in chips to $1200 *(I had a few more chips than her before the hand . . . more on that following)* and actually win the event about three hours later. Incredible.

First the hand. I'm the dealer and had 4 and 5 of Diamonds preflop, which came 6–7–Q with one Diamond. One of the three in the hand proceeds to bet about 1/2 of a decent-sized pot, which was called by player 2 and myself. *(I had grown my stack from the starting $4K to $8K, so the percent risk/reward seemed OK.)*

The turn then comes 3 of Diamonds. Bingo. I've got the straight, there's no full house possibility on the board, and on top of that, I've got a flush draw. *So, essentially, absent some kind of bizarre suck-out, I've got it.* Player 1 places a minimum bet (**yes!**), player 2 raises (**double yes!**), and I, of course, make the easy decision to push all-in . . . which was a mammoth raise over both the bet and raise. Player 1 calls *(he only had top pair . . . not a worry),* and then player 2 also calls holding 5–9 and is risking a mammoth chip stack chasing the 8 for the higher-end straight.

So, with three 8s already having been folded *(we found out later),* there's only a single card in the deck that can win it for player 2. The odds are heavily in my favor . . . more than 90 percent. And, of course, she hits the only remaining 8 . . . and it took all my sanity and professionalism not to launch the cards across the table and scream, "You bet your whole stack and risked your entire tourney on a chase?" *Keep in mind that most know I'm a pretty tight player and would never make that move with two others still in the hand unless I had the goods.*

Yet as they say, it's often darkest before the dawn, and like December's "Chip and a Chair" post few months ago, I somehow fought back from the brink to ultimately win the event when I was dealt pocket Aces and K–Q suited for the last two heads-up hands of the night.

The final hands played out like this: On the pocket Aces hand, I was the shorter stack and small blind, and simply called preflop *(although I'd raise with more players at the table, I was going for the monster trap play).* The flop then came K–8–9, my opponent checked, and I went all in. He then asked me if I hit the King, and I said no. After some discussion back and forth where he didn't believe me, I told him, "I didn't hit it and will show you." So, he called with his pocket 10s, and I took down the hand after two blanks hit the turn and river. *And true to my word, I said that I showed him that I didn't "hit the King"!*

That put me in the chip lead and I was then dealt K–Q suited for a flop that came K–10–8. I checked, he bet with a 10, and I went all-in and he immediately called. The turn and river again were of no help to him, and the odd night ended rather "easily" . . . at least compared to events a few hours earlier.

OK, so what are the trading lessons? I suppose the first one reflects a combination of perseverance and focus. Yesterday's trading was a good example. I entered a solid pullback shortly after 3pm with size and then had the rare "displeasure" of a late-day news item release touting interest rate risk that immediately shot the market down 4 points through the "previous resistance = new initial support" level . . . which is similar to the 90 percent poker play from last night. In both cases, I lost the "hand." Yet in both cases, I stayed focused and kept moving forward and ultimately more than made up for the far lesser probability occurrences. *As they say, stuff happens.*

The second may sound odd, but in my case it's highly relevant and all about momentum. You see, my trading and poker usually go hand in hand. I can't describe why, but they will forever be intertwined. For example, my poker game reached a peak in '08 and '09 when I won several local tourneys, and had both personal focus **and** good fortune on my side for a long period of time. And the same was true for my trading.

And then as I hit the mid-year 2009 bump, performance in both areas seemed to suffer. I'd often get hit by incredibly bad beats at the table while at the same time experiencing trading events where I had dentist appointments and critical phone calls at the worst possible moment.

Yet as I get ready to pursue a trading "stride" of sorts on 2010, my focus over the last few days feels, well, "sharp." It was sharp last night—especially in the hours that followed the bad beat where I frankly played my a$$ off—and it was sharp today on a trading day where early precision was mandatory.

Bad beats? They'll happen. Yet I believe one constant that will help keep you grounded when they do occur is **focus**. Focus on the long term in a business where time and probability do the heavy lifting. Focus on the short term as you play each hand or trade each sequence . . . both of which stand alone and aren't dependent on prior events. The rest is just a blur. An appropriate blur.

JAN
29
2010
Workplace Safety

Almost a year ago, I did one of my favorite posts entitled "Nine Lives" right after what was—until last week—my last brain-cramp day. I say favorite because I've always preferred to emphasize the pains and challenges of this business over the wins and successes, since the former still seems to get such little press despite a well-known high failure rate in this business.

At my end, I usually have 2–3 brain-cramp days a year, a count that has been fairly consistent over the years. And last week— although I haven't discussed it until now—I had one of my 2010 days after getting distracted overnight with a rather intense personal health scare. Simply put, my head was up my backside while trading that day.

So, how does one get through these driver's ed days? Well, I'd be flat out lying if I said I enjoyed them. I hate them. Yet two things keep me going. The first is that time and performance have shown that coming back from hits is one of my strengths, and I can point to several instances over the years—including the "Story of Grace" post referring back to a 2007 sequence—as well as that Monday in October 2008 when both major hits established the foundation and fortitude for record runs.

The second aspect that keeps me plugging away is my conceptual business plan ALLOWS for them. Yes, I hate 'em and work like heck to avoid them. But they **are** inevitable. And considering 250 trading days and a very high win/loss ratio, 2–3 instances out of a huge sample size quickly becomes a nonissue. Of course, the old adage that traders can't eat like a bird and poop like an elephant remains valid, so the consistency during the rest of the time **has** to be able to offset the messes.

Years ago, during my college years, I almost lost the tip of my thumb to a meat slicer when I got distracted in a kitchen. And every day I can see and feel the scar. Whether it's trading or slicing, rest assured that there's nothing wrong with you if you get "cut." *And for newer traders reading, yes, it happens to us **all**.* The first few days are typically painful, yet a poor memory (a strength of mine according to my wife, although she doesn't call it a "strength") can work with time to provide the inevitable healing.

Perhaps Jay Leno said it best the other day when asked if recent jokes about his displacing Conan O'Brien hurt him. He responded that being a comedian was like being a fighter and that it was his **job** to get hit in the head. For those who say that traders are like fighters, I'll simply restate it to say that traders **are** fighters. And I love a good fight. A good cut man in your corner doesn't hurt either.

Welcome to the human race.

Focusing on Life's Comma

If I had to summarize my beliefs about trading in a single word, it would be "perseverance." As I've often said, I make mistakes every day. Lots. Mistakes of judgment; mistakes of omission, mistakes of sub-optimal sizing, mistakes of entering or exiting too soon, mistakes of being a perfectionist, mistakes of allowed distractions, mistakes of self-doubt, and the list goes on.

On Friday, I had a strong day—and by P&L standards, it was the best of the year. Yet I awoke Saturday with a pit in my stomach, knowing there was one particular trade sequence after the final capitulation that I should have pressed as hard as I've ever pressed a trade.

It was one of my favorites and should have made the month right then and there. Yet I lost focus for a single moment, didn't have the Tom Cruise "Going for the Jack Nicholson Code Red Admission Kill" feeling, and by the time I realized that I'd missed the prime spot, the price rebounded so quickly that I couldn't chase the entry. And although not real financial loss, it was a costly opportunity loss . . . amounting in the tens of thousands.

So, I decided to clear the mind via a 12-hour poker marathon yesterday that started in Foxwoods among strangers and finished with a small local game until about 2am this morning amidst friends who regularly play together. And wouldn't you know it, I made several mistakes at the table yesterday, including letting up and folding preflop after winning a big hand (*I had pot odds and would have flopped a straight even with a sick 10–8*), simply not going with my instincts a few times, as well as ever so slightly suboptimizing a straight flush in which I couldn't induce a call from my opponent.

On the plus side, I correctly played pocket Aces in one particular hand both pre- and postflop, and took down the largest pot of the night just after midnight by going all in and getting called postflop . . . after which time it held up. And by the end of the day, I came out ahead. And the net result is all that matters.

I've often said that if I ever wrote a book, it would be titled *How to Make a Million by Making a Million Mistakes*. Feedback from a decade of trader educational efforts at this end would clearly show that one of the greatest "light bulb" moments for participants is when they see the number of mistakes I make as I share trades and thoughts on a moment-by-moment basis—and the subsequent actions taken to overcome them.

As I've stated dozens of times in this journal, I'll never understand why so many in this business refuse to acknowledge their—no, make that "our"—humanity instead of embracing it. For trading, poker, and life are **all** about making mistakes. And consider this: If there *were no mistakes, the market would never move!* We just have to make fewer than the other guy, as well as make sure the mistake ends with a comma instead of a period.

At this end, I don't believe in periods. It's the comma that allows us to continue. And profit.

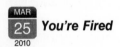 ### You're Fired

It's back. All of it. Charter blog onlookers will know them well: The countdown clock, the fictitious drawdown, the scorecard, and yes, even the **anger** . . . everything that kept me focused and motivated during the 2008–2009 run. *I'd even wear my old socks if my wife hadn't thrown them out. Remember, I'm a tightwad.*

Why? Simple. After sleepwalking through two days of market action, searching for a post-Jellie reason to trade, looking for every excuse in the book why not to make a trade, and simply not caring about trading just enough to cause me to loan some funds to the market with two stupid-a$$ unfocused and undisciplined sequences right after I reached a key equity mark, at 10:15am EDT I decided that I'd had enough. *Case in point, I was doing my taxes **during** market action the other day and then chose to sleep in during today's anticipated Europe breakout.*

So, I'm mad. And we're talking door-slamming, ticked-off mad. And so at 10:15am, I fired Don1 *(of the last session and a half)* and replaced him with Don2 *(head trader during 2008–2009)*. Don2 was, of course, a bit reluctant at first as he wanted to know what happened to his predecessor. But he said OK only after I agreed to provide him with his old tools . . . thus the countdown clock, etc. And wouldn't you know it, Don2 immediately sat down and fired off 12 consecutive profitable trades that more than made up for Don1's morning mess.

Word of caution: You **don't** want to be on the other side of Don2's trades over the coming weeks. My only question is whether he's any good at fixing doors.

P.S. Poker and massage night tonight. But only for Don2. And if Don1 asks for a trading job, don't even bother.

Current-Day Preface to the Following Flash Crash Journal Entry: At 2:45pm on May 6, 2010, the Dow Jones Industrial Average temporarily plunged about 1000 points, or about 9 percent, before quickly recovering within minutes. It was the second largest point swing and the largest one-day point decline on an intraday basis in the Dow's history. And although I won't go into the many theories on why it happened, which are better discussion during retirement cocktail parties, suffice it to say that the result was a liquidity crisis that had never been seen before.

As usual, I was trading in the context of providing market liquidity when, as they say, "the bottom fell out." Two days later, I summarized my thoughts in the following post.

MAY 08 2010 *The Flash Crash Autopsy*

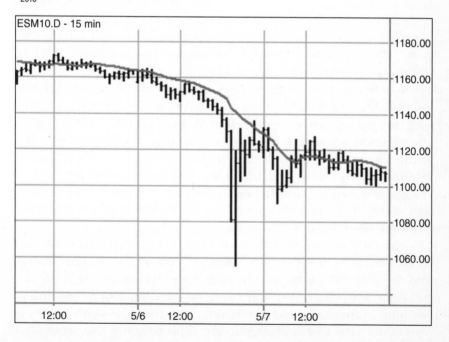

As of this writing, I'm still not sure whether to be perturbed or elated over how I handled the day. Yet perhaps the best description is a rather ironic combination of disappointment and satisfaction. This is because I could have (a) avoided the blindside hit *(the disappointment that I didn't)*, (b) handsomely profited from it *(another disappointment)*, and (c) gotten killed *(the satisfaction that I didn't)*. First, let me say that one regret is I wish that I'd captured and printed the day's actual trade auto-plot chart, which I didn't amidst the closing chaos, and they reset each day. But I do have my trade log and will walk through the sequence of events.

As I mentioned in Thursday's video and in several past posts, I have two trading strategies: providing liquidity *(the casino "house")* and speculating *(the guy walking into the casino)*. And as I've also said in the past, there's a fine line between the two and they actually tend to blur. Suffice it to say that speculating typically reflects longer-term-trend-type holds where I'm the aggressor.

Anyway, up until 2:30pm, I'd actually had a strong day going, keeping my sizes relatively light and providing liquidity on the long side near each barf point and exiting into the resistance. Then, with ES down 40–50 points and charts signaling what is usually extremely high probability, I began to step in to provide some short-term liquidity with a teeny (for me) 30-contract size on the long side near 1120, with a second teeny 30-contract size just north of 1100, so my average price was around 1110.

Now one important note about this strategy. As I teach, this was **not** doubling down. Rather, it's scaling into wholesale market points with very partial predetermined sizes and not putting a larger whole-sale position on **unless** the market confirms the expected move. Further, I purposely chose for this sequence to manage risk via partial position size vs. a hard stop, which is one of those elements that most "hang out a shingle" nontrading analysts never discuss. It's a strategy that in the long run and despite the rare hit like this has earned me well over seven figures.

Now I will say that looking back, I'm not quite sure why I only had 60 on, because my current "standard" trade size is 120, with a maximum of 480. Perhaps it was some inner feeling that it just didn't feel right, who knows. Yet there were **no** bottoming signs warranting anything more than a toe in the water and thus was in line with my plan that if 1100 **had** held after an initial probe south and rebound, I would have put the other 60 on upon confirmation with a hard stop then on a further break.

*Ironically, in hindsight it **still** would have worked . . . except that the 40-point plunge below 1100 made it difficult for me to conceptually rebuy when it finally traded back above 1100, as it would have been 40 points off the low. If liquidity hadn't taken its once-in-its-history 10-min near-death experience that required defibrillators to restart, it would have been a very profitable trade.*

Now those of us who have been around for a while have, of course, seen illiquid markets before, especially in the context of surprise interest rate cuts, employment reports, and FOMC decisions *(the latter two being anticipated).* And we know that some of the most illiquid markets can occur during the overnight trade.

Yet few if any of us have ever seen instances where liquidity was breached intraday to a point where some stocks momentarily lost **all** their value *(can you say Accenture?)* amidst the electronic trading chaos.

So, how do I feel I handled it? Perhaps the best analogy this poker-playing trader can reference is losing quad Aces to a royal flush. We'll start with what I did well.

- Partial sizing was a **huge** safety net. Who knows what I might have done if sized larger given the emotion of the situation. *(By the way, I **was** keenly aware of the intraday P&L during the plunge . . . I just tried to not let it affect my decisions.)* And despite the above trade plan rationale, why I didn't instinctively bet the quad Aces harder **before** the final plunge will perhaps forever be a mystery.
- Not selling it out at the lows for close to a 5 percent hit and instead waiting for a 30-point rebound to bail. *Don't get me wrong . . . it was and still is a bit painful and will take some time to heal, but if you had to make a choice between losing a sure finger versus a possible arm under extremely pressing conditions, the choice seemed clear.*

Here's what I didn't do so well:

- Trading the afternoon. I normally don't, due largely to lesser probability and increased pattern uncertainty. Plus, I'm usually tired by 2pm and simply either call it a day or trade incredibly small for fun. That was probably my largest mistake. Yet I sensed opportunity and usually have pretty good judgment in terms of when rules can be appropriately bypassed. I just didn't count on the royal flush.

- Not putting a trailing stop on my strong intraday P&L.
- Selling all 60 on the initial rebound instead of only 30, which I should have held to get more info on what was going on. *Again, risk would have been managed via sizing.* If I had done so, I would have had the option of selling the other 30 at a higher price or putting the other 30 back on after realizing what had happened.
- *By the way, in the heat of the battle I did consider buying the 1060–1080 area, yet had a concern of possible CME-busted trades lingering in my mind given the extraordinary conditions. That coupled with an impossible tape/DOM read at the time kept me from doing so. I was also concerned about the possibility of a 9/11-type market halt or the lock limit kicking in around 1050.*
- Not having a longer-term speculative short trade on to hedge the shorter-term liquidity trades. *Yet the risk/reward on doing so and getting decent wholesale entry prices simply seemed poor the farther the market fell, so that one's not a big issue.*
- Scaling back my aggression a bit on Friday morning. I was too apprehensive on Friday's MATD as I simply wanted to let the dust settle when I'd normally trade it hard. And I left far too much money on the table in doing so, and as a result will extend the recovery period. *Yet I got back on the horse the moment I got up, so that's a plus.*

In summary, some larger draws are the result of poor judgment, others the result of the lesser probability happening in which you only incur a small ding, and still others the result of some once-in-a-lifetime black swan. And if I had to weight 10 points to all three elements this time, I suppose I'd give the black swan a 7 or 8. Yet responsibility still lies with the trader to deal with the swan, and I still remain accountable for my actions from a stewardship perspective. In my daily job of providing a liquidity service for other traders, I lost a finger ($53.9 K, or 1.9 percent).

The bright side? Well, consider that the worst-case scenario of a hypothetical ill-timed and fully sized "leveraged" 480-contract position at my average purchase price sold at the lows would have cost me **$1.2 million**.

In the course of careers, traders get dinged like hockey players lose teeth. Yet nothing in this business worth pursuing comes without risk. And as Charles Sanford, retired chairman and CEO from Bankers Trust Corporation, once pointed out when addressing the

University of Georgia commencement in 1989, playing it safe over the long run can often be **more** dangerous.

Fortunately, with nine fingers I can still type—and trade—and the comeback has already begun. And in this business, the finger **does** grow back . . . but you **have** to protect the arm and hand. For those who aren't quite as fortunate, I hope that remembering that we are all only temporary stewards of whatever capital we have will provide some measure of relief. We simply do the best we can. A wise man once told me that. He's my father.

Current-Day Notes: The loss I incurred during the flash crash was one of the "broken bones" occurring in subsequent years. And as is the case with any real physical fall or tangible broken bones, time was needed after the flash crash for healing. It took me only eight trading days to recoup the loss, yet the emotional scars took longer to heal, and the memory of that event is always in the back of my mind, even if just a shadow.

SEP
21
2010
Money Never Sleeps

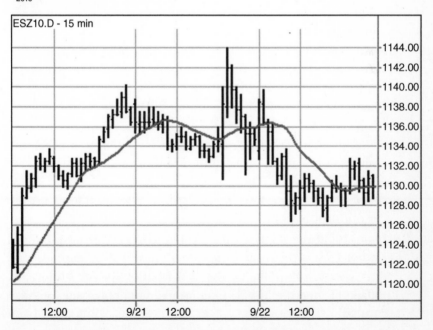

The purpose of this entry is to continue to remind all traders who are no-nonsense, buckle-down serious about this business that we have to continually work harder and sacrifice more than those against whom you're constantly competing. Today was probably as good as an example as I can provide. And since it's the end of a **very** long day, I'll skip right to the shorthand in the context of a time-stamped recap.

Monday 9:15pm   Expected a strong MATD on Tuesday morning and sensed that the best possible setup would likely be in the Europe session given how the day closed.

Monday 11:00pm   Had to decide whether to sacrifice a good night's sleep for the 3am Europe open. Decided given the significance of the close to set my alarm for 2:30am.

Tuesday 2:30am   First thought: *Damn . . . is it 2:30am already?* Second thought: Check the charts. If Europe opens on or near late day supports, trade. If not, go back to bed.

2:35am   Checked the charts and realized that the market was kind enough to set the golf ball on the tee, with the golf ball appearing as large as a watermelon. Cleared the eyes and mind and figured that I'd have enough energy for about 90 minutes of trading, which would hopefully be just enough to catch the first move up.

2:45am–4:00am   Traded Europe's opening MATD sequence by probing on support prior to open and adding upon Europe's confirmation of the up move.

4:05am   Back to bed for a few hours of shut-eye.

7:30am   Tossed and turned and only got about an hour's sleep. First thought: *Damn . . . is it 7:30am already?* Second thought: Make sure you're at least coherent until noon when you can take a pre-FOMC nap.

8:30am   Took the prehousing news move to support long, taking it out on the pop.

9:30am–10:30am   Traded the early tight MATD U.S. session oscillations *(the megaoscillations had already come in the Europe session as is often the case)*, nailing dang near each bottom and top.

11:00am   Faded the MATD first-hour range break back into the range.

12:00pm   Nap time . . . whew. Alarm set for 12:45pm.

1:00pm   First thought: *You guessed it. Damn . . . is it 1:00pm already?* Second thought: Prepare for the FOMC session, but don't plan to trade it given that (a) I specialize in morning rhythms and usually stink in the afternoons, and (b) I'll likely be running on fumes by then . . . **unless** the trades just "show up" and you get into a rhythm.

2:15pm–3:00pm   A solid 45-min zone, as the trades just started showing up, including the initial fade buy at 1131 (3 ticks off the low), a final long exit above 1142 (not the same trade but another one that I'd entered at 1137 and added at 38), a reversal short at 1143.25 (3 ticks off the high), and a final cover on the approach toward 1140 before exhaustion simply set in.

4:30pm   Hit the office sofa and didn't wake up for 3 hours.

When you think about it, it's actually rather simple. When we sacrifice and work our tails off, we win . . . consistently and in abundance. When we don't, we lose. It's our choice. Often, once you figure out the game, 95 percent of the effort is simply showing up. And last I checked, there is no "Easy Street" in the trader address directory. If you're looking for long-term success, I'd suggest checking "Sacrifice Blvd." But you likely won't find anyone home, as they'll be out working their tail off. Even if you call at 3am.

PART
VI

The MF Global Bankruptcy

Imagine that your life savings are tucked away in a fireproof safe, a safe secured with a series of chains and combination locks. The savings are the direct result of your correct decision to take charge of your own financial future by not relying on others to invest your capital. Now imagine that the safe is surrounded by a dozen people whose sole purpose in life is to guard it, all of whom are holding hands and staring at it. Now imagine that the safe is ransacked and burned beyond recognition without anyone noticing. Sound implausible or impossible?

Well, on October 31, 2011, such is essentially what happened to customer accounts at MF Global, when one of the largest derivatives brokerage firms in the world—**my** brokerage firm—experienced a colossal meltdown due to the combined ineptitude on the part of the company, its executives, industry regulators, and exchanges. At a minimum, the events that unfolded reflected pure recklessness and momentary loss of industry integrity and trust. At a maximum . . . well, suffice it to say that I'll leave that to the judicial system, although you can fill in the blanks using any number of verbs, adjectives, and pronouns.

This event had a profound effect on both me and the industry and shook our respective souls to their very cores. And like the flash crash of 2010, it's no exaggeration to say that the aftershocks of this earthquake are still reverberating and will likely be felt in some way as long as humanity and greed are involved in the financial markets.

Initially, it took me about a week to gather my thoughts on the situation, which led to the following journal entry as I recalled my thoughts as they unfolded.

NOV
04
2011

Frozen on the MF Global Iceberg

I've thought long and hard about whether, when, and how to write a post on the MF Global situation. One reason was because I wanted to avoid participating in the initial industry rumor mill that has been rampant beyond belief over the last four days and that often contains more inaccurate vs. accurate info. Another reason is that I have a lot of "skin" in this particular dilemma—*actually more of full torso, as I mention below*—and didn't want my personal emotion to dictate my words.

Yet this journal—even as it's evolved into more of a formal educational venue in recent times—has **always** been about the "good, bad, and ugly" of the truth behind the futures trading industry. *And oh, have **all three** been seen in spades this week.* And so I feel that the time has come to speak in the continuing spirit. So, here we go again with a deeply personal post with full transparency.

I'll begin by saying that I am one of the larger noninstitutional clients for whom MF Global cleared futures trades, with approximately $3 million in personal trading balances amidst three accounts. I'd been a customer of MF since 2003, and I'd rank their trade clearing, technical support, reporting, and yes—even the ethics of those with whom I **directly** worked (note the bold)—second to none.

I'll also quickly follow up these points by saying that I made two personal mistakes that led to more personal angst this week than should have ever occurred. The first was leaving too large an accumulated balance directly with the clearing firm. Ironically, I truly thought about significantly reducing the balance in recent days, but hadn't moved on it given what I viewed as higher priorities, not to mention the fundamental essence of "segregated accounts" with daily controls.

I'd also not given MF's European debt problems enough personal attention and thought during the preceding week as my focus was on my other businesses much of the time, including my obligation and fiduciary role to another firm. *And again, there was that "segregated account" protection where business segment A was supposed to have no relation to business segment B.*

The second error at my end was not having a back-up clearing firm with whom I could immediately clear new trades, which cost me dearly in opportunity loss this week, which in the "when it rains it pours" category turned out to be the most fertile trading environment in terms of concrete opening MATD or gap sequences we've had all year. So, before I jump on the MF dog pile, that's my own glass house for all to see.

Now, let's turn to the chronicle of my journey of this past week.

Monday: My plan—as it typically is on both the last day of the month **and** a Monday—was to trade lightly. And at 9:47:27am, I'd just closed out a small long trade for a modest profit. I then tried to place another order that the platform didn't accept. *"Great,"* I'd thought with some sarcasm, *"an order entry platform issue on a Monday morning."* So, I then checked to see if I could place a Eurex trade, which I could. *OK, must be an issue with the CME feed.* I then called the MF Global support desk and was told that the Merc had suspended MF's electronic access to the CME markets. *WTF? OK, let me trade Eurex as a derivative of the ES action. Hmmmm . . . on second thought, maybe not. Something has to be up.* The rest of the day is frankly a bit of a blur, but it included morning calls to my FCM FuturePath Trading *(the "Good," as I'll explain below)*, a decision to request an immediate wire of my full main account balance, and calls to my long-time contacts at MF *(more "Good")*.

Then an odd thing happened. For the electronic access to the CME—which I tested by placing orders outside the market—had been turned back **on**. A quick call to the MF support desk ensued: "What's going on?" I asked. "Liquidation/ orders only," they responded. "Are you aware I can place opening orders?" I shot back. Deathly silence at their end, followed by "We're only doing what we're told." I then turned my attention over the next several hours to babysitting the liquidating wire request as best I could from a distance. Of course, it turned out that the request—which was quickly joined by requests to liquidate my other two accounts—came after all outgoing activity had been frozen. It was during that time that the news began surfacing: A failed sale to interactive brokers, bankruptcy, frozen assets, and missing client money, which by law was segregated with controls that had tested the time of many failures over the last decade.

Tuesday–Friday: The rest of the week turned into a mix of constant phone calls to my broker *(God Bless them for putting up with me)*, calls to

MF Global, constant Internet searching, and a lot of personal and spiritual angst over what was or wasn't happening. And the news—along with my human emotion—shifted by hour as both fact and rumor battled for position in my mind.

$900 million missing. $600 million missing. $300 million missing. Nothing missing . . . it's all there and just an accounting issue. I've retained everything. I've lost everything. Sure, it's "only" 10 percent of client money as I grasped for silver linings—but what if my accounts were among the 10 percent . . . that's essentially 100 percent.

And then the personal regret kicked in. Why hadn't I pulled the balance down? Why did I allow myself to be distracted and "complacent" as to not see the writing on the wall during the preceding week and get the funds the heck out of there? *But they're segregated balances reported and monitored **daily**.*

OK, now the specific good, bad, and ugly categories:

The Good *(Much of It "Very")*

- God; my wife, Debra; and the entire team at FuturePath Trading—especially Damon, **all** of whom came to my support this week during those times when I was at best a pain in the neck and, at worst, unnerved.

  You see, the vast majority of the futures industry—while competitive on the one hand—is actually a very tight-knit family of sorts. And it was during the events of this week that we learned who were the true blue family members and who were the black sheep. *At one point, I even found myself comforting one of my MF Global friends—who was in tears over the prospect of damage to **my** account—despite her difficult personal situation.*

- Another "good" element was my decision to initially trade lightly—as a matter of general rule—and then to stop all trading completely on Monday as soon as I figured something was up, which left me with zero open positions as everything was unraveling. *Obviously, those with open position had to wrestle with both (1) somehow closing the positions and (2) exposing themselves to additional market time—perhaps days—and risk.*

The Bad

- My personal loss of spiritual perspective at times. *From dust to dust, Don. You're simply a temporary steward anyway.* Why it took me almost three days to finally put the situation in God's hands, I'll never know. For it wasn't until Thursday morning that Deb and I prayed together for God to directly intervene and unleash His full power and might to guide the regulators to ensure His assets remained in His kingdom. *Before that, Deb had been praying for me to regain my spiritual footing!*
- The loss of income as trader accounts have been temporarily frozen and inaccessible during a very fertile time.
- The lack of constant communication from the regulatory bodies to clients with accounts *(although I do understand their challenge, and the Trustee website was beginning to serve as a decent clearinghouse of sorts).*
- The quick—*under a week*—allowance for the transfer of accounts with positions and a portion of the underlying collateral to other brokers, but **not** for those accounts simply sitting in cash, which would be the case for most intraday or liquidity-providing traders. *At worst, initially moving 50 percent–75 percent of the cash **this week** would have been far more prudent, followed up with the rest in the near term as assets are redeployed, which by law should first go to making the customers 100 percent whole. I even phoned my senator's office—both the Washington and Boston offices—for the first time ever to discuss.*
- The resurrection of another reason for some politicians to rally the "transaction tax" charge during—of all things—the European summit that is addressing the same thing. *Talk about poor timing.*

The Ugly

To this point, I've not piled on the MF Global bandwagon. As in any "trade," I believe that the finger first points inward, and there are, of course, things that I could and should have done at my end. Having said that—and taking a deep breath—there is clearly a **lot** of ugly that has surfaced in recent days. Alleged violations in the sacred fiduciary and segregation principles along with alleged deceit with a trail requiring a team of forensic accountants and multiple regulatory agencies to unravel and which has drawn attention from the CFTC, SEC, SIPC, and FBI. This hits particularly close to home as we've tried our best in this small corner of the world to help this business become more transparent over time through "truth in blogging," bona fide education, and constant communication with fund clients via e-mail and weekly website briefings that involve trade sequence explanations. *And then the industry shroud reappears . . . talk about swimming upstream.* A man who was all smiles in giving a speech as his company was going south. I could go on with respect to the ugly, but will leave it at that . . . adding one more category called the irony.

The Irony

Indeed, there is tremendous irony that a firm catering toward traders—who should be taught tight risk-management principles in the event of a failed trade—would fail based on the excessive risk taken on by the firm itself. A few days ago, I posted "This too shall pass." In the end, there is absolutely no reason to believe that clients won't be either made 100 percent whole, or pretty darn close to it. So, this is truly a bump in the road, albeit a large one. Yet this week has reminded me why I don't like flying in planes. For unless I can see out the front window, can see what's ahead, and am flying the plane *(even though I'm **not** a pilot)*, I'm very, very uncomfortable. And this week I've had zero control . . . over everything. For some reason, I forgot who the real pilot is. And to Him I have to give my utmost trust. Have a blessed weekend.

Current-Day Notes: Over the course of the following year, I chose to temporarily shift my market efforts from trading and trader education to trader advocacy, using whatever tools I had at my disposal, including the blog, interviews, alliance with the Commodity Customer Coalition, and hundreds of phone calls and letters, to ensure that the voice of the customer wasn't buried under carpets, caught in needless red tape, or trampled on by the old Washington two-step.

Did I think that my 2008 marathon was grueling? It was nothing compared to this. In fact, 2008 and all its challenges seemed like a walk in the park compared to what would become a year-long advocacy effort of which I often had zero control.

Needless to say, and as I hinted in my initial "reactionary" post above, this period was a difficult one for me, just as it was for tens of thousands of farmers, ranchers, consumers, and small business traders who had trusted the system and its multiple layers of protective mechanisms. For years, I'd learned how **not** to let the market take my funds away, but dealing with the disappearance of our assets? Well, this was a whole new ballgame.

A Different Kind of Trade

As the MF Global saga continued to play out on both sides of the Atlantic in electronic print and congressional hearings, I discovered something very intriguing about bankruptcy claims: They're traded! Not only are they traded, but based on the dozens of e-mails and letters I'd receive over the next many months, there was a very liquid market of willing buyers *(albeit at extremely discounted prices)*. "OK, great," I thought, especially since I'd effectively managed my way out of various "trades gone extremely bad" before, including the flash crash of 2010, and this indeed qualified as a minicrash of sorts. The challenge, of course, was to ensure that any sale was not made emotionally and to use time as much to my advantage as price fluctuations.

There's no doubt that my years of trading experience helped me in this situation, as one cardinal rule of trading is realizing that any market in motion is always a "buy" or "sell" at any given time and that if there was a market of willing buyers, there was an expectation of further price increases from which the buyer would profit. As such, in the case where I owned not one, but three, MF Global claims, the objective wasn't to sell at discounted levels to ease the emotional pain; rather, it was to put myself in the perspective and mind-set of one who had just **bought** a series of bankruptcy claims *(my existing claims!)* and to look to sell only when market conditions dictated that further price upside would seem limited.

Suffice it to say that the next several months resulted in a watch-and-wait game, which isn't my strength as I don't typically care to have my capital in the market for very long. As such, you could call it one of my most difficult trades ever in terms of management. Yet I was somehow able to stay the course, keeping more than occupied with my other businesses while staying abreast of bankruptcy proceedings and claim prices through a constantly evolving network that included various brokers, attorneys, and the wonderful work performed by the Commodity Customer Coalition.

In the end, and despite an incredibly bad decision to place the bankruptcy into a Chapter 11 SIPC proceeding where customers found themselves battling with unsecured creditors, those of us who stayed on top of the evolving situation and knew the facts always felt strongly that we'd eventually get close to 100 percent of our funds back but that doing so would likely take time. So, taking all factors into consideration, I set a price between 97 percent and 98 percent at which I'd be more than comfortable selling.

Over time, the bids did increase as expected . . . beginning initially around 80 percent from a few less-than-reputable ambulance chasers, then more realistically toward 90 percent, then 95 percent, 96 percent, 97 percent . . . 97.5 percent. Of course you have to be careful how you interpret these percentages. For example, as we'd already had 80 percent of our assets returned earlier, selling at 95 percent was really selling for 15 percent of the remaining 20 percent, or 75 percent. *And boy, do the vulture funds attempting to buy claims from distressed sellers know that!* Nevertheless, as the price reached my target zone, I made preparations to sell to once and for all free my mind of what had become a major distraction and put the capital back to use in a manner where I would, I hoped, be able to recoup the small difference by trading the markets.

So, in mid-September 2012, I consummated the sale of my bankruptcy claims and summarized my thoughts in the following journal entry.

SEP 22 2011 *We Win*

They're only two words . . . but they're all that are needed to tell the story. Despite massive and pervasive self-interest, finger pointing, red tape, and regulatory ineptitude at every MF Global turn, we simply wouldn't back down. And we won.

For this trader, the MF Global saga—with all its twists and turns over the past 11 months—is over . . . and with a more than acceptable ending as by this time on Monday I will have completed the sale of my remaining MF Global claims and passed the risk of the last few pennies to the bond market. *And I hope the buyer profits from the purchase, as—borrowing from an old professional trader adage—it's always good to leave some for the other guy.*

And yes, I said pennies, as for all intents and purposes, bond market prices are screaming that MF Global customers will essentially get all their money back, and I was more than willing to "hit the bid" and give up a few cents to gain immediate access to the capital and grow it faster and farther than it ever would if it simply sat mired in bankruptcy red tape. *Heck, percentage-wise, it doesn't even rank among my largest trading losses.*

Yes, we won.

Many months ago, I mentioned in these pages that it would be incredibly wrong to underestimate the conviction of those who were harmed, whether traders, investors, hedgers, or farmers. And for traders . . . if the world hasn't noticed, we get knocked down every day in our business . . . **but** . . . we keep getting up.

We won because of people like James Koutoulas, John Roe, Trace Schmeltz, Greg Collett, and the entire Commodity Customer Coalition team, who when they saw the incredible ineptitude in dealing with this incredible wrong, stepped up to the plate big-time. We won because there were some in the press who didn't listen to the corporate spin machines and instead listened to our individual plights and granted interviews to help get our story out. And I could go on.

On a personal level, the last year has had a profound effect on how I've viewed life, both solidifying the incredible good and evil that are at work and in constant conflict in this world. *Before I go further, let me say that I'm extremely fortunate in that my accounts could have been transferred to PFG Best as some were, where lightning literally struck twice. So, my thoughts and prayers continue to go out to those still stuck in the mire.*

I suppose the greatest effect has been a stark reminder that we're simply stewards of whatever assets God has given us during our brief time here and that our true security lies in far greater places than a bank account.

For me, I still don't know why I was so richly blessed with exceptional performance in the late 2000s, just as I don't know why much of the last year transpired the way it did when my capital and incredible passion for this business were temporarily taken. Yet what I do know is that both instances are reminders not to get too high or too low as we travel life's roller coaster and that we should keep our eyes fixed on our true destination.

Another little-known tidbit in my personal story is that about a month prior to the MF Global Halloween fiasco, my business efforts were redirected toward a nonmarket endeavor. It was an interim effort that relied on past skills and relationships, with potential upside in terms of opportunity not unlike a trade. The downside? It would temporarily take my mind and focus off the markets and, as a result, bring in lower total income. Yet I thought that the change of pace would be good and accepted.

Looking back, it was as if the master plan went something like, "OK, you're heading for some incredible crap, but I've got a safe place in mind for you over here while that gets worked out. Just hang on tight and stay the course." Wow. And although some have suggested over the years that my writing skills were a strength, I could never have crafted such a plot. And even if I had, no one would have believed it.

The final moral? Life happens. It just does. As I told my daughter the other day after she was questioning a recent decision to separate from her boyfriend, there are no bad decisions. *Except that the only bad decision is no decision.* Every decision either teaches, reinforces, or redirects us to where we need to go.

As for my previous decision to rely on the dozens of protective mechanisms in place to safeguard customer futures funds when choosing where to deploy my capital? Well, suffice it to say that I'm now substantially diversified and have returned to my earlier days of trading leveraged ETFs as a part of my portfolio. And yes, I still trade and love trading the futures!

So another page turns . . . but the book remains the same. At the end of the story, right trumps wrong and good overcomes evil. It always has and always will. It's just that sometimes good has to stand up for itself to overcome the deafening roar coming from the other side. And although much work remains to fully restore confidence and rebuild this great industry, at this end—like Rob Petrie in the opening to *The Dick Van Dyke Show* of the 1960s—I don't plan on tripping over the ottoman a second time.

Current-Day Notes: Although both of these journal entries bookend that tumultuous year and attempt to put the 2011–2012 period in some sort of perspective, words cannot begin to aptly describe the industry and personal challenge that occurred during the nine months that elapsed between them. And although many of those interim thoughts are chronicled via interim posts at donmillerblog. com, including significant industry advocacy efforts, even those words can't shed enough light on the effect that this event had on my perspectives on money, humanity, and life itself.

As for the irony that one who emphasizes self-sufficient money management and ardently strives to protect his capital through effective trading strategies had the proverbial capital rug pulled out from under him? Using another analogy, I suppose that I was too busy chopping trees to notice that a forest fire was in the vicinity, as I had assumed that that's what multiple networks of forest rangers were for. And, I was apparently too busy putting my security in myself and a balance sheet instead of in the true assets of life, including God, family, and friends.

Mark Twain once said that if you put your eggs in one basket, you'd better watch that basket. I'd simply add to that by saying we should know whose basket it really is.

PART
VII

What Goes Up . . .

As I try to put the last decade in some sort of perspective, perhaps history can provide clues as to what it all means as well as what the future may hold and which dangers to avoid. After all, history is full of Internet stock moon shots, market bubbles, tulip crazes, and other bamboo-type performances that almost always succumb to gravity. So, perhaps the question of the day is whether such parabolic moves are **ever** maintained at their heights into the future, and if not, what can be done to minimize the risk of their ultimate demises. Said another way, does anyone **really** ever sell at the top, and if not, **why not?**

Let's begin with a review of three charts shown in Figure 7.1—we'll use "area" charts and omit the labels for now—each of which depicts real and exceptional financial performance in one manner or another.

To the naked eye, it appears that the item represented by each chart has gotten ahead of itself or at best might have one additional modest upward leg before reverting toward a more normal, gradual slope. After all, trees don't grow to the sky, and what goes up must come down. Or do they? Now let's fast forward in time to see how each chart played out as shown in Figure 7.2.

Amazing? Welcome to reality 101 and land of the bamboos. *Imagine shorting any one of these charts as it "appeared" to be extended?* As you can tell, each chart has several similarities, including a fairly pronounced base of either flat or modest growth, initial minisurges that appeared to peter out, followed by a seemingly unsustainable momentum-fueled move toward new heights with such power that all reason seems to have been abandoned. Yet each chart accurately

FIGURE 7.1   Area Performance Charts

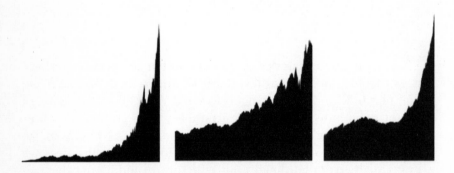

FIGURE 7.2   Area Performance Charts, Extended

depicts a bona fide occurrence that had occurred at some point in the past, and I could have literally chosen from hundreds of similar charts.

An Object in Motion Stays in Motion

Earlier, we discussed the concept of momentum, that powerful force that can turn snowballs into avalanches and launch space shuttles into the stratosphere, and there can be no better visual of market momentum than in these graphs. Probing further, there are so many decisions to ponder along the way, including determining what's causing the momentum, how to take advantage of it, and perhaps most importantly, knowing when the momentum will slow, end, or reverse. *Ask anyone shorting a market long before its peak and ask them how that worked out for them. Been there, done that.*

Newton's first law of motion states that an object in motion stays in motion with the same speed and in the same direction unless acted upon by an unbalanced force. So, perhaps one clue in determining how to take advantage of the move is not spending too much time understanding why it's moving and instead simply acknowledge that it **is** moving and likely will **continue** to move until such time the tide turns as the result of Newton's unbalanced force. But when will such an unbalanced force appear, and with what force? Unfortunately, no one can see into the future. Or can we?

Fortunately, history does provide us with the ability to see what happened in each of these cases, so let's now extend the charts a bit further to peek into their respective near-term futures and see how quickly they came down (Figure 7.3).

Wait, didn't I just say let's see "how quickly they came down"? Surely, these can't be real because **nothing** grows to the sky. *Can you say Cowabunga?* Yet although these charts may have even Sir Isaac scratching his head, they are indeed 100% real and further show the sheer power that momentum under the right conditions and with the right tailwind—real or proverbial—can have in markets and life.

Yet perhaps all good things indeed do come to an end as we fast-forward one last time while also revealing the depicted markets, beginning with the first two shown in Figure 7.4.

As you may have guessed, these charts depict markets from the Internet bubble era—in this case, the stock of data storage company EMC and the broader Nasdaq 100 index—where it was not uncommon to see moves approaching 1000% over a relatively short

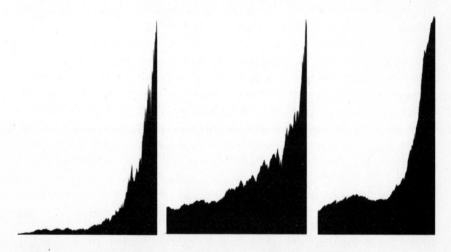

FIGURE 7.3 Area Performance Charts, Further Extended

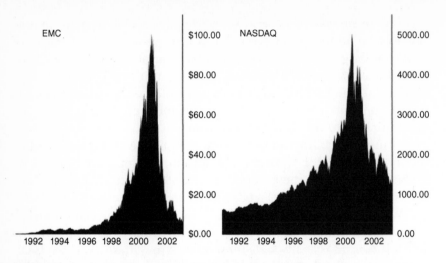

FIGURE 7.4   1992–2002 EMC and NASDAQ Weekly Charts

period of time, only to be followed by a **loss of most or all of the accumulated gains**, often in stomach-churning descents. *To this day, I still haven't met anyone who bought the Internet era near the bottom, sold near the top, and/or didn't get caught rebuying various early legs of the ultimate downturn. There are likely some out there—and if you did, major kudos—I just haven't met one.* And although I could have selected similar charts from other markets, eras, and industries—including tulips from the 1600s, tea from the 1700s, and Archie Karas's poker run and demise in the 1990s—the point that most such parabolic moves often end with an equally powerful thud would remain the same.

Ask any reputable professional poker player what the true secret to long-term success is, and the notion of knowing when to stop will likely surface in the first few minutes. Yes, that all-important decision of when to walk away. Walk away before the game starts, and you've given yourself no opportunity. Walk away too early in the game after a modest run, and you've caught the tip, but not the iceberg. Yet walk away too late, and you may lose everything you gained. It's such a fine, razor-thin line.

Trailing Stops at the Macro Level

Much has been written over the years about the need for protective trailing stop-loss triggers on individual market trades, yet I feel that very little has been written about the need for protective stops—or simply pauses—in the larger scheme of things such as an overall portfolio or non-market-related life endeavor. *And perhaps, ironically, it's the "larger scheme" that usually needs the protection more!* For example, imagine that the world's top trader (certainly not me) or athlete who effectively implements protective stop-loss mechanisms day in and day out on his or her trades or other daily activities only to have the results of tens of thousands of effective decisions over time wiped out simply by not applying the same protective control at a macro level. Exaggeration? History clearly shows otherwise.

As for what might cause such macrostops to trigger? In the context of financial market performance, changes in market rhythms resulting from shifts in supply and demand as depicted by the action of market participants might be one example, or in the case of personal performance, simply changes in individual dynamics, even if subtle.

So, knowing how history has played out time and time again, let's now add that third chart (Figure 7.5), which as you've probably guessed by now, reflects the equity curve of my self-directed futures retirement fund as chronicled in these pages.

For this chart, I've shown an eight-year performance period for my self-directed futures retirement fund, from January 1, 2004, to October 31, 2011—the night of the MF Global bankruptcy—and including the effect of the small loss subsequently absorbed as the result of selling my bankruptcy claim in 2012, which appears as an October 31, 2011, loss. And while the IRA chart reflects an eight-year period versus the EMC and Nasdaq eleven-year periods, the initial characteristics of each remain the same in terms of base and rapid parabolic growth, and we could show similar charts depicting far shorter or longer time frames.

As intriguing as it may have been reading about that magical ascent from 2007 to 2009, the subsequent "plateau" period could easily fill another book, as it produced as many challenges as those experienced in the momentum phase, including the flash crash, the MF Global meltdown, taking time to launch the Jellies, and pursuing other endeavors.

And while many questions remain in my mind as to how I've managed this period and why certain events unfolded the way they did—including why the MF Global debacle was timed just as I was reenergized and was beginning to launch a new upward leg—I'll say that I'm extremely grateful for the additional life lessons I've learned during this period. If I were asked to graph a chart depicting my

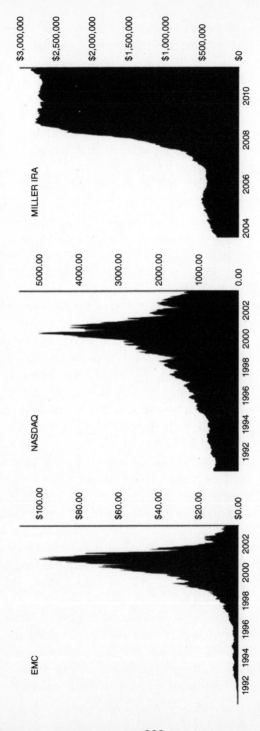

FIGURE 7.5 EMC and NASDAQ versus Miller IRA

lessons learned over time, that chart would also be parabolic, yet with no end in sight.

A Thousand Words

We'll conclude with Figure 7.6 that magnifies the Miller IRA chart of Figure 7.5. If it's true that a picture says a thousand words, this one may just have a few million. And lest this trader and author begin to get the least bit full of himself, I've highlighted the actual days and amounts of the largest fund losses experienced over these seven years for all the world to see.

Although it make take your eyes some adjusting to fully comprehend the multipurpose chart, here are the basics:

- The dots reflect each day's net account performance expressed in percent return on capital and align with the left vertical axis.

  Some dots include the effect of various account balance adjustments that affect the P&L, such as exchange commission rebates, currency fluctuations, and interest. With respect to exchange rebates, the exchange moved from daily to monthly processing in 2009. As such, daily net performance after that time will typically be understated throughout the month by the effect of member rebates, which would be offset by a single positive adjustment in the following month.
- Outlier performance dates—good and bad—are dated, often with a brief description. *Most are chronicled in these pages.*
- The shaded area to the right reflects the fund's actual accumulated balance and aligns with the right vertical axis.

Yes, this chart is indeed an eyeful. Yet from this trader's perspective, there are a few clear takeaways:

- First, although your eye may initially drift toward the isolated outlier performance dots, the vast majority of the cumulative gains are the result of those less noticeable "grinding" daily performances just above the middle "break-even" horizontal line that—believe it or not—number **more than 1300**. And although they may not be as "exhilarating" as the outlier days, the last time I checked, excitement wasn't on my list of objectives.
- Another observation might be in the form of a question along the lines of, "How could you have had all those large losses and

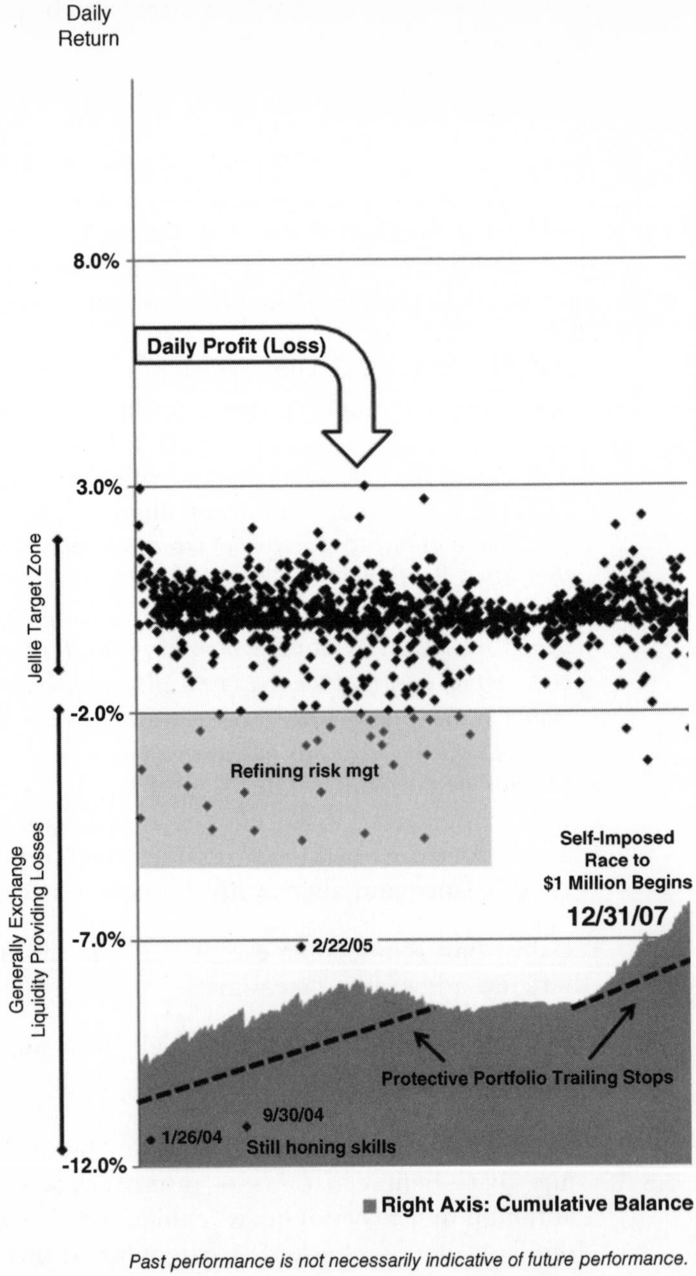

FIGURE 7.6   2004–2011 IRA Futures Fund Performance: Daily Profit and Cumulative Balance

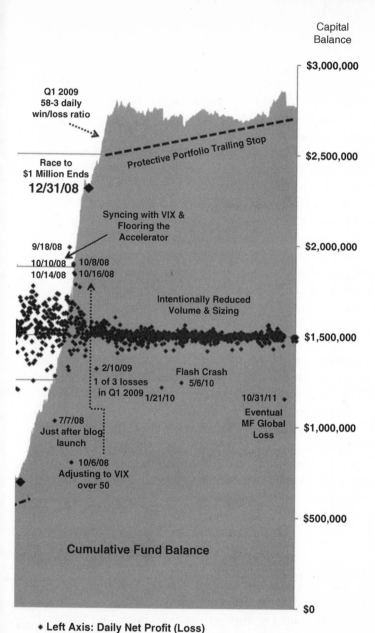

Capital
Balance

— $3,000,000

Q1 2009
58-3 daily
win/loss ratio

Protective Portfolio Trailing Stop

— $2,500,000

Race to
$1 Million Ends
12/31/08 ◆

Syncing with VIX &
Flooring the
Accelerator

9/18/08 ◆   — $2,000,000
10/10/08 ◆ 10/8/08
10/14/08 ◆ 10/16/08

Intentionally Reduced
Volume & Sizing

— $1,500,000

◆ 2/10/09   Flash Crash
1 of 3 losses   ◆ 5/6/10
in Q1 2009 1/21/10

◆ 7/7/08   10/31/11 ◆
Just after blog   Eventual   — $1,000,000
launch   MF Global
                                              Loss

◆ 10/6/08
Adjusting to VIX
over 50

◆   — $500,000

Cumulative Fund Balance

— $0

◆ **Left Axis: Daily Net Profit (Loss)**

still grow capital?" Frankly, the answer comes down to simple math as nine days at +1 plus one at −3 still equals a decent net +6. This is because modest results with higher probability will net the same amount as stronger results with lower probability, with the latter reflecting the often-quoted yet equally misunderstood "risk 1 to make 3" trader axiom. *And this trader prefers to go with the higher probability, accepting the rare negative outliers.*

- With respect to those larger losses, most of them were the result of providing liquidity during extreme moves as noted in the lower sidebar next to the left axis, trading intentionally at times during market extremes before turn triggers activated. As noted in the rising slope of outlier losses over time—such as the 2010 flash crash resulting in less than one-fifth of the loss of an early 2004 loss when I was still cutting my teeth on futures—the risk decreased over time as my timing and understanding of market rhythms improved.

- Note the use of rising protective stop triggers on overall capital in 2004–2005, 2006–2008, and 2009–2011. *And yes, they were also in place during 2007–2008, but the chart is already complex!*

- Tightly bunched performance dots around the zero line may be caused by several factors, including intentional breaks in personal trading volume due to desire or circumstance, changes in risk management, and perceived decrease in opportunity. 2006 and 2010 are examples, as is the forced break thanks to MF Global in late 2011.

- Learn what your performance and the market are telling you. Specifically, note that the largest daily percentage loss in the six years between March 2005 and October 2011 *(October 6, 2008, as chronicled in these pages)* was immediately followed by the **four** largest performance days during the same period.

The most astonishing aspects of this chart from my perspective? (1) I somehow managed to **not** underestimate the potential of personal momentum and slow down in early 2008, which would have caused me to miss out on most of the increase in equity; and (2) I somehow managed to survive both the flash crash **and** MF Global bankruptcy without violating the protective macrostop in place during those times, as each barely made a nick in the protective armor.

With respect to the first point, I strongly believe that use of the daily fictional drawdown concept and monthly "dig-out-of-the-hole"

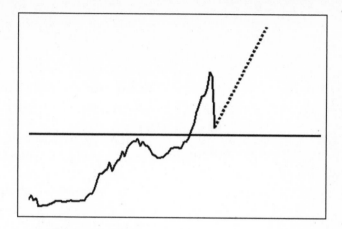

FIGURE 7.7   Visualization Chart

equity curve charts helped me sustain that essential sense of urgency and focus regardless of the reality that was unfolding, while making me unaware of the heights being attained during the ascent. Add to these two concepts a trader who admittedly has a fear of heights, and you can see how important maintaining such a mind-set was for me.

As far as surviving the flash crash and MF Global with merely a scratch, although I'll take at least some small solace in how I managed each of them once I found myself fully embedded in their respective "claws," I consider myself extremely fortunate that both events occurred during a time when I was less active in the market. From that perspective, perhaps it's indeed better sometimes to be fortunate than good.

Nevertheless, despite history that may suggest otherwise, Figure 7.7 will remain my "virtual reality," forever frozen in time because, in my view, I've fallen from grace after getting complacent and need to work on another comeback. Such must be the never-changing mind-set when cultivating bamboos.

VIII

PART

Final Thoughts

More than 10 years have passed since what I often refer to as my personal abyss, and almost 5 years have passed since I embarked on my inner self-actualization journey. It's often said that timing is everything—in the markets as well as in life—and such certainly appears to be the case for consolidating and formalizing my thoughts in these pages. As I approach the age of 52, my perspectives on life and trading have come into even clearer focus given the events of recent years, without which would have likely resulted in a compilation that, although perhaps helpful, would have been incomplete.

I consider myself extremely fortunate to have been given thus far five decades in which to grow, make mistakes, and adjust for course corrections, especially in a world where lives too often seem to be cut short before so many can rise to their fullest potential. Why some are given the blessing of time to cultivate and fully develop while others aren't will forever remain a mystery.

As I reviewed my experiences in great detail in preparation for this book, one theme that seemed constant throughout my life and career was **imperfection** in the form of less-than-perfect markets, trade sequences, traders, brokers, regulators, and humans amid the backdrop of an imperfect world. Yet perhaps it's our very humanity and imperfections that combine to form our greatest strengths and lead to our greatest discoveries, for most accomplishments or advances in the history of this world seem to have their footings held strong by the once-wet concrete of extreme or multiple failures that over time hardened to provide a foundation that could withstand the future winds of time.

Another theme is **flexibility** in terms of both trading style and business plan that the financial markets provide. Just as there is no single "right" way to trade—as long as gains exceed losses and costs—there are also multiple ways in which to incorporate a trading plan into one's life. For example, the $2 million I earned via intentional and extreme dedication over a short period of time—and have preserved via a portfolio stop loss—could have similarly been generated by a far less intensive plan over a longer period of time if better suited to one's career choice or life circumstances. Consider that $50,000 per year over 40 years, $100,000 per year over 20 years, or $2 million over 18 months all add to the same figure. None of them are "correct," yet all are correct. And such is the beauty of participating in the financial markets. For me, the short-term intensive strategy simply fit nicely into my life and career mix.

In terms of my immediate future, one wonderful aspect about acquiring the skill to profit from the financial markets and subsequently growing a portfolio to one's full objective is that it provides the freedom to enter and exit the larger market race at the time and place—and with the intensity—of one's choosing, with protective mechanisms fully in place. And although I anticipate continuing to be involved as a short-term sprinter, longer-term marathoner, or simply one who provides support for other "racers" through increased education and industry awareness, I must admit that compiling this collection has tempted me to once again tighten up the laces and turn up the intensity as a racer. For just as runners love to run, I simply love to trade. *Of course, I also owe it to my wife, Debra, to enjoy our empty-nest years to the extent that time and grace permit!*

As I first mentioned when we began this journey together, this is a true story that I hope showed that despite the tremendous imperfections of humanity—and this trader specifically—anything is possible when years of extreme dedication and motivation collide with that special window of opportunity where personal rhythm and external circumstances fully align. I also mentioned that if some of these words increased your perspective on life as much as they did on trading, we'll call it mission accomplished. Although I'll let time provide the ultimate verdict, I'm hopeful that these words have stirred your soul to diligently strive to maximize your gifts and talents and jump through that window of opportunity with full force when it appears—regardless of age, endeavor, or field—while keeping your successes in perspective and your friends and family far, far closer than your bank account.

Is this a book about trading or life? I'll let you decide.

Journal and Jellie Shorthand and Acronyms

3LB—Three-Line Break. A Japanese candlestick chart that ignores time and only changes when prices move a certain amount. 3LB often neutralizes the inherent price chop and reflects one of our trend detection and turn signals. We use it primarily on a one-minute basis, and it's often an outstanding SOOT indicator during extreme trends to avoid premature reversal attempts. Further explained in *Beyond Candlesticks* (Nison 1994).

Air on XX—Reflects that price is stretched on the stated time-frame ("XX") such that visual "air" exists between price or VIX and defined trend support.

DAX—The futures contract based on the the primary index of the Deutsche Boerse in Europe representing 30 of the largest and most liquid German companies that trade on the Frankfurt Exchange.

DMI—Don Miller Indicator. Coined by the first Jellie team to reflect my general interest in trading current market conditions. A low value often coincides with SOOT and SOH conditions.

EESM—Emergency and Extended Scalp Mode. Reflects "get back in the saddle" conditions after a poorly executed trade sequence or day.

ES—The commodity ticker symbol designating the "E-Mini" Standard and Poors futures contract traded on the CME's

Globex electronic trading platform. The letters "ES" are often followed by subsequent letters and numbers indicating the month and year of expiration. For example, "ESU08" reflects the S&P E-Mini contract expiring in September 2008. Expiration months are designated by the letters H (March), M (June), U (September), and Z (December).

IFT—Inverse Fade Theory. Reflects some of the Jellies' desire to ride the immediate short-term trend during times when we issue "No Fade" warnings, as is often the case late in the day when we warn of potentially disastrous late-day fade entries.

IIAGD (or IIAGU)—If It Ain't Going Down (or Up) conditions. Reflects the current path of least resistance, often defined by bull and bear tails and traps indicating trapped longs or shorts whose exits will help fuel price movement in the opposite direction.

LOD, HOD—Low of Day, High of Day. Can apply to price, TICK, or VIX.

MATD—Morning-After Trend Day. Reflects expected tradable oscillations as the market adjusts to new price levels. Its relatives include MATC (Morning-After Trend Close) and MATN (Morning-After Trend Night).

NML—No-Man's Land. Reflects an "efficient" market that is trading midrange where minimal opportunity exists for wholesale entries and subsequent profit potential. Often best defined by our 1500 Tick Range chart.

NQ—The commodity ticker symbol designating the "E-Mini" NASDAQ 100 futures contract traded on the CME's Globex electronic trading platform. The letters "NQ" are often followed by subsequent letters and numbers indicating the month and year of expiration. For example, "NQU08" reflects the NASDAQ E-Mini contract expiring in September 2008.

PJO—Prime Jellie Opportunity. Reflects those one to three trades sought over the course of the day that reflect the highest probability and opportunity to profit.

POLR—Path of Least Resistance. Reflects the current market "current" that Jellies attempt to ride based on prevailing trends and timeframes.

SOH—Sitting on Hands. Describes what Don and Jellies should do while SOOTing.

SOOT—Stay Out of Trouble mode. Reflects conditions reflective of minimal trading opportunity.

TD—Divergence between the NYSE TICK and market price. TD is usually accompanied by the applicable timeframe, as in five-minute TD.

TMAR—Take the Money and Run. Reflects immediate limited expected potential.

TUB—Trust Until Broken. Reflects trade support premises such as key swing highs or lows, taking into consideration that such a level is a "zone" only as the market is famous for probing stop levels.

VIX—Chicago Board of Options Volatility Index designed to track market volatility and used as an indicator of market sentiment. The VIX typically trades inversely to ES.

About the Author

Don Miller is an independent fund trader who has created numerous instructional tools for individual investors and professional traders. In the process, he has mentored hundreds of traders on the technical and psychological aspects of the financial markets.

In 2008, after years of suboptimal futures trading results due to his lack of focus, lack of motivation, and an imbalanced career mix, Don began an online trading journal at donmillerjournal.blogspot.com (later merged with donmillerblog.com) that chronicled his successful attempt to grow his self-directed retirement fund by $1 million in a single year through intraday futures trading, ultimately earning $2 million over 18 months. In 2009, he created the in-depth Jellie trader training program in an effort to reinvigorate his passion, give back to the industry, and support various charities, including the American Diabetes Association, which is of particular significance to him, as his daughter was diagnosed with type 1 diabetes at age 10. In 2012, as one of the clients affected by the MF Global bankruptcy, Don assumed a prominent industry role as customer advocate, working closely with several media outlets and the Commodity Customer Coalition to fight for the speedy and safe return of client assets.

Don's online trading journal has been listed in the top 10 trading blogs at TraderInterviews.com, and his journal entries have appeared in the International Traders Expo Resource Directory and via syndication on MoneyShow.com. He has spoken at numerous industry forums, including the International Traders Expo and American Association of Individual Investors. His market insights have been published in multiple periodicals and online publications, including *Technical Analysis of Stocks and Commodities, SFO* magazine, MoneyShow.com, and TradingMarkets.com. Don graduated summa cum laude from Bryant College, receiving a bachelor of science in business administration with a major in accounting, and earned an executive master of business administration degree from the University of Wisconsin.

Don and his wife, Debra, have been married since 1985 and have two children, Courtney and Chelsea.

E-mail: don@donmillereducation.com
Trading Blog: donmillerblog.com
Trader Education Website: donmillereducation.com
Twitter Handle: @millerdon

Bibliography

Aronson, Eric. "Keep Watering Your Bamboo Tree." www.dashlive.com, October 4, 2004.

Bourquin, Tim. "10 Trading Blogs Every Trader Should Be Reading." www.traderinterviews .com.

Bourquin, Tim. "Trader Don Miller's Philosophy on the Markets." www.Moneyshow .com, March 26, 2009.

Child, Julia. *Mastering the Art of French Cooking*. New York: Alfred A. Knopf, 1961.

Commodity Customer Coalition. www.commoditycustomercoalition.org.

Covey, Steven. *The Seven Habits of Highly Effective People*. New York: Free Press, 1989.

Collins, Daniel. "MF Global: Where's the Money?" www.futuresmag.com, November 1, 2012.

Collins, Daniel. "MF Global Debacle Grows More Outrageous: Where's the Money?" *Futures*, www.futuresmag.com, June 15, 2012.

Dash, Mike. "When the Tulip Bubble Burst." www.businessweek.com, April 24, 2000.

Edgerton, Brett. "Henin Joins Growing List of Athletes Departing before Their Time Is Up." ESPN.com, May 14, 2008.

Gladwell, Malcolm. *Outliers: The Story of Success*. New York: Little, Brown, 2008.

Grossman, Lev. "Outliers: Malcolm Gladwell's Success Story." *Time*, www.time.com, November 13, 2008.

Hill, Napoleon. *Think and Grow Rich*. New York: Random House, 1963.

Koppenheffer, Matt. "The Astonishing Lack of Progress at MF Global." *The Motley Fool*, www.fool.com, January 23, 2012.

Lefevre, Edwin. *Reminiscences of a Stock Operator*. New York: John Wiley & Sons, [1923] 1994.

Levine, David. "PFG Collapse Hits Some MF Global Victims." www.huffingtonpost .com, July 12, 2012.

Miller, Donald. *Don Miller Trader Education*. www.donmillereducation.com.

Miller, Donald. *Don Miller Trading Journal*. donmillerjournal.blogspot.com and donmillerblog.com, July 4, 2008–December 24, 2012.

McCluskey, Molly, and Tim Beyers. "MF Global: Who Knew What, and When?" *The Motley Fool*, www.fool.com, December 16, 2011.

Nison, Steve. *Beyond Candlesticks*. New York: John Wiley & Sons, 1994.

Phillips, Larry. *The Tao of Poker*. Avon, MA: Adams Media Corporation, 2003.

Penn, David. "TradingMarkets Ten Traders' Resolutions for 2009." www.tradingmarkets .com, January 12, 2009.

Rotella, Bob. *Golf Is Not a Game of Perfect.* New York: Simon & Schuster, 1995.

Sanford, Charles S. "Life Value and the Paradoxes of Risk." Commencement speech to the University of Georgia Class of 1989, www.terry.uga.edu, June 1989.

Schwager, Jack D. *Schwager on Futures: Technical Analysis.* New York: John Wiley & Sons, 1996.

Shinzawa, Fluto. "Bruins Get Great Equalizer." *Boston Globe,* www.boston.com, April 18, 2010.

"The SIPA Liquidation of MF Global Inc." dm.epiq11.com, November 1, 2011–December 24, 2012.

Steenbarger, Brett N. *The Psychology of Trading.* Hoboken, NJ: John Wiley & Sons, 2003.

Szala, Ginger. "MF Global: One Year and Counting." *Futures,* www.futuresmag.com, November 1, 2012.

Tichy, Noel, and Ram Charan. "Speed, Simplicity, Self-Confidence: An Interview with Jack Welch." *Harvard Business Review,* www.hbr.org, September 1989.

Twain, Mark. *Pudd'nhead Wilson and Other Tales.* 1894.

van Loon, Hendrik Willem. *The Story of Mankind.* New York: H. Boni and Liveright, 1921.

Vischer, Phil. *Me, Myself, and Bob.* Nashville: Thomas Nelson, 2006.

Whitehouse, Kaja. "Bank Chased Out: MF Global Victims Start Boycott of JPMorgan." *New York Post,* www.nypost.com, December 21, 2012.

Whitehouse, Kaja, and Anelia Dimitrova. "Peregrine Financial Group Founder Wasendorf Is the Madoff of Iowa." *New York Post,* www.nypost.com, July 13, 2012.

Index